The
Craft
of
Music
Teaching

**in
the
elementary
school**

INEZ SCHUBERT
LUCILLE WOOD

Los Angeles State College

 SILVER BURDETT COMPANY
the educational publishing subsidiary of Time Inc.
Morristown, New Jersey
Park Ridge, Ill. • Palo Alto • Dallas • Atlanta

Contents

Music

Foreword

TO THE PROFESSOR OF MUSIC EDUCATION

This textbook is designed to help you guide your students through the "front door" of musical learning and to set an example of artistic teaching that they can follow when working with children. **In the "front-door" approach, students first experience music well within their performing ability and understanding.** They respond to the total effect of music, recognize obvious characteristics that create this effect, and are guided to a beginning knowledge of the elements of music. After they have entered the front door — and only then — students begin to learn the more technical aspects of musical structure and notation.

This book makes artistic teaching possible because it contains carefully structured lessons based on music materials appropriate for the elementary school. **It frees you to create an atmosphere of enjoyment and appreciation and to work with your students in creating expressive musical performances.** It permits you to be a demonstration teacher, presenting model lessons that are colorful, clear, and meaningful.

The pattern for each lesson includes an introduction, a "problem" to be solved, a climactic point, and the resolution. Lessons are spiced with variety and the spirit of enjoyable participation. They provide for incidental learnings through student reactions and questions. They use classroom instruments to their fullest potential and encourage students to use many senses to gain understanding of musical concepts. Students actually participate in the music through singing, rhythmic activities, and instrumental accompaniments, pausing after each activity to discuss and clarify what they have learned. **Most time is given to musical performance, but proper emphasis is given to explanation, review, and evaluation.** Unique marginal notes in the lessons define and emphasize important teaching concepts. The accompanying record, *Songs from The Craft of Music Teaching*, may be used to teach many of the songs or as examples of interpretation.

The Appendix, which contains forty-nine songs, provides additional practice and learning experiences. These songs may be used for review and for individual performances on the recorder and autoharp.

Through the material in the lessons and the Appendix, students develop a music repertory of their own, which includes songs, related orchestral selections, and ways of presenting them in the elementary classroom. Your students are given the materials needed to begin their careers in music teaching with confidence as well as the techniques that will enable them to become competent and enthusiastic teachers.

TO THE COLLEGE STUDENT

Familiar songs have been chosen for your initial classroom experiences in music. You and your class will "make music" immediately; you will actually experience music, not just talk about it! Later lessons are planned to help you become aware of the effects of songs and orchestral compositions and to understand how these effects are achieved.

Each lesson offers guidance for musical performance and listening. Focus points (▬) place special emphasis on important musical terms and concepts that are being studied in each lesson. Notes in the page margins tell you about the techniques and philosophies of music education — the "how" and "why" of teaching — in a clear and practical form. **You will learn the essence of the art of music, and you will learn how to teach music to children.**

The enjoyment of toe-tapping rhythms, catchy melodies, and dramatic musical effects is part of musical learning. In the lessons in this book, you feel this enjoyment by singing simple folk tunes and familiar songs. Through experience with these songs you learn about melody, rhythm, harmony, and form; about tempo, dynamics, and musical moods; about the elements and basic characteristics of music.

In this atmosphere, you identify and master the skills necessary for creating and teaching music in the elementary classroom. **You are guided in your study of background information and fact, and you acquire the ability to continue your musical growth independently.** You follow a complete, practical guide that helps you learn every step of the teaching procedure. Later, the book becomes an invaluable source book when you are ready to teach your own music classes.

As you progress through this book, you will be developing your musical taste. Through recognition and discovery, you will learn that the nature of musical expression is unique — that music is a mode of expression and reveals in tone and rhythm what man does, what he thinks, and how he feels. You will discover that music can enrich your personal life and give you deep aesthetic satisfaction.

TO THE TEACHER IN SERVICE

To teach music effectively, it is necessary to bring to the classroom a spirit of adventure and a willingness to discover what music has to offer. The best teaching procedures are those that permit children to explore the excitement of music for themselves and to become involved in the tonal and rhythmic drama of music. In the beginning, you will need the careful guidance and support offered by this book. When you become aware of your own musical potential and have developed general understandings of the language, vocabulary, and symbols of music, you will be ready to strike out on your own.

Start at the beginning of the book. Follow the sequence of activities in each lesson. **Many of the lessons can be taught to your children; you and your class can learn together!** Other lessons are for your own study and will help develop your musical knowledge and skill. Be especially mindful of the marginal notes. They express principles you can apply to all your music teaching.

Begin to develop your own ideas and ideals of music education in the elementary classroom. Translate these ideas and ideals into action, realizing that it is the process of the translation, not its completion, that is important. Develop skill in musical performance and in reading the musical score by practicing on your own. There is no other way to develop these skills. Use the songs in the Appendix for extra practice on the autoharp and recorder and for developing additional music lessons especially suited to the children in your classroom.

When you have completed this book, you will have developed a high degree of confidence and independence in music teaching. You will know a great deal about music and about how to teach music to children. Most important, you will be ready to guide your class through enjoyable and fruitful musical experiences.

Twenty-two of the songs presented in this book are recorded on a 12-inch long-playing record, *Songs from The Craft of Music Teaching*. This recording is designed for specific lessons and is an integral part of the teaching approach of the book. Most of the instrumental music studied in this book is included in the *Bowmar Orchestral Library*. Other recordings are available in *Musical Sound Books, Adventures in Music*, and on numerous long-playing records.

LESSON 1

BROTHER JOHN *(Frère Jacques)*

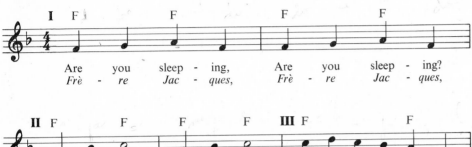

I F F F F
Are you sleep - ing, Are you sleep - ing?
Frè - re Jac - ques, Frè - re Jac - ques,

II F F F F III F F
Broth - er John, Broth - er John? Morn - ing bells are ring - ing,
Dor - mez vous, Dor - mez vous? Son - nez les ma - ti - nes,

F F IV F F F F
Morn - ing bells are ring - ing, Ding ding dong, Ding ding dong.
Son - nez les ma - ti - nes, Din din don, Din din don.

Traditional

BECOMING ACQUAINTED WITH THE MUSIC

With the index finger of the left hand, press the F-major chord button on the autoharp. With the right hand, strum across the strings in the direction away from the body. Continue strumming in an even rhythm at a moderate **tempo** (rate of speed). *Listen* to the sound.

Sing "Brother John" with this autoharp accompaniment.

Develop the habit of *listening* to the sounds of music.

 TONALITY The sound of the F-major chord on the autoharp establishes the key of F major, the key in which "Brother John" has been sung.

The autoharp provides a harmonic accompaniment that can be played successfully by those with little or no previous musical experience.

SINGING EXPRESSIVELY

The words of a song often suggest the style in which it should be sung. Study the words of "Brother John." Decide whether the song should begin

- softly and increase in volume (**crescendo**) *or*
- loudly and decrease in volume (**decrescendo**)

Any song worth singing should be sung expressively.

1

Notice that the high point of the melody coincides with the words "Morning bells are ringing."

Sing "Brother John" again and make appropriate changes in dynamics.

 One aspect of musical interpretation is the expressive use of **dynamics** (degrees of loudness and softness). Dynamics is to music what perspective and intensity of color are to art. Soft sound conveys an illusion of distance or peace; loud sound gives an illusion of nearness or excitement.

PLAYING AN APPROPRIATE ACCOMPANIMENT

Play the last two measures of "Brother John" (illustration 1) on the melody bells or on the piano. This melodic figure may be used as an accompaniment for the entire song.

Illustration 1

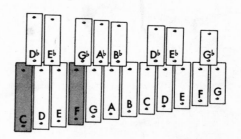

Sing "Brother John" with autoharp and melody bell accompaniment. Hear how the tone color of the accompanying instruments adds new sounds to the performance.

Listen for the distinctive sounds created by playing a variety of musical instruments.

 Every musical instrument has a distinctive sound — a characteristic **tone color** or **timbre.** When melody bells are used with the autoharp, a new sound is created. It is possible to create an endless variety of tone colors by using combinations of different instruments, voices, or instruments and voices together.

PLAYING AN INTRODUCTION

Develop skill in creating good introductions for songs. It is often possible to use patterns found in the songs themselves.

An effective introduction for "Brother John" may be created by playing two measures of the combined melody bell and autoharp accompaniments shown in illustration 2.

2

Illustration 2

The introduction is an integral part of the structure, or *form,* of a song. It establishes the tempo and key and often suggests the style of performance.

SINGING A ROUND

Sing "Brother John" as a two-, three-, and four-part round with autoharp and melody bell accompaniment. Listen to the sound that results when this melody is sung as a round. Think of words to describe the difference between this sound and that of singing in **unison** (all voices singing the same melody).

When a melody is sung in the form of a round, the music changes from a single-voiced texture (**monophonic**) to a many-voiced texture (**polyphonic**). As each voice enters in succession, the effect is that of weaving a new and richer rhythmic and harmonic texture.

Singing a round is a more complex musical experience than singing in unison. Singing a round demands from the performers a greater degree of concentration and closer attention to the director in order to keep all parts together.

MOVING TO MUSIC

The words of "Brother John" suggest an appropriate movement to accompany each of the four sections in the song — for example, swinging like a big bell or pulling the bell rope. The movements should be big and vigorous and done in time with the music.

A sequence of rhythmic movements can be planned to dramatize the story of "Brother John." Sing the song in unison with the accompanying motions; then, dividing into four groups, sing, and move to "Brother John" as a four-part round.

Bodily movement is a natural response to music and a vital way of interpreting music.

CREATING VARIATIONS

Several effective variations can be created for "Brother John." Pretend that the action takes place in a village where a group of townsfolk is trying to awaken Brother John.

Variation 1 — The Town Crier. Half of the class sings the melody in unison. The other half of the class sings the town crier's descant, or counter melody (illustration 3).

Working out variations leads to concrete knowledge about the elements of music (rhythm, melody, harmony) and gives experience in making decisions about musical interpretation (tempo, dynamic level, instrumentation).

3

Where, in this lesson, has the town crier's pattern been used before?

Illustration 3

Are you sleep - ing,

Broth - er John, Broth - er John, Broth - er John,

HARMONY A simple two-part harmony is created when a melody and a counter melody are sung together.

Variation 2 — The Marching Band. The class sings "Brother John" in the style of a march. The following percussion instruments create the sound of a marching band.

In working out a percussion accompaniment to be used with a specific song, use only those instruments whose tone color will add to the spirit of the music.

Small drums in the rhythm of briskly marching feet

Large drums on the first beat of each measure

Cymbals at the beginning of each of the four parts of the song

A suggested rhythm pattern for each instrument appears in illustration 4.

Illustration 4

Study the symbols of musical notation to discover with the eye what has been heard (sound) and felt (rhythm).

SMALL DRUM

Meter signature: The top number indicates that the beats are grouped in fours — four beats in a measure.

LARGE DRUM

Bar line: This vertical line indicates the beginning and end of a measure.

Rest: This symbol indicates silence.

CYMBALS

Repeat sign: The repeat sign indicates that this rhythm pattern is to be repeated throughout the song.

How can dynamics be used to create the effect of a marching band coming from a distance, marching through the heart of the village, then marching away again?

DYNAMICS It is possible to create the illusion of distance and nearness through the use of dynamics.

Variation 3 — The Village Band. The class sings "Brother John" in the style of a waltz. As preparation, clap the beat pattern of a waltz, accenting the first note in each measure.

4

Illustration 5

Then sing "Brother John" in $\frac{3}{4}$ meter, using the autoharp accompaniment (one strum to a measure) shown in illustration 6.

Illustration 6

Are you sleep - ing, Are you sleep - ing?

RHYTHM When the meter of a song is changed, the character of the music is altered.

An "oom-pah-pah" accompaniment (illustration 7), often associated with a village band, may be simulated by using a low-pitched instrument on the "oom" and a high-pitched instrument on the "pah-pah." Observe that in this rhythm pattern the accent on the first beat is reinforced by the drum.

Illustration 7

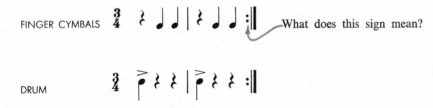

FINGER CYMBALS   What does this sign mean?

DRUM

RHYTHM In $\frac{3}{4}$ meter, the top number indicates that the beats are grouped in threes — three beats in a measure.

Practice this percussion accompaniment, decide how dynamics will be used, and establish the tempo. Then sing and play "Brother John" with the instrumental accompaniments shown in illustrations 6 and 7.

Variation 4 — Lamentation. The class sings "Brother John" in a more serious mood. Find the D-minor chord button on the autoharp. Strum the D-minor chord and sing the song slowly (illustration 8). Compare the sound of this variation with the sound of the original song. Think of adjectives to describe this variation.

Illustration 8

Slowly

Are you sleep-ing, Are you sleep-ing, Broth-er John, Broth-er John?

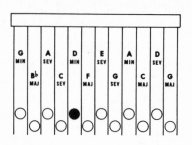

Analysis of tonality be-comes meaningful only after music has been ex-perienced. At first, naming the key is all that is necessary.

TONALITY The sound of the D-minor chord on the autoharp establishes the key of D minor, the key in which "Brother John" has been sung.

Play the melody bell descant in illustration 9. Compare this descant with the descant in illustration 1.

Illustration 9

D   A   D   D   A   D
Broth - er John,   Broth - er   John

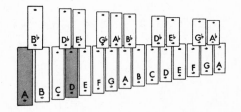

To heighten the dirgelike effect of the variation, add the sound of a deep-pitched drum in slow tempo.

PLANNING A PERFORMANCE

Organize a chorus and orchestra for a performance of "Variations on the Theme of 'Brother John.'" The class may create an original sequence of varia-tions or use the following outline.

Autoharp introduction
Statement of the theme (Sing in unison with autoharp accompaniment.)
Add melody bell descant.
Sing as a four-part round.
Variation 1 — The Town Crier
Variation 2 — The Marching Band
Variation 3 — The Village Band
Variation 4 — Lamentation

To move smoothly from one part of the performance to the next, it will be necessary to play short instrumental interludes between the variations. The autoharp, melody bells, and a variety of percussion instruments may be used for these interludes.

LISTENING TO ORCHESTRAL MUSIC

Listen to a recording of the third movement (first section) of Gustav Mahler's *Symphony No. 1.*

What familiar melody has the composer used?

What instrument is played in the introduction?

How is Mahler's introduction similar to the introduction used in the class performance of "Brother John"?

When a listener can identify some element of the music, he is better able to understand and to participate actively in the listening experience.

Listen to the recording again, then compare Mahler's music with the "Variations on the Theme of 'Brother John' " created by the class.

How were melody, rhythm, harmony, and tone color varied in the class performance? in Mahler's music?

How did Mahler change the melody?

Listen for contrasts in music. Comparisons lead to interesting and meaningful class discussions.

How were tempo, dynamics, and tone color used in the class performance? in Mahler's music?

Listen to Mahler's music again to identify (through the ear and with the eye) the musical ideas notated in illustration 10.

Illustration 10

(a)

(b)

(c)

Mahler's inspiration for the third movement of his first symphony was a painting called "The Hunter's Funeral Procession," well known to children in southern Germany. The painting depicts animals of the forest, in comic posture, escorting the dead hunter's coffin to the grave.

Listen again to the music to discover how Mahler portrayed this subject.

Only background information that contributes to musical understanding is important to the listener.

7

LESSON 2

BELLS

I F   F   C₇   F

Church bells at noon go ding dong ding,

II F   F   C₇   F

Church bells at noon go cling clang cling.

III F   F   C₇   F

Hear them as they ring through the sun - shine of morn - ing,

IV F   F   C₇   F

Hear them as they sing o - ver streets of the town.

V F   F   C₇   F

Ring - ing, sing - ing bells that go ding ding dong.

French round. Words by Vivian Cooper

BECOMING ACQUAINTED WITH THE MUSIC

Recordings are a valuable asset in presenting and learning a new song.

Listen to the recording of "Bells" several times while following the score. After becoming familiar with the melody, sing along with the recording.

Now learn to sing the song *without* the support of a recording.

The pattern in illustration 1 was played on the melody bells as an accompaniment for "Brother John."

Illustration 1

F   C   F

Compare illustrations 1 and 2. Notice that all the notes in illustration 2 are half notes (♩). Each note is held for two beats. Play this pattern on the melody bells:

Illustration 2

F   F   C   F

RHYTHM   An important aspect of rhythm is the relationship among notes of different duration. In $\frac{4}{4}$ meter, a quarter note (♩) represents one beat, and a half note (♩) represents two beats.

Compare the two rhythm patterns in illustration 3.

Illustration 3

Beats   1 2 3 4   1 2 3 4

What tells that there are four beats in each measure?

An unfamiliar musical pattern may be learned more quickly if it is compared with a familiar one.

Sing "Bells" again, using only the bell pattern in illustration 2 as an introduction and as an accompaniment.

SINGING A ROUND

Sing "Bells" as a three-part round, then as a five-part round, using the bell pattern as an introduction and as an accompaniment.

CREATING APPROPRIATE ACCOMPANIMENTS

Choose the most effective tempo and dynamic level, then sing the song again with bell and autoharp accompaniment. Notice that the same autoharp pattern (illustration 4) is used for each of the five parts of the song.

Illustration 4

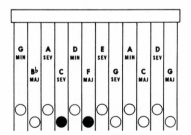

Recognition of repeated patterns aids learning. Look for repetition of *chord* patterns.

Hum the melody and study the score of "Bells." Notice the similarity between part I (first phrase) and part II (second phrase); between part III (third phrase) and part IV (fourth phrase).

FORM   A **phrase** is a melodic unit comparable to a sentence in speech.

Repetition and sequence are among the most important devices used in music. When a phrase or shorter melodic pattern is repeated from the same pitch, it is called **repetition.** When the melodic pattern is repeated at a higher or lower pitch, it is called **sequence.**

Study the score of "Bells" and locate each melodic figure shown in illustration 5. Sing the song in unison and play each figure on the bells as it occurs in the melody. Notice carefully the direction in which the notes in these melodic figures move (up, down, or stay the same).

Illustration 5

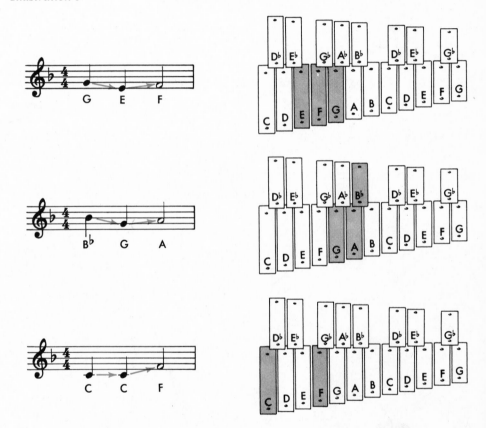

Create another effective accompaniment by playing a two-chord autoharp pattern on the resonator bells, as shown in illustrations 6 and 7.

The three notes of the F chord (illustration 6) are played simultaneously, each note by one student.

Illustration 6

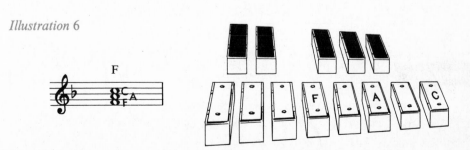

The four notes of the C_7 chord (illustration 7) are played simultaneously, each note by one student.

Illustration 7

Practice playing the two-chord pattern (illustration 8) on the resonator bells. Play this pattern as an introduction and as an accompaniment while the class sings "Bells," first in unison, then as a five-part round. Listen carefully to the difference in quality between the F chord and the C_7 chord.

Illustration 8

Hum the melody of "Bells." Notice that it seems natural to take a breath at the end of each phrase. A chord pattern that ends a phrase and indicates a resting point (momentary or final) is called a **cadence.**

Listen as each chord pattern in illustration 9 is played on the autoharp or resonator bells.

Which cadence gives the listener a feeling of conclusion or repose?

Which cadence suggests there is more music to follow?

Listen for the distinctive quality of the cadence.

Illustration 9

HARMONY In these patterns, the F chord gives the feeling of repose. It may be called the "passive" chord. The C_7 chord gives the feeling of inconclusiveness. It may be called the "active" chord. This striving of the active chord — its urge for movement to a passive chord — is a dynamic force in music.

THE GERMAN BAND

Oh, we are two mu-si-cians who come from Ger-man-y.

Oh, we are two mu-si-cians who come from Ger-man-y.

We can play the vi-o, vi-o, vi-o-lin;

We can play the bull fid-dle and flute.

And we can al-so dance hop-sa, hop-sa-sa, hop-sa-sa,

And we can al-so dance hop-sa, hop-sa-sa.

German folk song

BECOMING ACQUAINTED WITH THE MUSIC

The score becomes meaningful when the eye helps the ear discover like (or similar) and unlike phrases.

Listen to the recording of "The German Band." When the melody has become familiar, sing the song with the recording to discover

* which phrases are similar
* where a sequence occurs

Sing "The German Band" with only the autoharp accompaniment — one strum to a measure. Notice that the same chord pattern is repeated throughout the song — once in every four-measure phrase (illustration 1). How is this chord pattern similar to the chord pattern used in "Bells"?

Illustration 1

Recognizing familiar patterns aids music learning.

 The sound of the G-major chord and the active D₇ chord establishes the key of G major — the key in which "The German Band" is sung.

PLAYING APPROPRIATE ACCOMPANIMENTS

Study the score of "The German Band" and locate the melodic pattern shown in illustration 2. In which phrase does it occur? Notice the direction in which the notes of this pattern move (up, down, or stay the same).

Illustration 2

B B B   A A A   G G

Learn to play this pattern on the melody bells.

Sing the song again with autoharp accompaniment, playing the pattern on the bells where it occurs in the melody. Listen to discover that the bells simulate the sound of the glockenspiel, an instrument often associated with a German band.

Choosing accompanying instruments appropriate to the music helps develop judgment and musical taste.

 Melodic patterns composed of repeated notes or notes that move by steps (line-space-line on the music staff) are easy to play on the bells or piano.

Study the fingering chart in illustration 3 and locate on the recorder the three notes, B, A, and G. Learn the melodic pattern in illustration 2. A few students may be chosen to play the recorder where this pattern occurs in the melody while the class sings the song with autoharp accompaniment.

Illustration 3

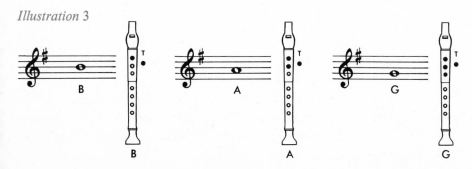

B   A   G

B   A   G

Playing an easy accompaniment on an orchestral instrument such as the bass viol affords an opportunity to become acquainted with the instrument.

Create another instrumental accompaniment by plucking the open G and D strings on the bass viol or the low G and D strings on the autoharp. Use the rhythm pattern shown in illustration 4. Notice that this pattern is based on the roots of the G and D₇ chords.

Illustration 4

HARMONY The note on which a chord is built is called the **root.** G is the root of the G chord, and D is the root of the D₇ chord.

Study illustration 5 and make observations about the general structure of chords.

Illustration 5

G chord   D7 chord

HARMONY A chord is built by adding thirds above a root. If two thirds are added, the chord is called a **triad;** if three thirds are added, the chord is called a **seventh chord.**

Making a musical notation chart of rhythm patterns used in a percussion accompaniment helps to identify visually what has been played. Visual experience deepens musical understanding.

Use percussion instruments (large and small drums and cymbals) to help create the sound of a German band. Make up original drum rhythms or use the patterns suggested below.

Illustration 6

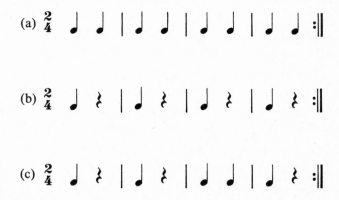

SYMBOLS Meter signatures are music symbols that indicate the rhythmic flow of the music. In $\frac{2}{4}$ meter, the top figure (**2**) indicates that the underlying pulses, or beats, of the music are grouped in twos. The lower figure (**4**) indicates that the quarter note is the symbol for one beat.

RHYTHM

The rhythmic flow of music never stops, even when there is no sound. Silences in music are indicated on the score by rests, which correspond to notes in time value.

SYMBOLS

There is a rest symbol corresponding to every note symbol. The quarter rest (𝄽) is equivalent to the quarter note (♩).

Play "The German Band," using all the instrumental accompaniments that have been practiced. The class divides into singers and instrumentalists (autoharp, melody bell, recorder players, and so on). Students who play other instruments, such as the flute, clarinet, or violin, may want to play them as a part of the class orchestra.

Devise an introduction and decide which instrumentalists will play it.

It is important that all the singers and players keep together and that the recorder and bell players come in at the right time (on cue).

Use all available resources for "making music" in the classroom.

When planning an instrumental accompaniment, use only those instruments that enhance the spirit of the music.

For artistic musical performance, it is essential to play in rhythm and to come in on cue.

CREATING A DANCE

The polka is a dance that reflects the gaiety of the people who created "The German Band." Invite a class member who is familiar with the dance to teach it to a small group of students. One polka step is outlined below.

Dancing is a vital way of becoming involved in the music, a dynamic way of bringing the music to life.

Illustration 7

hop	step	step	step	hop	step	step	step
R	L	R	L	L	R	L	R

PLANNING A PERFORMANCE

Imagine that the class is a troupe of traveling musicians who have been invited to perform at a country fair. Plan to use "The German Band" in a variety of ways. Some suggestions for organizing such a performance are listed below.

Work out an introduction. To establish the key of G major, the key in which the song will be sung, use at least one of these instruments: autoharp, melody bells, piano, bass viol, recorder.

Decide which percussion instruments should be used in the introduction. Select only those instruments that are appropriate to the spirit of the music.

Decide which instruments will be played throughout the performance.

Begin the performance by singing the song through with only autoharp and simple percussion accompaniment.

Feature a single instrument (bass viol, melody bells, recorder, and so on) in each repetition of the song.

Use musical judgment in deciding on dynamics to add drama to the music.

Decide in which part of the performance the dance will be most effective.

Plan a grand finale — perhaps a parade of all the performers.

End the performance with a **coda** (a section of a composition that is added to the form as a conclusion). Decide whether the coda should be loud or soft.

Develop skill in creating codas, using rhythmic, melodic, or harmonic patterns from the song.

15

LESSON 4

DU, DU LIEGST MIR IM HERZEN

German folk song

BECOMING ACQUAINTED WITH THE MUSIC

A comparison of two songs oftens leads to a better understanding of the musical elements in each.

"Du, du liegst mir im Herzen" is a popular German folk song. The tune is typical of the music played by German bands. Sing the song, preferably in German, and compare it with "The German Band." Find adjectives to describe the differences between the two songs.

If the class had difficulty with the German words, they may try singing this less lyrical English translation:

You, you are in my heart,
You, you are in my mind,
You, you cause me much sorrow,
Though to you I am so kind.
Yes, yes, yes, yes,
Though to you I am so kind.

Study the score of "Du, du liegst mir im Herzen" and observe that three chords are used in the autoharp accompaniment (C, G₇, F). Determine where the chord changes occur.

Illustration 1

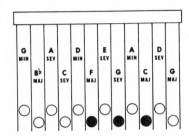

Sing the song with autoharp accompaniment, strumming on the strong beats of the rhythm. (A study of illustration 2 will reveal visually how the strong beat in "Du, du liegst mir im Herzen" is different from that of "The German Band.")

Illustration 2

THE GERMAN BAND

What kind of note is this?

DU, DU LIEGST MIR IM HERZEN

Observe that the music of "Du, du liegst mir im Herzen" is made up of six four-measure phrases. Sing the song again to discover

- which phrases are alike
- which phrases are similar
- which phrase is different from the others

Study the score to discover the element of form in a piece of music. Look for like (or similar) and unlike phrases.

CREATING APPROPRIATE ACCOMPANIMENTS

Simulate an "oom-pah-pah" accompaniment, often associated with a village band, by playing the drum and finger cymbals in the rhythm patterns shown in illustration 3. Which pattern shows the underlying beat?

Perform each song in a manner or style that will bring out the individual qualities of the song.

17

Illustration 3

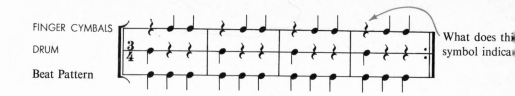

FINGER CYMBALS

DRUM

Beat Pattern

What does this symbol indicate?

RHYTHM A waltz moves in groups of three: ONE-two-three; ONE-two-three. The strongest of these pulses is the first beat of each group.

SYMBOLS In $\frac{3}{4}$ meter, the top figure (**3**) indicates that the underlying pulses, or beats, are grouped in threes. The bottom number (**4**) tells that the symbol for one beat is a quarter note (♩).

Study the score of "Du, du liegst mir im Herzen" and locate the melodic pattern shown in illustration 4. In which phrase does it occur?

Learn to play the pattern on the melody bells. The sound of the bells creates the effect of a glockenspiel. Why is this phrase easy to play on your melody instruments?

Illustration 4

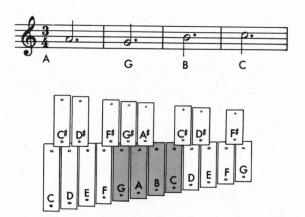

Now learn to play the melodic pattern in illustration 4 on the recorder. Study the fingering chart in illustration 5 and learn how to locate on the instrument the four notes of the pattern.

Illustration 5

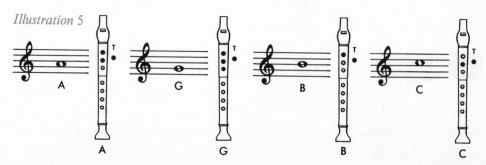

Some students may be chosen to play the percussion patterns (illustration 3), a few others to play the melody bell and recorder part (illustration 4) where it occurs in the melody, while the class sings the song with autoharp accompaniment.

GOING DEEPER INTO STRUCTURE

Out of the performance of "Du, du liegst mir im Herzen," what observations can be made about the time duration of the quarter note (♩)? the half note (𝅗𝅥)? the dotted half (𝅗𝅥.)?

Which is the shortest?
Which is the longest?

SYMBOLS   A dot adds to a note one half of the note's rhythmic value.

Develop the skill of recognizing in music symbols the rhythmic movement of music.

"Du, du liegst mir im Herzen" has been sung and played in the key of C major. This means that all the notes in the song belong to a family of tones called the **C-major scale.** The word "scale" comes from the Italian word *scala*, which means "ladder."

TERM   A **scale** is a family of pitches organized in ascending or descending order according to a specific pattern of musical intervals.

Study illustration 6. Sing the scale on the letter names and on the numbers. Determine with ear and eye why "scale" is a good descriptive name for this family group.

Illustration 6

C	D	E	F	G	A	B	C
1	2	3	4	5	6	7	8

What can be determined about the key in which "Du, du liegst mir im Herzen" is written?

On what note does the song end?
On what chord does the song end?
What other chords are used in the accompaniment?

TONALITY   Of all the tones in a scale, the first tone (**tonic**) is the most important. This tone is also known by other names — the "first degree," the "keynote," and the "home tone." Songs sometimes start, and almost always end, with the tonic note. Two other important tones in a scale are the fifth tone (**dominant**) and the fourth tone (**subdominant**).

19

Study the C-major scale in illustration 6 and learn the letter name of the first tone in this scale; the fifth tone; the fourth tone.

The chords in illustration 7 are those used in the autoharp accompaniment of "Du, du liegst mir im Herzen." Observe that the chord built on the first degree of the scale is identified by the Roman numeral I. Determine why the F and the G₇ chords are identified by the Roman numerals IV and V₇.

Illustration 7

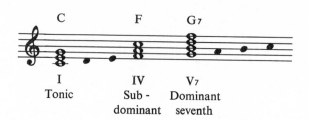

Observe that the V₇ chord includes a fourth tone, seven notes above its root.

LESSON 5

BARCAROLLE

Listen to a recording of "Barcarolle" from *The Tales of Hoffman,* an opera by Jacques Offenbach. Find adjectives to describe the general effect or mood of the music.

Listen to "Barcarolle" again, using the listening skill developed in previous lessons to discover

- how the character of the rhythm helps create the specific mood of the music (What movement does the rhythm suggest? Find adjectives to describe the rhythm.)
- how the tempo helps to establish the mood
- how the dynamic level enhances the mood (Are the changes in dynamics obvious or subtle?)
- how the composer's choice of instrumental tone color contributes to the total effect
- why "Barcarolle," which means "boat song," is an appropriate title for this music

When the mood of a piece has been determined, try to discover how the composer created this mood.

PLAYING IN HARMONY

After becoming familiar with the music, learn to perform the first theme (illustration 1) on the recorder, on the melody bells, or on the piano. Observe and play the harmony part in the last two phrases. The charts in illustration 2 will help in finding the notes on the instruments.

The best way to learn music is to become personally involved in it — that is, to sing, to play, or to dance to it.

Illustration 1

21

Illustration 2

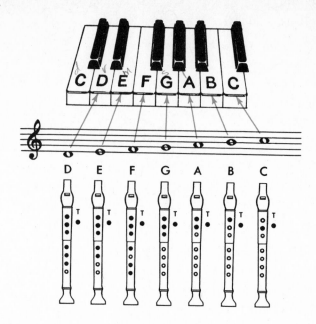

Organize a classroom orchestra and play the first theme of "Barcarolle." Strum the autoharp chords to imitate the **arpeggios** (broken chords) played on the harp in the recording. In the performance, follow the tempo, changes in dynamic levels, and the general musical style heard in the recording.

STUDYING THE SCORE

Follow the score (illustration 1) while listening to that portion of "Barcarolle." How does the appearance of the score reflect the mood of the music?

Learn to identify the characteristics of a piece of music through the eye (from notation) as well as through the ear.

Are the notes in the melody line "close together" or "far apart"?

Is the chord pattern in the accompaniment simple or complex?

What rhythm pattern is repeated most often in the melody line?

After class discussion of melody, harmony, and rhythm, compare class discoveries with these general conclusions:

MELODY Scale-wise movement (notes "close together") of a melody in slow tempo may help to establish a quiet mood.

HARMONY Simplicity of harmonic pattern may bring a feeling of serenity.

RHYTHM Repetition of the pattern in a melody in slow tempo gives a calm, rocking rhythm to the music.

EXPLORING ⁶⁄₈ METER

"Barcarolle" is heard in the second act of *The Tales of Hoffman,* which takes place in Venice. It is first sung as a vocal duet in a gondola, and the rhythm of the music suggests the gentle, rocking movement of the boat.

Sing the first theme of "Barcarolle" on the syllable "loo" or listen to it on the recording and imitate with bodily movements the
- long, sweeping motions of the gondolier as he rows the boat down the canal
- gentle sway of the gondola as it rocks from side to side

How many movements of the gondolier are felt in each measure? How many rocking motions of the gondola are felt in each measure?

Study the diagram in illustration 3 to find the
- rhythm pattern identified with the movement of the gondolier
- rhythm pattern identified with the motion of the gondola
- rhythm pattern played in the autoharp accompaniment
- rhythm patterns played on the melody instruments

Illustration 3

This curved line is called a tie.

A curved line connecting two or more notes of the same pitch is called a **tie.** When several notes are tied, the tone they represent is held for a length of time equal to the sum of the value of the tied notes.

When the rhythm pattern ♩ ♪♪ ♪ , frequently found in ⁶⁄₈ meter, is played in a quick tempo, the result is vigorous, as in march and dance music. When the same rhythm pattern is played in a slow tempo, the effect is gentle and flowing.

In ⁶⁄₈ meter, the top number (**6**) indicates that there are six beats in a measure; the bottom number (**8**) indicates that the eighth note (♪) is the symbol for one beat.

To get the gentle, rocking effect of the rhythm in "Barcarolle," think of each measure as containing *two* dotted quarter notes (each equal to three eighth notes), as in illustration 4.

Illustration 4

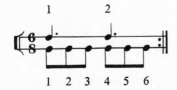

LEARNING TO RECOGNIZE FORM

The realization that all music has form heightens intellectual appreciation; the discovery of the form in a particular piece of music deepens understanding.

Every work of art has form. To grasp the form of a composition, it is necessary to cultivate "musical memory." Listen again to the recording of "Barcarolle" to determine how many times the melody of illustration 1 is heard.

Give the theme (illustration 1) the letter name "A" whenever it occurs.

Give the contrasting section the letter name "B."

Listen for an introduction and a coda.

 **Form** in music is a specific arrangement of musical ideas based on the principles of unity (repetition or recurrence of theme) and variety (presentation of contrasting themes).

How does "Barcarolle" reveal good musical form?

LESSON 6

NINNA NANNA

Nin - na   nan - na,   nin - na   nan - na.

Words or phrases retained from the foreign language in which a folk song is written help to keep some of the original flavor of the song.

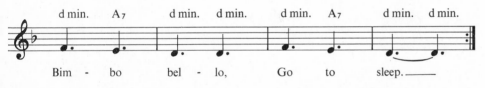

1. Go____ to sleep,____ my lit - tle ba - by,
2. All____ the birds____ have closed____ their eyes,____

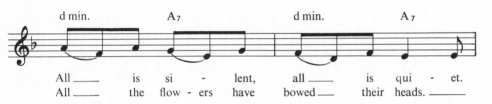

All____ is si - lent, all____ is qui - et.
All____ the flow - ers have bowed____ their heads.____

Bim - bo bel - lo, Go to sleep.____

From *Ninne Nanne, Giochi, Scherzi, Favolette, Filastrocche, Danze* by Achille Schinelli, Casa Editrice Carlo Signorelli, S.p.A.

Music by Achille Schinelli
English words by Inez Schubert

BECOMING ACQUAINTED WITH THE MUSIC

Follow the score while singing "Ninna Nanna" and find adjectives to describe the sound of the music.

How is "Ninna Nanna" different from the songs learned in previous lessons?

What is the effect of the minor mode in this song?

How is this music similar to "Barcarolle"?

What musical characteristics identify "Ninna Nanna" as a lullaby?

Follow the score as the song is sung again to discover the

- general contour of the melodic line (the downward and upward movement of the notes)
- phrase-wise structure of the song
- chord pattern of each phrase

 The constantly recurring downward movement of notes in a melody in a slow tempo often suggests a mood of peace and quiet.

CREATING APPROPRIATE ACCOMPANIMENTS

Prepare to accompany "Ninna Nanna" on the autoharp by locating the D-minor and A₇ chords on the instrument. Practice the chord pattern of the song outlined below.

Phrase A (measures 1–4):   D minor   A₇   D minor   D minor :‖

Phrase B (measures 5–8):   D minor   A₇   D minor   A₇   :‖

Phrase A (measures 9–12):   D minor   A₇   D minor   D minor :‖

The wide variety of musical effects that may be produced on the autoharp makes it possible to adapt an autoharp accompaniment to the specific mood and style of many different kinds of songs.

Sing the song with autoharp accompaniment, strumming with long, slow strokes to produce a harplike sound. The accompaniment will help create the mood usually associated with a lullaby.

Now study the melodic pattern in illustration 1.

Do the notes move up or down?

Do the notes move in a scale-wise progression?

Is the rhythm even or uneven?

The charts in illustration 1 will help you locate the first three pitches of the song on the melody bells and on the recorder. Learn to play the pattern.

Illustration 1

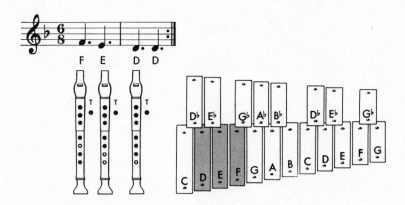

Sing "Ninna Nanna" with autoharp accompaniment while a few students play the bell and recorder parts in the first and last phrases of the song.

SINGING EXPRESSIVELY

One important principle of good singing is that the performer must interpret the song musically. An expressive interpretation of "Ninna Nanna" requires that each downward-flowing phrase be sung smoothly and in one breath. Breathing should always be related to the phrases of a song.

Practice singing "Ninna Nanna" with correct phrasing. To improve vocal production, follow the suggestions below.

Keep the body erect (not stiff) and alert.

Hold the chest up comfortably; breathe easily and deeply.

Hold the head naturally.

Sing with an attitude of listening.

Feel the mood of the song. Let the meaning of the text color the singing tone.

When a beginner becomes sensitive to mood and style in music, he is encouraged to develop the skills and techniques necessary for expressive performance.

PLANNING A PERFORMANCE

Plan a performance of "Ninna Nanna," using the suggestions listed below.

Decide on the tempo and the dynamic level that will be most effective in sustaining the mood of the song.

Devise an introduction that will suggest a quiet mood. Use appropriate instruments to establish the D-minor tonality and the rocking rhythm of a lullaby (♩ ♪♩ ♪).

Use a bell or recorder solo as an interlude between the verses of the song. The solos may be played by students who have learned to play the entire melody.

Create a coda to suggest that the "Bimbo bello" has gone to sleep.

Develop skill in creating good introductions from the material of the song itself.

Provide opportunities for members of the class who have developed additional skill in performance to contribute to the musical experience of the whole class.

GOING DEEPER INTO STRUCTURE

Study the rhythm patterns used in the performance of "Ninna Nanna" (illustration 2) and identify the

- pattern of the autoharp accompaniment
- pattern that creates the rocking motion of a lullaby
- pattern that shows the rhythmic movement of the melody

Both "Ninna Nanna" and "Barcarolle" are written in $\frac{6}{8}$ meter. How many of the rhythm patterns in illustration 2 were used in the performance of "Barcarolle"?

Illustration 2

27

Study the score of "Ninna Nanna" to discover the name of the key in which the melody is written.

On what note does the song end?

On what chord does the song end?

What chords are used in the accompaniment?

TONALITY The note D is the tonic in the key of D minor.

HARMONY The D-minor and A₇ chords are built on the tonic (D) and dominant (A) tones of the D-minor scale.

Illustration 3

Locate the flat-sign (♭) at the beginning of the staff in illustration 3. This symbol is the key signature.

SYMBOLS A flat-sign (♭) is the music symbol that lowers a pitch by a half step, the smallest interval normally used in Western music.

SYMBOLS The **key signature** is a sign composed of one or more flats or sharps (♯) placed after the clef at the beginning of a staff to indicate the key in which the music is to be performed. All notes that are flatted or sharped in the key signature will be flatted or sharped throughout the score unless otherwise indicated.

The last two measures of "Brother John" and "Ninna Nanna" are notated in illustration 4. Observe that the key signature at the beginning of each staff is the same, although "Brother John" is written in the key of F major and "Ninna Nanna" is written in the key of D minor.

Illustration 4

F major

D minor

TONALITY A given key signature may indicate either of two keys, a major key or its relative minor key. A key is called **major** when it is based on the major scale; **minor** when it is based on a minor scale.

28

The F-major scale and its relative minor scale, D minor, are notated in illustration 5. Notice that both scales have the same key signature. An important difference between the two scales is that they begin on different tones. Listen as each scale is played on the piano and think of words to describe the sound of the major scale; of the minor scale.

Analysis of the basic materials of music becomes meaningful only after music has been experienced. At first, identifying major and minor scales *by ear* is all that is necessary.

Illustration 5

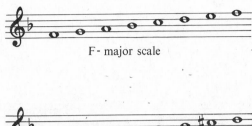

F- major scale

D - minor scale

MODE The most important aspect of the mode (major or minor) is the color it gives the music and the emotional response it evokes in the listener.

LESSON 7

TIC-TÌ, TIC-TÀ

Sun - shine is smil - ing o - ver hill, o - ver dale,
Doves on the wing are float - ing down from on high,

O - ver vine - yards and or - chards to - day;
Gen - tly coo - ing, they light___ here and there,

Boun - te - ous har - vest, ev - 'ry bas - ket and pail,
Bring - ing the az - ure from the hue of the sky,

1. Brim - ming full___ for the fes - ti - val ar - ray.
Mak - ing

2. har - vest and fes - ti - val more fair.

Refrain

Turn and re - turn, like the flow'r and the fern,
Sing like a king, let the gay danc - ers swing

To my heart, tic - a - tì, tic - a - tà,
To the tune, tic - a - tì, tic - a - tà,

Play and be gay in the mer - ri - est way,
See, ev - 'ry tree nod - ding sweet mel - o - dy,

Cel - e - brate, tic - a - tì, tic - a - tà.
Cel - e -

brate, tic - a - tì, tic - a - tà.

Music by Gaetano Lama
Words adapted from the Italian

BECOMING ACQUAINTED WITH THE MUSIC

Sing the Italian harvest song "Tic-Tì, Tic-Tà" and compare its musical characteristics with those of "Barcarolle," the quiet, flowing boat song. Find adjectives to describe the difference between the two songs in

- the general character of the rhythm
- the tempo
- the over-all effect or mood of the music

To follow the score accurately, notice the symbols called "first and second endings." These signs occur twice, once in the first section of the song and again in the second section.

SYMBOLS The symbols ⌐1. :‖ ⌐2. ⌐ direct the reader to follow the score through the first ending, ⌐1. :‖ , to the repeat sign, then to go back to the beginning of the music and to follow the score through again, this time skipping the first ending and proceeding through the second ending.

Sing "Tic-Tì, Tic-Tà" again and notice that it seems natural to take a breath at the end of each phrase. Pay particular attention to the phrase endings. Each phrase, with the exception of the last, ends with a whole note (o).

RHYTHM An important aspect of rhythm is the relationship among notes of different duration. The whole note (o) is equal to four quarter notes (♩).

A comparison of two musical compositions often leads to a better understanding of the elements in each piece of music.

The meaning of musical symbols should never be learned as isolated facts. Learn to interpret these signs as they are encountered in a musical experience.

A true understanding of musical notation grows out of many experiences with music.

31

CREATING APPROPRIATE ACCOMPANIMENTS

In working out a percussion accompaniment for a specific song, use only those instrumental tone qualities that add to the spirit of the music.

A tambourine accompaniment will lend color to a performance of "Tic-Tì, Tic-Tà." This percussion instrument adds to the spirit of festive gaiety suggested by the words of the song.

Two distinctive sounds may be produced with the tambourine. To produce the sound of a small drum, hold the instrument in one hand and rap the tambourine head with the heel of the other hand. To produce a jingling sound, shake the instrument.

Learn to play the tambourine pattern that appears in illustration 1.

Illustration 1

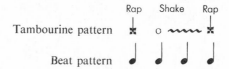

Study the score of "Tic-Tì, Tic-Tà" to discover
  • that C is the home tone of the song and that the music is written in the key of C major
  • the letter names of the I and V₇ chords in the key of C major
  • the chord pattern of each phrase (Does the pattern change at the beginning or at the end of each phrase?)
  • that the chord pattern of the first section (phrases 1 and 2) is repeated in the second section (phrases 3 and 4)

Recognition of repeated patterns aids learning. Look for repetition in the harmonic scheme (chord pattern).

 Repetition of harmonic (chord) patterns creates a feeling of unity in a musical composition.

Use the autoharp introduction in illustration 2 to suggest a procedure for cuing in the singers at the right time.

Illustration 2

Decide on an effective tempo; play the autoharp introduction; then, sing "Tic-Tì, Tic-Tà" with autoharp and tambourine accompaniment.

STUDYING THE SCORE

Study musical notation to discover with the eye what has been heard (sound) and sensed (rhythm).

As "Tic-Tì, Tic-Tà" is sung again, listen carefully and study the score to determine whether the
  • notes of the melodic line are "close together" (moving scale-wise) or "far apart"
  • melody is made up mostly of "long" or "short" notes
  • second phrase of the song, beginning "Bounteous harvest," is similar to the first phrase
  • third and fourth phrases of the song are similar (What musical term describes this similarity?)

32

How do the characteristics of melody, rhythm, and tempo each contribute to the mood of the music?

LEARNING TO RECOGNIZE FORM

Review what has been learned about form in music, then analyze the phrasewise structure of "Tic-Tì, Tic-Tà." Compare class findings with the diagram below.

Develop the habit of analyzing the over-all structure of a song. This will help in learning new material more quickly.

Illustration 3

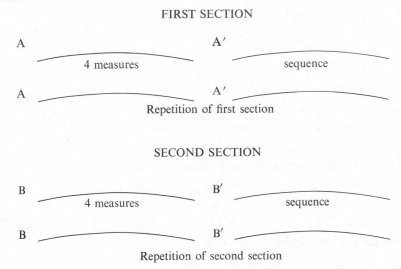

FIRST SECTION

A _____ 4 measures _____ A′ _____ sequence _____

A _____ A′ _____
Repetition of first section

SECOND SECTION

B _____ 4 measures _____ B′ _____ sequence _____

B _____ B′ _____
Repetition of second section

FORM The form of a song is determined by the arrangement of its phrases. Order is brought to the music through the repetition and contrast of phrases. Repetition and contrast give unity, variety, and balance to a song.

SINGING IN HARMONY

Study the harmony part (the line of notes under the melody). Observe that the notes in this part follow, almost exactly, the contour of the melody line. Observe, also, that the harmony lies three or six notes (intervals of thirds or sixths) below the melody (illustration 4).

Learn to sing the harmony part.

Much experience and success in unison singing is necessary before a harmony part can be carried independently.

Illustration 4

Melody note
Harmony note

Melody note
Harmony note

After the harmony part has been learned, half of the class may sing the melody and the other half the harmony part.

HARMONY Harmony adds richness and color to a melody line and gives depth to the music. Thirds and sixths are **consonant** intervals; that is, they are restful and pleasing to the ear.

CREATING A DANCE

Dancing is a vital way of becoming involved in music and can help to clarify the form of the song.

Study and perform the dance below to discover how the floor patterns point up the form of "Tic-Tì, Tic-Tà."

Dancers form a circle and join hands.

Verse: Phrase 1 — Move in a circle to the left.

Phrase 2 — Move in a circle to the right.

Phrase 3 — Move in a circle to the left.

Phrase 4 — Move in a circle to the right.

Refrain: Phrase 5 — Move to the center of the circle, raising hands.

Phrase 6 — Move away from the center of the circle, lowering hands.

Phrase 7 — Move to the center of the circle, raising hands.

Phrase 8 — Move away from the center of the circle, lowering hands.

Develop other floor patterns that reflect the form of "Tic-Tì, Tic-Tà."

LESSON 8

FENG YANG SONG

1. Sing the Feng Yang Song; Sing it loud and long.
2. Gifts for you have I, Kites that swoop and fly;

Clash cym - bals, beat the drum, Strike the met - al gong!
Small trin - kets, man - y toys, All of you may buy.

We are the ven - dors who trav - el all day long,
Pa - per of gold shin - ing, Bam - boo smooth and strong,

Call - ing our wares to the Feng___ Yang___ Song.
Call - ing the clear, ring - ing toy - man's___ song.

Coda, after last verse

Feng yang, fong yong, beat the gong,___ Strike the clap - pers well.

Clash cym - bals, byah yah yang, Clash cym - bals, byah yah yang!

Brr dong! Brr dong!

Brr dong yah feng yang, fong yong, Brr, beat the drum!

3. Shave I have for you,
   Smooth-neat and true.
   Trimming and cutting hair,
   All of that I do.
   Keenness and skill
   To my instruments belong,
   Calling the clear, ringing
   Barber's song.

4. Fortune's magic spell
   I know very well;
   Dry sticks of ancient wood
   Always good foretell.
   Come, try your luck
   For the sticks are never wrong,
   Calling the clear, ringing
   Fortune teller's song.

Chinese folk song

BECOMING ACQUAINTED WITH THE MUSIC

The study and performance of folk music from foreign lands often creates warmth of feeling and understanding of other peoples.

Listen to the recording of "Feng Yang Song" to discover why the music may be identified as Oriental. What can be said about the
- tone color of the instruments used in the accompaniment?
- sound of the melody?
- rhythmic movement of the song?
- style of the performance?

An outline of the recorded version of "Feng Yang Song" appears below. Study the outline, then sing the song with the recording, letting the text suggest the spirit of the music.

Introduction — instrumental

Verse 1 — vocal and instrumental

Interlude — instrumental

Verse 2 — vocal and instrumental

Coda — vocal and instrumental

If any part of a song proves difficult, isolate the part and practice it separately.

It may be necessary to practice certain parts of the coda separately. Read these words aloud in rhythm:

Illustration 1

To discover how some of the exotic sounds of Oriental music are created, use percussion instruments often associated with this type of music.

CREATING APPROPRIATE ACCOMPANIMENTS

Sing "Feng Yang Song" again with the recording. In the coda, play the gong, the clappers (two wood blocks struck together), the cymbals, and the drum where the names of these percussion instruments occur in the song.

Now create an accompaniment characteristic of Oriental music, using the first five words of the song. Select five percussion instruments, such as small and large drums, high and low tone blocks, and gong, and assign each instrument to a different word (illustration 2).

Illustration 2

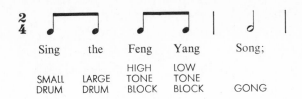

		HIGH	LOW	
Sing	the	Feng	Yang	Song;
SMALL	LARGE	TONE	TONE	
DRUM	DRUM	BLOCK	BLOCK	GONG

RHYTHM An important aspect of rhythm is the relationship among notes of different duration. The quarter note (♩) is equal to two eighth notes (♪). The half note (♩) is equal to two quarter notes.

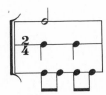

Each of the five instruments is played by a different student. To facilitate learning the accompaniment (illustration 2), the students should line up in the order in which the instruments are to be played (small drum, large drum, and so on).

Sing the song with the recording again. Play the instrumental accompaniment (illustration 2) throughout the verse of the song and play the gong, clappers, cymbals, and drum where the names of these instruments occur in the words of the coda. Listen especially to the percussion accompaniment and find words to describe the effect it creates in the music.

Learn to play the pattern in illustration 3 on the melody bells or on the piano and use it, instead of the recording, as introduction and accompaniment for "Feng Yang Song." When the class has learned to sing the song with this accompaniment, the percussion accompaniment may be added to the performance.

An authentic accompaniment adds to the original flavor of a song.

Illustration 3

Bb Eb

Listen to the sound of a **pentatonic scale** (five-tone scale) as it is played on the melody bells or on the piano. Describe the sound of this scale.

The experience of hearing and performing the pentatonic scale, upon which much Oriental music is based, leads to an understanding of the differences between the music of the Eastern and Western worlds.

Illustration 4

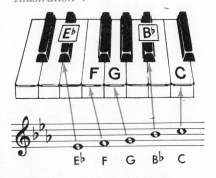

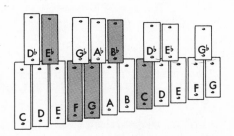

37

Learn to play the pentatonic scale in illustration 4 on the bells or on the piano. "Feng Yang Song" is based on this scale.

Sing the pentatonic scale, ascending and descending, on the syllable "loo."

Use all or some of the notes of the pentatonic scale (illustration 4) to improvise an accompaniment on the bells or the piano. Experiment with simple rhythm patterns in $\frac{2}{4}$ meter.

Since the melody of "Feng Yang Song" contains the notes of the pentatonic scale exclusively, any choice of pitches of the scale will sound well as an accompaniment for the song. If several patterns are played simultaneously, they must be played softly.

PLANNING A PERFORMANCE

Many songs such as "Feng Yang Song" originated in the Chinese province of Feng Yang. Famine often struck the people of this province, and the farmers were forced to wander over the countryside, begging for food. They sang their native songs to attract attention. In time, the Feng Yang songs were adopted by street vendors in Chinese communities. "Feng Yang Song" is one of the popular street songs still sung by Chinese vendors to advertise their wares.

The history of the Feng Yang songs suggests ideas for an authentic re-creation of the music.

The class divides into groups of instrumental accompanists and singers, some of whom may be chosen to represent particular characters in the story.

Work out an introduction. Use a pitched instrument (melody bells, piano) to establish the proper key. Plan to use suitable percussion instruments to bring authentic tone color to the performance and to emphasize the rhythmic movement of the music.

Play a melody or piano accompaniment such as throughout the song to keep the singers in tune.

A solo voice or a small group of voices may sing verses 2, 3, and 4.

Use the rhythmic accompaniment (illustration 2) at some time during the performance.

Use the notes of the pentatonic scale (illustration 4) to improvise a melody bell or piano accompaniment.

Use the cymbals, clappers, gong, and drum as sound effects in the coda.

GOING DEEPER INTO STRUCTURE

As has been learned, the notes used in a particular song belong to a family of tones called a scale. Study the scales in illustration 5. Notice that both scales start on the same pitch. Listen first as the scales are played on the piano or on the bells, then sing each scale on the syllable "loo."

Illustration 5

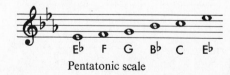

Eb F G Ab Bb C D Eb
Major scale

Eb F G Bb C Eb
Pentatonic scale

Discuss the difference between the *sound* of the major scale and the *sound* of the pentatonic scale. What can be discovered about the *structure* of the two scales? Compare class responses with these general observations:

The major scale has seven different pitches. The first pitch is repeated as the eighth degree — an octave (eight notes) higher.

The pentatonic scale has five different pitches.

The fourth and seventh degrees of a major scale are omitted in a pentatonic scale.

Sing the major scale, ascending and descending, first with numbers, then with syllables. Observe where half steps occur in the scale by following the steplike diagram in illustration 6.

Illustration 6

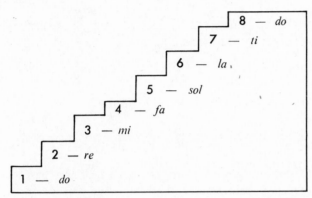

Sing the ascending scale again and stop on the seventh pitch (*ti*). Then sing the descending scale and stop on the fourth pitch of the scale (*fa*). What feeling is created when the singing stops on either the fourth or seventh tones and does not go on to complete the scale?

In a major scale, the tendency of the fourth tone to resolve to the third, and the seventh to resolve to the eighth, is called **tonal magnetism.**

The strong pull of the fourth and seventh tones in a major scale accounts for the distinctive sound of music written in the major mode. The exclusion of the fourth and seventh tones in a pentatonic scale creates what might be called its "exotic" quality.

PANAMAM TOMBÉ

Calypso song as sung by The Carib Singers. Collected by Massie Patterson

BECOMING ACQUAINTED WITH THE MUSIC

Music with a particularly prominent characteristic is easy to identify.

One approach toward understanding a musical composition is to recognize its outstanding musical element.

Listen to the recording of "Panamam Tombé." What element of the music (melody, rhythm, harmony) accounts for the song's distinctive Latin American flavor?

"Panamam Tombé" has a special kind of rhythm called syncopation ("off-the-beat" rhythm). Although syncopated patterns are often difficult to read, particularly for children, the rhythm patterns in "Panamam Tombé" are quite easily learned by rote (through the ear).

Play on the conga drum (a large, one-headed drum) the rhythm pattern notated in illustration 1. Notice that there is an accent mark (>) on the last beat of the measure. To *feel* this accent more strongly, reach out to strike the drum on the fourth beat. Allow the body to move forward with the reaching-out motion. Students who do not have access to a conga drum may play the pattern on their desks.

Illustration 1

LH   RH   LH   RH

RHYTHM   **Syncopation** is a variation of a rhythm pattern in which the expected accent on a strong beat is replaced by an unexpected accent on a weak beat or between two beats — thus the term "off-the-beat." This rhythmic device adds interest and an element of surprise to music.

Listen to the recording again and play the conga drum pattern as an accompaniment.

An outline of the recorded version of "Panamam Tombé" appears below. Study the outline, then follow the score as the recording is played. Pay particular attention to the first and second ending signs.

Introduction — instrumental

First time (excluding last eight measures) — vocal and instrumental

Second time (excluding last eight measures) — instrumental

Third time (including last eight measures) — vocal and instrumental

After becoming familiar with "Panamam Tombé" through the ear, prepare to sing with the recording by observing

• the first and second ending signs (as experienced in "Tic-Tì, Tic-Tà")

• that each part of the song is repeated before the next part is sung

• the *D.C. al Fine* at the end of the score

SYMBOLS   *D.C. al Fine (da capo al fine)* is the sign that indicates repetition of the music from the beginning to the word *Fine*.

Sing "Panamam Tombé" with the recording while a few students play the conga drum accompaniment.

CREATING APPROPRIATE ACCOMPANIMENTS

Develop a typical Calypso percussion accompaniment by learning to play the rhythm patterns in illustration 2. Notice that the basic beat pattern is played on the conga drum ($\frac{4}{4}$ ♩ ♩ ♩ ♩). The other two patterns (bongo drums, maracas) include eighth notes (♪).

SYMBOLS   In $\frac{4}{4}$ meter, two eighth notes equal one beat (♫ = ♩), or (♪ ♪ = ♩).

The tone colors of certain instruments are often identified with the music of a particular nation. If authentic instruments are not available, experiment with all available classroom "sound-makers" to find the instrument whose tone color approximates the "right" sound.

41

Illustration 2

Latin American rhythms

Study the diagram of the form of "Panamam Tombé" (illustration 3). Keep in mind that each phrase is four measures long. Use the diagram as a guide and create a percussion score for the song. Use rhythm patterns created by the class or use the ones shown in illustration 2.

Illustration 3

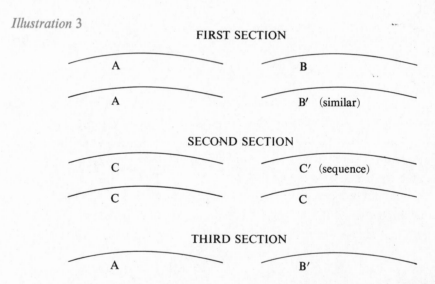

FIRST SECTION

A   B

A   B′ (similar)

SECOND SECTION

C   C′ (sequence)

C   C

THIRD SECTION

A   B′

A performance is apt to be more successful if percussion players are free to concentrate on playing their parts in the accompaniment while the rest of the class sings the song.

The class sings "Panamam Tombé" with the recording while a few students play the percussion accompaniment. Listen for the musical effect produced by the percussion instruments.

RHYTHM   When several contrasting rhythm patterns are played simultaneously, the rhythmic texture of the music becomes more interesting.

"Panamam Tombé" is a Calypso song, and it is appropriate to add the cowbell, an authentic Calypso instrument, to the percussion accompaniment. If a cowbell is not available, substitute a large cymbal and a metal striker to produce a clanging sound. Decide on a rhythm pattern for the cowbell, keeping in mind that it should be used sparingly.

Practice time should always be allowed for a difficult rhythm pattern before it is used as an accompaniment.

Some students may be able to play the syncopated rhythm pattern in illustration 4 on the claves (two hardwood sticks). Practice chanting the rhythm patterns on the words before attempting to play the pattern on the claves.

Illustration 4

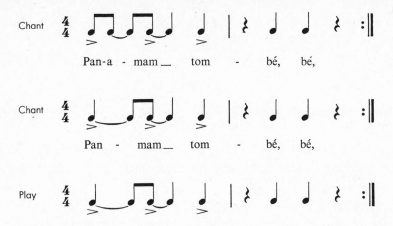

Add the claves and the cowbell to the percussion accompaniment and sing "Panamam Tombé" with the recording.

Now learn to play the autoharp accompaniment for "Panamam Tombé." Simulate the sound of a guitar by using short, quick strokes. Study the score to discover

* the home tone and the key of the song
* the letter names of the tonic (I) and dominant seventh (V_7) chords used in the autoharp accompaniment
* the chord pattern of each phrase (In which part of the song does the chord change occur at the end of the phrase only?)
* in which part of the song the autoharp accompaniment is easiest to play, and why

Play a simple introduction, such as $\frac{4}{4}$ 𝅗𝅥 𝅗𝅥 | 𝅗𝅥 𝅗𝅥 (F F F F), and sing "Panamam Tombé" with autoharp accompaniment.

PLANNING A PERFORMANCE

In a role much like that of a wandering minstrel in Old England, a Calypso singer in the West Indies improvises songs on almost any subject — from local gossip to contemporary news events. The songs are often humorous, sometimes satirical in character. The words are intriguing mixtures of French, Spanish, and English, the languages of the people who live on the Islands. The innovation of accenting certain syllables of words (syllables that are not usually accented) to accommodate the rhythm of the music is peculiar to Calypso singers.

"Panamam Tombé" *(My Hat Fell Off)* may have been improvised for a Calypso song contest during carnival time. Song contests are popular and are held frequently throughout the Islands.

To re-create "Panamam Tombé" as it might be performed in the West Indies, the class divides into groups of singers, percussionists, and autoharp players.

Use an autoharp introduction and accompaniment. This instrument will help to keep the singers in tune.

Background information is important if it leads to a more authentic style of performance.

To be interesting and effective, folk music must be interpreted in the spirit and style in which it was created.

43

The second part of the song may be sung by a solo voice or by a small group of singers.

Repeat the song so that each percussion instrument or combination of percussion instruments is used to full advantage.

Improvise an additional set of words for the second part of the song.

LISTENING TO ORCHESTRAL MUSIC

Listen to a recording of "Dansa brasileira" by the Brazilian composer Camargo Guarnieri to determine the specific musical quality that identifies this composition as Latin American.

The rhythmic scheme of "Dansa brasileira" is based on the rhythms of the samba, a popular dance of Brazil. A samba often includes a characteristic pattern of fast, even notes in the melody line.

Listen to the recording again and study the themes notated in illustration 5. Listen to determine

- in which theme a fast, even-note pattern occurs
- in which theme a syncopated pattern occurs
- the orchestral instrument that introduces each theme and contributes to the quality of excitement in the music
- where the two themes are played simultaneously in the composition

Illustration 5

(a)

(b)

Compare the rhythm patterns heard in "Dansa brasileira" with the rhythm pattern played in the percussion accompaniment of "Panamam Tombé." Study illustration 6 and identify the rhythm pattern played or heard

- on the maracas in "Panamam Tombé"
- on the claves in "Panamam Tombé"
- on the conga drum in "Panamam Tombé"
- on the cowbell in "Panamam Tombé"
- in the melody of the first theme of "Dansa brasileira"
- in the melody of the second theme of "Dansa brasileira"
- in the accompaniment in "Dansa brasileira"

Illustration 6

Practice playing the rhythm patterns in illustration 6 on the maracas, the claves, the bongo drums, the conga drum, and the cowbell; then play the patterns with the recording of "Dansa brasileira." If the rhythm pattern for the claves (illustration 6c) proves difficult to play, the class may practice it first without the tie (♩. ♪♩♩).

LESSON 10

TAFTA HINDI

1. Taf - ta Hin - di, Taf - ta Hin - di. Come and buy, oh,

la - dies___ fair. Shin - ing sat - in, love - ly lac - es,

Pea - cock feath - ers for your hair. Pea - cock feath - ers for___your___hair.

2. *Tafta Hindi, Tafta Hindi.*
   Dark eyes peek through silken veil.
   Finger waving, voices calling,
   "Bring inside your goods for sale."

3. *Tafta Hindi, Tafta Hindi.*
   Come and buy, oh little maid!
   "I want satin, I want laces,
   Mother, please buy rich brocade."

Arabic folk song.
Words by Louise Barker

BECOMING ACQUAINTED WITH THE MUSIC

Try to imitate the "musical sounds" of a particular country; these sounds are as characteristic of a culture as are the arts, crafts, clothes and homes of that culture.

Prepare to read the score of "Tafta Hindi" by learning to play
  • the first two measures of the song, to be used as an introduction, on the recorder (illustration 1) (The sound of the recorder will simulate the sound of the *arghool,* an Arabian wind instrument.)
  • the autoharp accompaniment (illustration 2) (Play the instrument with light, short strokes to imitate the sound of the *'ud,* an Arabian stringed instrument that was the forerunner of the European lute. Observe the signs that indicate the last four measures should be repeated.)

Illustration 1

Illustration 2

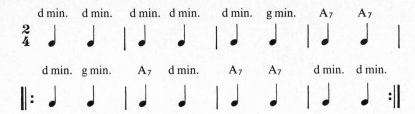

A few students may be chosen to play the recorder introduction and the auto-harp accompaniment while the rest of the class follows the score.

Listen for the beginning pitches of the song as they are played in the introduction.

Follow the contour of the melody line and listen carefully to hear the harmonic structure of the song as it is revealed in the accompaniment.

STUDYING THE SCORE

Study the score to discover the rhythmic figures used in the melody of "Tafta Hindi."

Notice that, for the most part, the melody moves in an even rhythm of eighth notes (♫ ♫).

Notice that the rhythmic figure appears twice in the melody:

Develop the skill of seeing rhythm patterns in the notation.

Illustration 3

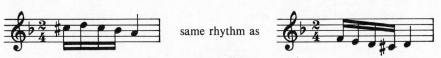

same rhythm as

Notice that the rhythmic figure appears twice in the melody:

Illustration 4

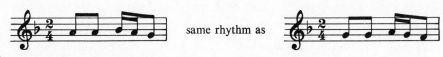

same rhythm as

 An important aspect of rhythm is the relationship among notes of different duration. The eighth note (♪) is equal to two sixteenth notes (♬).

$$♪ = ♪ + ♪ = ♫ = ♬$$

Chant the words of "Tafta Hindi" in rhythm.

Study the score again and notice that the notes in the melody move, for the most part, on repeated tones and in scale-wise progression. With the exception of measures 1 and 2, the first pitch of each measure is the same as, or very close to, the last pitch of the preceding measure.

Sing "Tafta Hindi" with the help of the recorder introduction (illustration 1) and the autoharp accompaniment (illustration 2).

Let the eye help the ear read the score by observing consecutive notes on the same pitch, notes that move in scale-wise progression, and consecutive notes that encompass larger intervals.

CREATING APPROPRIATE ACCOMPANIMENTS

The contrast between the relatively high pitch of the finger cymbals and the relatively low pitch of the drum creates an effect typical of Eastern music.

Create rhythm patterns to be played on the drum and the finger cymbals or learn the patterns below.

Illustration 5

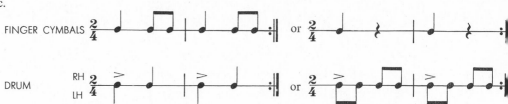

Irregular rhythms are characteristic of much Eastern music. Use regular patterns in accompaniments to this type of music only if irregular rhythms prove too difficult to master.

Combine the drum and finger cymbal patterns that best complement each other, then sing "Tafta Hindi" with the recorder introduction and the autoharp and percussion accompaniment.

Now study the drum patterns in illustration 6. Notice that eighth notes are used exclusively in both patterns.

In the first pattern, accent marks group the eighth notes into a regular rhythm.

In the second pattern, accent marks group the eighth notes into an irregular rhythm. Irregular rhythms are used frequently in the music of the East.

Illustration 6

Some students may be able to play the irregular rhythm pattern shown in illustration 6b. Those students may accompany "Tafta Hindi," using the drum pattern in illustration 7, which combines regular and irregular rhythm patterns.

Illustration 7

PLANNING A PERFORMANCE

It is possible that "Tafta Hindi" was first heard in a market place or a bazaar in Arabia.

To re-create the song as it might have been heard in its original setting, the class divides into groups of singers and instrumentalists.

Play a D-minor chord on the autoharp to give the beginning pitches.

Chant the first two measures of the song five or six times to imitate an Arab vendor calling attention to his wares.

Decide on the order in which the percussion instruments will be used.

Devise an instrumental interlude for recorder and drum and play this interlude between the verses of the song.

Create a coda for instruments or for voices. Which will be more effective?

Vary the dynamics of the introduction, the verse parts, the interludes, and the coda to enhance the dramatic intensity of each part.

GOING DEEPER INTO STRUCTURE

Sing "Tafta Hindi" with autoharp accompaniment. Pay particular attention to the melodic figure in the fourth measure of the song.

Sing the tonal pattern in illustration 8 several times, using the syllable "loo." Locate the pattern in "Tafta Hindi." This tonal pattern helps to identify the music as Eastern in origin.

Illustration 8

The exotic sound of Eastern music can be attributed in part to the scale upon which the music is based.

Study the scales in illustration 9. Notice that both scales start on the same pitch. Listen first as the scales are played on the piano or on the melody bells, then sing each scale on the syllable "loo."

Illustration 9

D - major scale   D harmonic minor scale

Discuss the difference between the sound of the D-major scale and the sound of the D harmonic minor scale. Upon which scale is "Tafta Hindi" based?

Sing the ascending and descending form of the D-major and D harmonic minor scales on "loo." Follow the structure of each scale (illustration 10) as it is sung. Notice the distribution of whole steps and half steps.

Illustration 10

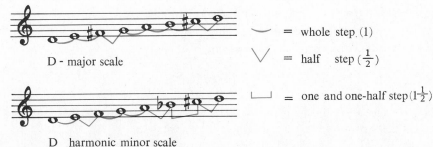

D - major scale

D harmonic minor scale

⌣ = whole step (1)

∨ = half step ($\frac{1}{2}$)

⊔ = one and one-half step ($1\frac{1}{2}$)

SCALE The interval of one and one-half steps between the sixth and seventh degrees is one of the identifying features of the **harmonic minor scale.**

49

Examining and playing a keyboard helps to clarify the concept of intervals in music. Illustration 11 shows a section of the keyboard from C to C (an octave). Study the piano keys to learn about whole steps and half steps.

The distance between any two keys with a single key between them is called a **whole step.**

The distance between two keys with no key between them is called a **half step.**

Illustration 11

The tonal pattern in illustration 12 consists of the upper four notes of a harmonic minor scale.

Illustration 12

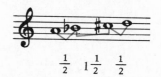

A short melody may be created by using the notes of the tonal pattern in illustration 12. Play the melody in illustration 13 on the piano or on the bells.

Illustration 13

The pattern of the upper four notes of a harmonic minor scale (half step, one and one-half steps, half step) may be played starting from any key on the keyboard. Play the pattern, starting from the following notes; then create melodies using the notes of the patterns that have been played.

Illustration 14

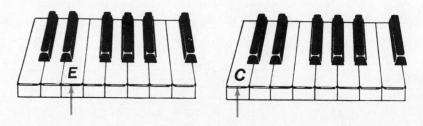

LISTENING TO ORCHESTRAL MUSIC

The Nutcracker Suite by Peter Ilyich Tchaikovsky tells an old Russian fairy tale in eight compositions, three of which suggest dances of different countries.

Listen to a recording of one of these compositions, "Arabian Dance," and discover how Tchaikovsky captures the sounds of the East. Compare this music with "Tafta Hindi" and describe its

- mode
- melody
- rhythm
- tone color
- tempo
- dynamics

When the listener discovers the music materials and ideas with which composers work, he shares with them the delight of creativity.

Listen to the brief introduction, played by violas and cellos. Observe that the pitches played make a simple design when shown in blank notation (illustration 15a). Compare it to the musical notation (illustration 15b).

Illustration 15

Use high- and low-pitched drums to imitate the sound of the violas and cellos and play along softly with the music.

Illustration 16

Compare class discoveries of the qualities that identify Eastern music with these general observations about "Arabian Dance":

The harmonic minor, G minor, contributes to the exotic sound of "Arabian Dance." Review the scale discovered in "Tafta Hindi."

Illustration 17

The interval of one and one-half steps between the sixth and seventh pitches is prevalent in Eastern melodies. Eastern melodies often make use of another interval of one and one-half steps between the third and fourth pitches (illustration 18). Tchaikovsky uses this interval in "Arabian Dance." Play the scale shown below and listen to its exotic effect.

Illustration 18

51

The mood of the music is often changed when the structure of a scale is varied.

The short five-note trill heard in "Arabian Dance" is typical of Oriental music.

A **trill** is the rapid alternation of a tone and its upper neighbor.

The persistently repeated rhythm pattern **(ostinato)** in the accompaniment provides a hypnotic effect.

The muted strings, oboe, and tambourine contribute instrumental color typical of Eastern music.

Follow the score of the two themes:

Illustration 19

(a)

(b)

Observe that the characteristics of the melody that contribute to the languorous and exotic mood of the music are the
- limited range and simple scale-wise patterns
- flowing movement, indicated by a legato sign (‿‿‿‿), gently interrupted by a lift or pause, indicated by the staccato sign (•).

The sign for legato (‿‿‿‿) indicates that the music is to be performed in a smooth, flowing manner. The sign for staccato (•) indicates that the music is to be performed in a crisp, detached manner.

LESSON 11

THE MAN ON THE FLYING TRAPEZE

He'd fly through the air with the great-est of ease,

This dar-ing young man on the fly-ing tra-peze,

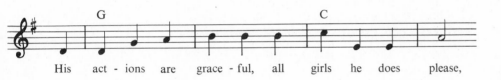

His act-ions are grace-ful, all girls he does please,

And my love he has sto-len a - way. _____

Traditional American song

BECOMING ACQUAINTED WITH THE MUSIC

Sing "The Man on the Flying Trapeze" to discover
- how the rhythm of the song expresses the swinging of the trapeze
- how the contour of the melody depicts the movements of the trapeze artist

Look for the drama of a song in its rhythm and melodic line as well as in its words.

 RHYTHM The rhythmic movement of a song often describes the activity told about in the text.

 MELODY The rise and fall of a melodic line is a musical means of expressing dramatic tension and release.

53

MOVING TO MUSIC

Appropriate bodily movement deepens understanding of rhythm and provides variety in musical activities.

While singing this song to an autoharp accompaniment, use large arm and body movements to imitate the rhythmic motion of the trapeze artist.

Illustration 1 shows how these sweeping motions are reflected in the contour of the melody. How does the melody suggest that the trapeze hesitates briefly before beginning its downward swing? What notation pattern creates these hesitations?

It is important to feel the rhythmic swing of a song before picking out the particular note patterns that characterize its musical idea.

Illustration 1

RHYTHM A feeling of hesitation is created by placing a short note after a long one (and ♩. ♪), increasing the variety and rhythmic interest of the music.

SYMBOLS A dot after a note increases the length of that note by half its original value (♩. = ♩ + ♩ and ♩. = ♩ + ♪).

Sing "The Man on the Flying Trapeze," giving special attention to reading correctly the notes of longer duration (♩ and ♩.). Observe how correct interpretation of note values enhances the effect of the song.

CREATING APPROPRIATE ACCOMPANIMENTS

Recall the clues that indicate in what key a song is written, then determine the key of "The Man on the Flying Trapeze."

On what pitch does the song end?

On what chord does the song end?

This accompaniment uses the three **primary chords** (I, IV, V_7) of the key of G — G, C, D_7. Find them on the autoharp.

Intellectual understanding of harmonic progression follows and reinforces aural experience.

Study the harmonic progression in this song. Observe that the chord progression of the last two phrases is like that of the first two. Accompany "The Man on the Flying Trapeze," strumming once for each measure.

HARMONY The chord progression IV to V_7 creates a strong feeling of forward movement.

Learn to create and perform song introductions with taste and skill.

Use a keyboard instrument (piano, melody or resonator bells) with the autoharp to create the introduction in illustration 2. Describe the melodic and rhythmic movement of this introduction.

Illustration 2

One ——— two ——— read - y sing He'd

The calliope is often heard at circuses and fairs. This instrument consists of steam-blown whistles (played from a keyboard). To simulate the sound of the calliope, divide into three groups, using recorders to play the three-part accompaniment shown below.

Taste in music develops with the realization that songs should be performed only in appropriate musical settings.

Illustration 3

SINGING IN HARMONY

"The Man on the Flying Trapeze" is popular with barbershop quartets. Use a keyboard instrument or the recorder to learn the simple barbershop harmony in illustration 4.

How many different pitches are there in the top staff of the score?

How many different pitches are there in the bottom staff of the score?

Observe the sharp-sign (♯) in the key signature and the natural-sign (♮) in the bottom staff.

A sense of musical style develops with the realization that songs should be performed in traditionally correct ways.

 A sharp-sign (♯) is the music symbol that raises a pitch by a half step, the smallest interval normally used in Western music.

 A natural-sign (♮) is a symbol used to cancel a sharp or a flat. Naturals, sharps, and flats are often used to add color to melody lines and harmony.

Word definitions of musical symbols should follow, not precede, aural experience with musical sounds.

Illustration 4

PLANNING A PERFORMANCE

Create a production number by performing various interpretations of "The Man on the Flying Trapeze" in sequence.

Decide on an effective introduction.

Set the stage by singing the song in unison with autoharp accompaniment.

Class members who are interested in interpretive dance may dramatize a trapeze act while the "spectators" sing and sway to the music.

Sing the barbershop arrangement with autoharp accompaniment.

Play the three-part accompaniment for recorder, adding bells or piano to emphasize the melody.

Create vocal or instrumental interludes and an appropriate coda.

Skills and knowledge are necessary to a musical performance, but they are not substitutes for imaginative interpretation.

GOING DEEPER INTO STRUCTURE

The pattern of a major scale remains the same no matter which pitch is the tonic. "The Man on the Flying Trapeze" is written in the key of G major — its melody notes are those of the G-major scale.

Experiment with the scale in illustration 5 to discover which pitch must be changed to fit the pattern of the G-major scale.

Play the scale and decide which pitch sounds wrong.

Play the scale again, correcting the one wrong note.

Illustration 5

Examine the ladder picture of the G-major scale in illustration 6. It is easy to see that the F must be raised (sharped) to create the half step between the seventh and eighth pitches.

Illustration 6

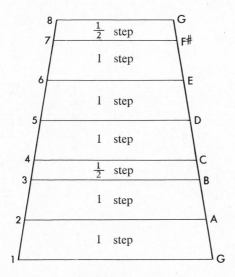

SYMBOLS A short cut in musical notation is the use of the necessary sharps or flats in a key signature at the beginning of the score

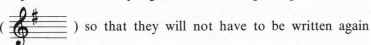) so that they will not have to be written again

every time they are needed in the music.

It is aural and intellectual understanding, not memorization of key signatures, that is meaningful and practical.

CIRCUS PARADE

1. Oh, here comes the cir - cus band,
2. Oh, here come the el - e - phants,
3. Oh, here come the mer - ry clowns,

Ta - ra - ra - ra, ta - ra - ra - ra - ra,
Clump, clump - ta - ra, clump, clump - ta - ra - ra,
Ha - ha - ta - ra, ha - ha - ta - ra - ra,

Here comes the cir - cus band,
Here come the el - e - phants,
Here come the mer - ry clowns,

Ta - ra - ra - ra - ra - ra - ra!
Clump, clump - ta - ra - ra - ra.
Ha - ha - ta - ra - ra - ra.

Refrain

Zing! Zing! _____ Zing! Zing! _____

Ta - ra - ra - ra, Ta - ra - ra.

Oh, how much I love the cir - cus, Ta - ra - ra! Boom! Boom!

4. Oh, here comes the dancing bear,
   Thump, thump-ta-ra, thump, thump-ta-ra,
   Here comes the dancing bear,
   Thump, thump-ta-ra-ra-ra.

5. We're off to the circus now,
   Hooray, ta-ra, hooray-ta-ra,
   We're off to the circus now,
   Hooray, ta-ra-ra-ra.

Words and music by Milton Kaye

58

BECOMING ACQUAINTED WITH THE MUSIC

A particular kind of music can often be identified through the sound produced by the musical instruments used in the orchestration. Listen to the recording of "Circus Parade" to discover the musical sounds and effects that give the music a distinctive quality.

What orchestral instruments are used?

What family of instruments (woodwind, string, brass, or percussion) is *not* heard in this music?

How do the tempo and rhythm contribute to the descriptive qualities of the music?

What melody pattern within the song is typical of band music in general?

Sing the first and last verses of the song with the recording. Decide what available percussion instruments may be used to simulate the sound of the band. Which would be most effective for the words "Zing! Zing!" of the refrain — drums, large cymbals, or rhythm sticks?

Dramatic instrumental tone color captures the attention of the listener because he can respond physically and emotionally to the sound.

Only one or two listening suggestions should be made when a recording is played for the first time. A second hearing will lead to clarification and further discovery.

A band song calls for band instruments.

CREATING APPROPRIATE ACCOMPANIMENTS

Sing the first and last verses again with the recording, playing the big cymbals on the "Zing! Zing!" of the refrain. The tone color of this instrument approximates the sound of the words.

TONE COLOR Percussion instruments, such as the cymbals, are dramatic in tone color and, like spice, are more effective when used sparingly. They add excitement to climactic points in the music.

The recognition of simple, traditional uses of tone color is a basis for understanding the more sophisticated use of tone color in the symphony orchestra.

Experiment with drums to create rhythm patterns that point up the decisive march rhythm of the music.

Decide whether a large drum, used to simulate the bass drum of a band, is more effective played on the strong beats only or played on every beat of the music.

Decide whether the small drums, simulating the snare drums of a band, are more effective played on every beat or played in another, more intricate rhythm.

Create drum rhythms while singing the song with the recording. Then compare these rhythms with the typical drum rhythms shown below.

The experience of creating rhythm patterns is both satisfying and worthwhile. Identifying and reading rhythm patterns are steps toward learning to interpret a score.

Illustration 1

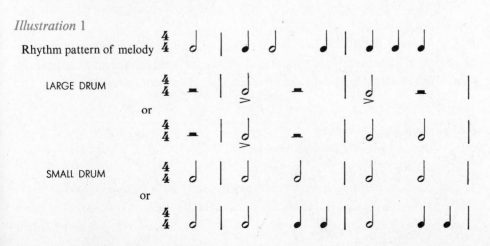

59

The in the score is a rest sign and is equal to the half note (♩). It is called a **half rest.**

From the rhythm patterns in illustration 1 or from one of those created by the class, choose the drum accompaniments most effective for "Circus Parade." A few students may play the drum and cymbal accompaniments while the rest of the class sings the song with the recording.

Now sing all the verses of the song without the recording. Discover aurally and visually the short, easy-to-play melody pattern that could be performed on the melody bells to simulate the sound of the glockenspiel.

Look for the dramatic high point of a song and learn to make the most effective use of it.

On the melody bells, practice the short downward-moving scale pattern (illustration 2) found in the refrain and combine it with the cymbal accompaniment.

Sing the refrain without the recording, playing the cymbals and melody bells as an accompaniment. Listen for the colorful effect created by these instruments.

Illustration 2

Learn the autoharp accompaniment.

Remember the visual clues on the score that indicate the key and decide in what key the song is written.

On the autoharp, locate the chords used in the accompaniment.

Devise an introduction on the autoharp, such as the one in illustration 3, that will set the tempo, suggest the mood, and establish the key of the song.

Illustration 3

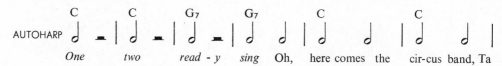

Experiment to determine why one strum to the measure is more effective than two strums to the measure.

Meaningful repetition is needed in a lesson, especially when a song has many phrases or verses.

Sing "Circus Parade" with autoharp, melody bell, cymbal, and drum accompaniment. Take turns practicing and playing the various instrumental accompaniments. Learn all the verses of the song during this practice session.

Music and drama are a natural combination. The song that moves in a strong rhythm and tells a colorful story lends itself especially well to meaningful dramatization and enlivened musical performance.

PLANNING A PERFORMANCE

Plan a circus parade.

The class divides into instrumentalists, circus performers, and vocalists.

Decide who will play drums, cymbals, and melody bells in the marching band. Choose a bandmaster.

Students who will play autoharp accompaniments and those who sing the five verses should stay in their seats. It is difficult to perform and sing at the same time, except perhaps on the simple refrain.

Students who will interpret circus animals and clowns must decide what movements they will use in their acts.

Learn the new introduction in illustration 4 on melody bells and autoharp. Observe how the introduction emphasizes the vigorous quality of the song. This pattern can also be used effectively as an interlude between each verse. Such interludes give singers and performers a chance to catch their breath.

Illustration 4

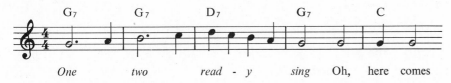

Decide on a different activity for each verse. Consider these ideas in re-creating the circus parade:

First verse: A grand march around the classroom by the circus band (drums, cymbals, melody bells). The band should finish its march in front of the room and form a background for the circus acts that follow.

Second verse: Performance of the elephants. Their slow, cumbersome movements make a sharp contrast to the brisk march rhythm of the band.

Third verse: Performance of the merry clowns. The lively, comical antics of the clowns are in contrast, both in tempo and in mood, to the band and the elephants. Tambourines would add color to the clown act.

Fourth verse: Solo act of a dancing bear. This would give an imaginative student interested in interpretive dance an opportunity to experiment with angular, awkward movements.

Fifth verse: Grand finale. The circus band might lead the retinue of animals and clowns, each moving in his own style, in a grand march around the classroom.

GOING DEEPER INTO STRUCTURE

Study the varied rhythmic ideas used in the song.

Sing the uneven rhythmic figure used on the "Ta-ra-ra-ra" of the verse, then sing the same melody written in an even rhythm. Both are shown in illustration 5. Compare the effect of the two rhythmic figures.

Illustration 5

Dotted rhythms break up the smooth flow of a rhythm pattern and bring points of tension to the music.

Compare the two measures shown in illustration 6. Notice that in the first example the emphasis is placed on the second beat of the measure, creating a syncopated rhythm.

Illustration 6

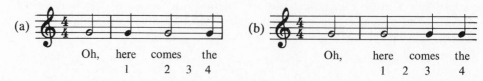

Study the especially colorful points in the melody.

Compare the two melodic figures in illustration 7 by singing them or playing them on the melody bells. Notice that the first melodic figure has an F-sharp (♯), while the second figure has an F-natural (♮). What is the difference in the sound of these two melodic figures?

Illustration 7

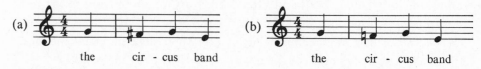

Sharps (♯), flats (♭), and naturals (♮) that do not belong to a prevailing key are called **accidentals.** They are used to color or embellish a melody or harmony line.

Sing and compare the two phrases shown in illustration 8. Why is the phrase used to conclude "Circus Parade" more effective than the alternate shown here? Point out the accidental.

Illustration 8

Final phrase

Alternate phrase

LESSON 13

CIRCUS MUSIC

Listen to a recording of "Circus Music" from *The Red Pony* by Aaron Copland for another musical interpretation of the circus. How many circus sounds and rhythms are suggested in the music? How do these sounds and rhythms compare with those in "Circus Parade"?

One approach to program music is to listen for the sounds and rhythms that reveal the subject told about in the music.

LISTENING TO ORCHESTRAL MUSIC

Imagine that the class has been asked to create an accompaniment for "Circus Music" with classroom percussion instruments. Listen to the recording again to discover circus sounds and rhythms unnoticed in the first hearing and to decide on percussion instruments that might be appropriate to the different parts of the music. Why is it easy to determine that the music has three sections?

Before making final decisions on percussion accompaniment, listen to the recording again and study the themes in illustration 1. Follow the themes on a chart or chalkboard as the teacher points out the notes. What can be discovered about each theme?

Illustration 1

Students need opportunities to hear music and to see its notation on the score at the same time.

Section A

Section B, Theme 1

Section B, Theme 2

While the recording is played again, follow these listening guides and compare them with class discoveries:

Band instruments — woodwinds, brass, and percussion — are used throughout.

In *Section A,* the music is in $\frac{3}{4}$ meter, with an underlying "oom-pah-pah" accompaniment. Notice that sometimes the accent falls on the third beat instead of the first, giving the music a humorous, slightly unstable quality. Listen for dissonance in the harmony and for awkward interruptions in the struggling melody line. The over-all effect is of an out-of-tune (perhaps out-of-practice!) circus band.

HARMONY **Consonance** and **dissonance** are two basic elements of harmony in music. Consonance gives a feeling of repose, while dissonance creates a feeling of disturbance and restless activity. The more dissonance used, the higher the tension and conflict in the music.

Knowledge and understanding of music grows with the ability to recognize the contrasts and similarities in the sections of a musical composition.

In *Section B, Theme 1,* listen for the high, fluttering sound of the woodwinds and the agitated, uneven movement of the melody line. There is frequent repetition and rapid twisting and turning in the melody.

In *Section B, Theme 2,* listen for the sprightly tune played down and up a pentatonic scale.

The third part of the music is a repetition of *Section A.*

CREATING APPROPRIATE ACCOMPANIMENTS

Adding appropriate percussion accompaniments to recorded music is a meaningful way to increase skill in performance and to become more sensitive to instrumental tone color and rhythmic effects. But playing inappropriate instruments for the sake of teaching names of instruments or note values should never be encouraged.

Decide what percussion instruments would make an appropriate accompaniment to the recording of "Circus Music." In creating these accompaniments, keep in mind the special qualities discovered in each of the three themes.

In *Section A,* for example, an "oom-pah-pah" accompaniment on small and large drums might be used.

Illustration 2

A loud clapping sound, which might be produced by striking a wood block with a rhythm stick, can be used to mark the end of phrases and unexpected accents.

Between *Section A* and *Section B,* there is a pause followed by loud chords, which suggests that another and different kind of act is about to take place. Use a large drum and large cymbals to work out a pattern to play at this point.

In *Section B, Theme 1,* try using triangles on each accented beat and finger cymbals for jingling effects.

In *Section B, Theme 2,* experiment with tambourines on each accented beat and with jingle bells throughout.

Between *Section B* and the repeat of *Section A,* use the same pattern as before on the loud chords.

Make final decisions on the percussion instruments and rhythms to be played and use them as an accompaniment for Copland's music.

Students become more discriminating in their use of percussion instruments and rhythm patterns when they understand the structure of a composition.

PLANNING A PERFORMANCE

"Circus Music" is a part of the music Aaron Copland wrote for *The Red Pony,* a movie based on a novel by John Steinbeck. The plot centers around a little boy named Jody, whose father gave him a red pony. Besides his real-life experiences, Jody enjoyed a dream world in which he and his pony Gabilan shared many marvelous adventures — one of them in a circus. "Circus Music" was written for that scene in the movie and later became a part of a suite for children.

Plan a circus act that could be used in a classroom.

A ringmaster is chosen to direct the act, and the rest of the class is divided into ponies and musicians.

Remembering various trained-pony acts, decide on a set of movements appropriate to the comparatively slow tempo of *Section A.* Create a floor pattern for these movements, using a large circle and a figure eight.

Decide on another set of movements for the music in *Section B.* Smaller movements and a correspondingly smaller floor pattern are more appropriate for this music.

Repeat the movements and floor pattern of *Section A* when the section is repeated.

The ringmaster and ponies take bows on the loud chords heard between sections.

After the dramatization has been decided upon and practiced, add the percussion accompaniments to the circus pony act.

Under the guidance of a skillful teacher, the creative imagination of children can turn descriptive rhythmic movements into a meaningful artistic performance.

LESSON 14

RIDING ON AN ELEPHANT

I'm rid - ing on_____ an el - e - phant,

So high!_____ so high!_____

I'm rid - ing on_____ an el - e - phant,

Oh, I am up so high!_____

French folk song

By permission of Folkways Records & Service Corp.

PREPARING TO TEACH THE SONG TO GRADE TWO*

"Riding on an Elephant" is a good song to teach to Grade Two. Children quickly become involved in the words and music, and they can easily identify its obvious musical characteristics.

Grow familiar with the rhythmic movement of the song by practicing on the drum the slow, swaying rhythm (of an elephant walking), illustration 1. Think of the unfamiliar $\frac{6}{4}$ meter as being two measures of $\frac{3}{4}$ meter.

Illustration 1

1 2 3   4 5 6   1 2 3   4 5 6

---

*This is the first of a number of lessons designed to acquaint the student with techniques of teaching music at specific levels in the elementary school. The college class plays the roles of both teacher and children and participates fully in the activities of the lesson. Each of the sentences in quotation marks serves the dual purpose of suggesting both the teacher's comments to an elementary-school group and a learning experience for the college class.

Keeping in mind the $\frac{6}{4}$ meter, study the rhythm pattern of the melody. Observe that the drum pattern in illustration 1 appears in several places in the melody.

Be careful to distinguish between a curved line over two notes of the same pitch (♪), which is a tie (studied in "Barcarolle," Lesson 5) and a curved line over two notes of different pitches (♪), which is a slur.

SYMBOLS A curved line over or under two or more notes of *different* pitches is a **slur.** It indicates that the notes connected by it should be played or sung as smoothly as possible. In a vocal score, a slur indicates that two or more notes are sung on the same word or syllable.

Study the contour of the melody. The patterns will be easy to learn on a keyboard instrument. On the score, locate the large intervals shown in illustration 2 and practice them.

Illustration 2

Obtain recordings of Anatol Liadov's "Dance of the Mosquito" and Camille Saint-Saëns' "The Elephant" from *Carnival of the Animals*. Listen to the music and be prepared to answer the questions asked later in the lesson script. (For help on "Dance of the Mosquito," refer to Lesson 17.)

Obtain pictures of a violin, bass viol, trumpet, and clarinet.

Identify the ABA form in "The Elephant."

TEACHING THE SONG TO GRADE TWO

Before presenting a song, remember to plan the music lesson carefully. A well-organized teacher can create the warm, relaxed atmosphere so necessary for a successful lesson. Following are suggestions for presenting "Riding on an Elephant" to a second-grade class.

Introduce this song through its most obvious characteristics — the slow tempo, swaying rhythm, and heavy accents descriptive of an elephant. Help the children to recognize these characteristics in the drum pattern.

A beginning song repertory should be composed largely of songs closely related to the child's experiences, actual or vicarious.

> "My drum is going to tell you what circus animal plays a big part
> in our music lesson. Listen and guess which one it is."

Play the drum accompaniment slowly (illustration 1), heavily accenting the first beat of each measure.

> "How did the drum help you decide which animal is told about?"

Although children should hear a song several times in order to learn it, do not discourage the child who joins in quickly.

Teach the song by singing it several times. Suggest an appropriate activity or make an attention-getting request with each repetition. Children develop the habit of listening attentively if a teacher takes advantage of their natural curiosity by asking pertinent questions or by suggesting activities that result in appropriate responses.

"Johnny may play the slow, heavy sound on the drum while I sing the song. You will discover in the words which animal the drum tells about."

"As I sing the song again, pretend that you are sitting on the elephant's back. The slow, heavy drum rhythm tells how the elephant moves. Show how you would move when the elephant walks."

"Now sing along with me when you can and discover how the melody tells that the elephant is very tall."

Every well-planned lesson should include purposeful repetition.

Before the children attempt more difficult instrumental accompaniments, devise interesting and worthwhile practice sessions that give them a chance to become familiar with the song.

"Sing along with me and show with your hands the highest part of the melody."

"As we sing the song again, discover which part of the song is sung two times."

Children become aware of tone color when they are guided in selecting appropriate instruments for "making music."

Help the children to develop musical taste by guiding them in choosing instrumental sounds appropriate for the elephant song.

"In countries where people ride in chairs fastened on top of elephants' backs, the elephant wears little bells for decoration. Decide which of these percussion instruments sounds most like the elephant bells."

Play the rhythm sticks, tambourine, and finger cymbals — one at a time.

Ideas for a more vivid interpretation of a song add interest to the music lesson.

"While we continue to practice the song, Ann will add the sound of elephant bells by playing the finger cymbals with drum accompaniment."

Help children develop sensitivity to the musical effects that can be created by the ascending and by the descending melody line.

A well-planned lesson will provide experiences in which children become aware of the melodic movement of the music.

"We can use the melody bells for a 'musical ladder' to climb up on the elephant's back before we sing the song. Listen while I play this introduction and discover how the music shows we are climbing up."

Play the melody bells from middle C to the C above (illustration 3), holding the instrument in a vertical position.

Illustration 3

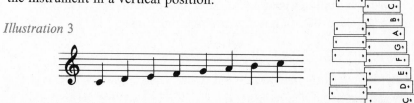

"Look and listen while I draw this 'musical ladder' on the chalkboard. Show with your hands its upward movement."

On the chalkboard, draw a scale pattern in blank notation as the class sings the
scale.

Illustration 4

‾C ‾D ‾E ‾F ‾G ‾A ‾B ‾C

"Jimmy wants to play the 'musical ladder' on the melody bells.
After this introduction, we will sing the song with the drum and finger cymbal accompaniment."

Point out to the children that playing the melody bells downward from C to
C would make a good ending (coda) for the song. Let them use it in performing
the song.

"How can the melody bells show that we get down from the elephant's back after we have sung the song?"

Give children the pleasure of "making music" by letting them sing "Riding
on an Elephant" many times with instrumental introduction, accompaniment,
and coda. Children never tire of taking turns playing the different instruments
and participating in the various activities.

"Now we can put together all the sounds and activities discovered
for 'Riding on an Elephant.'"
"David may play the bell introduction."
"Johnny may play the drum — the sound and rhythm of the ele-
phant's walk."
"Ann may play the finger cymbals — the sound of the elephant's
bell."
"Steve may play the bell coda."
"Everyone can pretend he is riding on an elephant and rock back
and forth as the animal sways from side to side."
"Anyone who wishes may pretend he is an elephant and move to
the music while we sing."

Encourage children to tell in their own words their reactions to, and discoveries of, the musical experience. Some children may discover such musical
characteristics as slow tempo, swaying rhythm, contrasting tone colors of heavy
drum and light finger cymbals, the high point in the melody, and the special effect created by the ascending and descending melodic pattern played on the
melody bells.

"What did you hear or do in the music lesson that you think best
describes the elephant ride?"
"How did we make the music more like a song about an elephant
ride?"
"How did the music describe the elephant?"
"How did the introduction and coda, both played on the melody
bells, make the ride more real?"

When a child performs in front of his classmates, give him the support he needs. Avoid situations that could result in failure or embarrassment.

Through practice, each child must be given the opportunity to play with confidence the part of the performance for which he is responsible.

Evaluate the success of a musical experience by studying children's personal reactions to the music and their responses to questions about the musical activities. Consider these reactions and responses in planning further musical experiences.

Each activity should be extended beyond the immediate experience into periods of individual or group experimentation and exploration.

Chart (or write on the chalkboard) in blank notation the introduction and coda played on melody bells.

Illustration 5

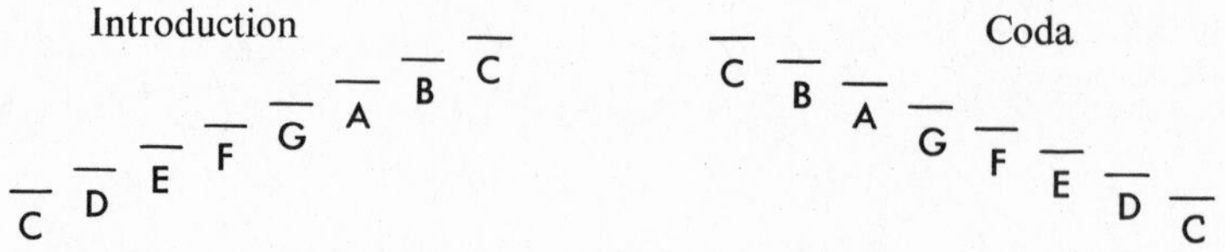

Introduction   Coda

C D E F G A B C   C B A G F E D C

"We will put this chart above the music table, and everyone who wishes may practice the introduction and coda on the melody bells.

"David and Steve will help you learn these patterns."

PRESENTING ORCHESTRAL MUSIC TO GRADE TWO

Listening to orchestral music that can be related to a song lesson is not only an enjoyable experience for a second-grade class but reinforces the discoveries of the lesson. Select recordings that are appropriate in length, interest, and content for children. Two such recordings are "The Elephant" from *Carnival of the Animals* and "Dance of the Mosquito."

A child's interest in orchestral music is stimulated when it is related to a recent experience.

"Yesterday we discovered musical sounds that describe an elephant. Today we will hear parts of two compositions, played by an orchestra, and decide which one was composed to describe an elephant."

Encourage a discussion of the contrasts between "The Elephant" and "Dance of the Mosquito."

The general qualities of music are best perceived by children in two sharply contrasting pieces of music.

"Which composition is low; high? light; heavy? sprightly; clumsy? fast; slow? Which of these words describe an elephant?"

Ask the children to identify the instrument that effects the sound of the elephant's movements.

Children enjoy and understand music best when they become involved in it.

"Here are pictures of four instruments — the violin, trumpet, bass viol, and clarinet. As you listen again to "The Elephant," discover which one of the instruments plays the melody and gives the music a low sound."

After children have identified the general qualities of a piece of music, help them discover the sounds that create these qualities.

Because of the tempo and form (ABA) of the music, this song provides opportunity for rhythmic activity.

"Remember some of the tricks that elephants can do and plan an elephant circus act. Elephants often perform in a ring. When the bass viol plays solo, or alone, one 'elephant' can make up a solo act."

LESSON 15

THIS IS HALLOWEEN

1. One lit - tle skel - e - ton hop - ping up and down,
2. Two lit - tle witch - es fly - ing through the air,

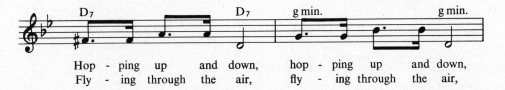

Hop - ping up and down, hop - ping up and down,
Fly - ing through the air, fly - ing through the air,

One lit - tle skel - e - ton hop - ping up and down,
Two lit - tle witch - es fly - ing through the air,

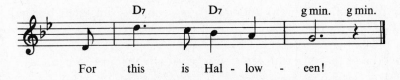

For this is Hal - low - een!

3. Three little pumpkins walking in a row,

4. Four little goblins skipping down the street,

5. Five little children playing trick or treat,

Words and music by Lucille Wood

TEACHING THE SONG TO THE KINDERGARTEN

Halloween is always an exciting time for children, and there are many songs for this occasion. This lesson shows how one such song, "This Is Halloween," might be presented to a Kindergarten class.

Take advantage of the repetition provided by a song with five verses and sing them all.

"Who are some of the make-believe people of Halloween?"
"Which ones do you hear about in this song?"

Little children will naturally join in the singing when they are ready.

Encourage children to join in on the repeated phrases. Children are more attentive while listening to and learning a song when they can sing a part of it almost immediately. The last line of a song is the part that children often learn most quickly.

"There are many verses, and some of you sang the last line of each verse with me. Let us sing it together":

Illustration 1

For this is Hal - low - een!

Kindergarten children can learn to identify and demonstrate the up-and-down movement of melody.

"Did the tune go up or down?"
"Sing it again and show with your hand how it goes."

Kindergarten children learn songs by hearing them many times. Rhythmic activities may be used to make the repeated hearings more interesting and to facilitate learning the song.

The first suggestion to young children for adding dramatization or rhythmic movement to a song should be a casual invitation.

"While we sing the song this time, decide whether you would like to be a skeleton, a witch, a pumpkin, a goblin, or a trick-or-treater."

Organize rhythmic movement by following the sequence suggested by the words of the song.

Some children feel more secure when their rhythmic activities are guided.

"The words of the song will tell you when it is your turn to hop, fly, walk, skip, or play trick or treat."

Take advantage of the drama in this song to inspire children to create the most descriptive movements possible.

Encourage children to be the best of whatever they decide to be.

"I saw witches who flew very high, goblins who were ugly and awkward, and pumpkins that were round. Who would like to describe what the children were doing to look like real witches?"

On another day Let the children organize a dramatization based on the text of each verse. Add a percussion accompaniment that will suggest the sound of each character.

As children select percussion instruments to provide sound effects, they will learn to discriminate between sounds that are high or low, long or short, swishing or clicking, ringing or jingling.

"While Tom is hopping like a skeleton, Mary may find and play an instrument that she thinks will sound like a skeleton hopping."

"Why was the sound that the sand blocks made a good sound for the witches flying? Was it a long or short sound? soft or loud?"

This song has been learned as a Kindergarten class might have learned it. But before planning the lesson, the teacher should know the musical characteristics that give the song its Halloween-like mood. Study the score for clues. Look for

- indications of the mode
- the over-all contour of the melody
- patterns in the melody, rhythm, form, and harmony

The ability to interpret a score will increase as the student develops the habit of observing musical characteristics in notation.

Compare class discoveries with these observations:

The last note and chord of the song indicate that the song is in the minor mode, as are many Halloween songs.

The contour of the melody is angular.

The melody has an up-and-down pattern made up of notes that move chord-wise.

Discovering patterns in music provides a short cut to learning.

The rhythm has an uneven pattern (♩. ♪ ♩. ♪). This dotted rhythm usually indicates a vigorous movement in the melody.

The form is ABAC.

The harmony is based on the G-minor and D₇ chords. The phrase-wise pattern is

Phrase A:	G minor	G minor	D₇	D₇
Phrase B:	D₇	D₇	G minor	G minor
Phrase A:	G minor	G minor	D₇	D₇
Phrase C:	D₇	D₇	G minor	G minor

Patterns in music should be experienced and identified before they are analyzed.

GOING DEEPER INTO STRUCTURE

Minor Mode   When determining the key of a song, remember that every key signature may indicate either a minor key or its relative major. The last note and chord of this song suggests that the song is in the key of G minor. However, the key signature of G minor (𝄞♭♭) is also that of the relative B-flat major.

Illustration 2

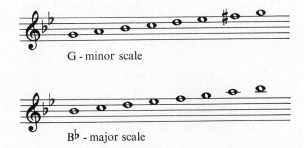

G - minor scale

B♭ - major scale

Melody   Observe in illustration 3 that the angular melody line of the first three phrases is built on the notes of the two chords played on the autoharp.

73

Illustration 3

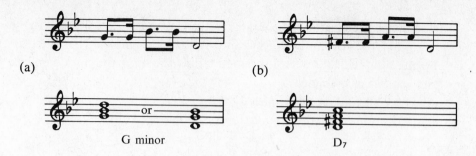

(a)　　　　　　　　　　　　　(b)

G minor　　　　　　　　　　　D₇

Play the G-minor chord on the autoharp and listen to the sound.

Sing one pitch that is heard in the chord, then listen and sing the other two pitches in the chord.

Play and sing the pitches of the D₇ chord.

Compare the melody of the first three phrases with the melody of the last phrase.

Learn to sing major and minor tonic chords as an aid in establishing a feeling for the key and tonality of an unfamiliar song.

MELODY The notes of a melody can move in three ways — scale-wise, chord-wise, and on repeated tones.

To capture the spirit of a song accurately, interpret the notation precisely.

Rhythm The uneven rhythm is notated as dotted eighths followed by sixteenths ( ). The sixteenth note in such a pattern should be short and incisive.

RHYTHM The dot after the eighth note increases its value by half ( ).

Pretend that every uneven dotted rhythm ( ) in this song is an even rhythm ( ) and sing the first phrase. Compare the effect.

Notice that the vigor of the song is lessened when the even rhythm pattern is sung in the melody.

Harmony In the autoharp accompaniment, the G-minor chord is built on the tonic (G) and the D₇ chord is built on the dominant (D).

Illustration 4

G minor　　　　　　D₇

74

LESSON 16

BEA

WITCHES' DANCE

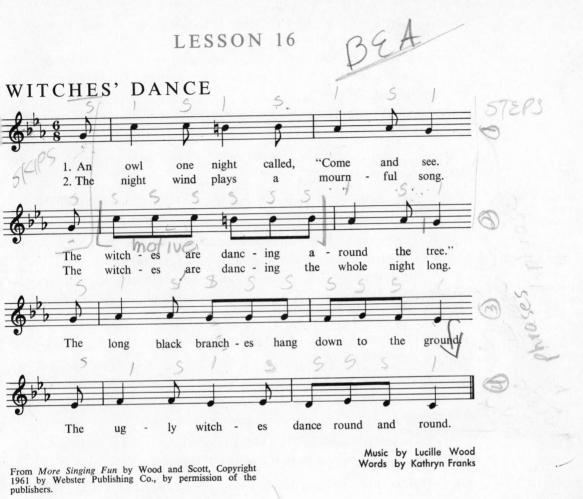

1. An owl one night called, "Come and see.
2. The night wind plays a mourn - ful song.

The witch - es are danc - ing a - round the tree."
The witch - es are danc - ing the whole night long.

The long black branch - es hang down to the ground

The ug - ly witch - es dance round and round.

Music by Lucille Wood
Words by Kathryn Franks

TEACHING THE SONG TO GRADE THREE

Another song for Halloween, "Witches' Dance," is presented here as it might be taught to a third-grade class.

Sing the song slowly for the class with an air of suspense and with the spooky quality of the make-believe world.

> "Listen for words that describe a mysterious sight or sound of Halloween."

A good technique for teaching the words of a song is to relate children's responses to phrases in songs. For example, if a child says, "There is an owl in the song," the teacher might reply with the line; "An owl one night called, 'Come and see.' " She should then invite the children to repeat the phrase.

After the words of the song have been discussed and are understood, focus attention on the melody.

> "Listen to the melody this time and describe the sounds that re-mind you of Halloween."

A poem, picture, story, or darkened room can heighten the mood and dramatic appeal of a song.

Take advantage of information that a child who has had instrumental lessons can contribute to the class.

Children should learn to hear and name the difference between major and minor chords before they learn *why* the chords sound different.

"Your words — 'weird,' 'creepy,' 'strange' — are descriptive and colorful. Andy [who takes piano lessons] says that the song has a minor sound. Perhaps you can hear this minor sound on the autoharp. Listen to these chords [G minor and G major] and guess which one has the minor sound."

"Think of words to describe the difference in the major and minor sound."

Help the children discover that the melody moves on a downward-scale line (notes "close together").

A visual image of a melody quickens learning and memorization.

"Sing along when you can and discover how the shape of the melody suggests the sound and movement of the wind."

"Design the melody with your hand as you sing."

Give children reasons for developing good singing habits.

The techniques of correct breathing should be considered as a means to expressive interpretation of a song, never as ends in themselves. Constant repetition of "sit tall" or "breathe deeply" is boring to children.

"What do we need to remember about singing habits that will help us sing each phrase with the long, unbroken sound of the mournful wind?"

Invite the children to join in on the repeated or easier phrases and help them learn the more difficult ones.

Although a song should be presented as an expressive whole, drill on difficult parts is effective when children recognize the need for it.

"You sang the first two phrases well. The third was more difficult. Let us practice it together, then sing the entire song. As you sing, listen for the weird, creepy sounds that you described."

At an appropriate time, let the children organize a dance dramatization, following the sequence suggested in the words of the song.

Collect scarves, bits of fabric, and paper from which children may make simple costumes to wear in their dramatizations.

"Now that you have decided who will be the trees, witches, and wind, choose scarves or crepe paper of an appropriate color to make the dance more real. The singers may choose sound effects that will make the music more mysterious."

One way of broadening and deepening an experience in music is to give children the opportunity to use what they have learned to interpret a piece of related music.

A successful music lesson will motivate children to explore other music.

"Now we will listen to orchestral music that suggests another Halloween dance."

PRESENTING ORCHESTRAL MUSIC TO GRADE THREE

Play portions of a recording of "Morning" and "In the Hall of the Mountain King" from *Peer Gynt:* Suite No. 1 by Edvard Grieg.

Children begin to recognize contrasts in music when they are given an opportunity to choose a composition for a specific purpose. The reason for their choice is as important as the choice itself.

"Listen to a short part of each of these compositions and decide which is more appropriate for another Halloween dance."

When children know that they will have an opportunity to give reasons for their choices, they will listen more attentively.

"Explain why you chose the second composition."
"Why does it sound like a Halloween dance?"

Incorporate the children's ideas of the music of "In the Hall of the Mountain King" into the planning of dramatic movement.

Using children's ideas for rhythmic movement is a significant way of involving them in the music.

"Listen all the way through to the composition you have chosen. Decide what Halloween characters might be dancing."

The children may suggest witches, goblins, or skeletons.

In the limited space of a classroom, group activities are more successful if they are guided. You might suggest that the children pretend to be

goblins dancing around a tree

witches dancing around a cauldron

skeletons in a haunted house, dancing around a chair or table

Children move more freely and imaginatively in a large area. However, by organizing groups and taking turns, many worthwhile rhythmic activities may be carried on in the classroom.

"The children who would like to try their dancing ideas may find something in the room that they can pretend is a tree, cauldron, or table."

Guide the children in listening for clues in the music that suggest dramatic interpretation.

"I noticed that Ann danced slowly when the music started and then went faster and faster. Let us discover other ways that the music tells the Halloween characters to change their movement by listening particularly to the recording while the dancers do their dance again."

Guide the children to an awareness of the contrasts in the music that they have sensed aurally and through movement.

Only after children have experienced and described in their own language the materials of music should the musical terms that name these materials be introduced.

"Name the changes you found in the music while I write them on the chalkboard."

Illustration 1

Tempo	Slow — Fast
Dynamics	Soft — Loud
Pitch	Low — High
Instruments	Few — Many

"We have discovered how composers change music in order to describe the different things that happen in a musical story."

LISTENING TO ORCHESTRAL MUSIC

At an appropriate time, play the recording again to explore further the descriptive quality and mood of "In the Hall of the Mountain King."

After children have interpreted an orchestral composition in their own way, broaden their understanding of the music by giving them appropriate information, or program notes, about it.

"We have used this composition to accompany a Halloween dance, but the music was not composed for Halloween. The composer, Edvard Grieg, who lived in Norway, enjoyed the make-believe people in the folk tales of his country and described them in his music. Guess whether he was describing little elves, clumsy trolls, or light fairies. Explain how the music and dancing helped you decide."

An experience in music should provide a maximum of music and a minimum of talking. Program notes should be presented in as few words as possible.

Acquaint the children with the story of "In the Hall of the Mountain King" and play the recording once more.

"The music of 'In the Hall of the Mountain King' describes ugly trolls dancing angrily around Peer Gynt. Peer has caused their ill temper by refusing to marry the troll princess. With this story in mind, listen to the music and find several ways in which the music suggests that the trolls become more and more angry."

Visual experiences clarify aural experiences. Children become aware of melodic contour and form (repetition and contrast) by following the score of themes.

Whenever possible, the teacher should put a large reproduction of the musical themes on the chalkboard or on a chart.

"Look at the shape of the melody on the chart. This is the first melody you heard. Listen to the music again and count the melodies that have this same shape."

Illustration 2

GOING DEEPER INTO STRUCTURE

"Witches' Dance" has been learned as a third-grade child might learn it. Now, as an adult, observe that the
- sound of the song identifies the mode as minor
- song ends on C, a clue that the key *may* be C minor
- key signature of E-flat major is also that of its relative C minor

( )

Play and sing the C-minor scale up and down:

Illustration 3

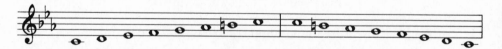

Sing the song again and follow the score, observing that the melody follows the downward movement of the C-minor scale.

Determine why the sound of the harmonic minor is especially appropriate for a Halloween song.

LESSON 17

DANCE OF THE MOSQUITO

Many composers have captured in orchestral music the sounds and movements of nature. Pretend that the class is planning a musical composition that suggests the dance of a mosquito. Select a

- tempo (fast or slow)
- pitch (high or low)
- melody (simple or complex, wide or restricted in range)
- rhythm (notes of long or short duration)
- tone color (subdued or piercing)

Planning an imaginary musical composition provides insight into the way a composer plans a successful composition.

LISTENING TO ORCHESTRAL MUSIC

Listen to a recording of "Dance of the Mosquito" by Liadov and compare the musical characteristics chosen by the composer with those selected by the class.

Listen again to "Dance of the Mosquito" and discover how Liadov achieved a "miniature" musical quality by using

- fast tempo
- high pitch
- simple melody with a restricted range
- notes of short duration
- piercing tone color of piccolo and flute
- muted violins to imitate the buzz of the mosquito
- repetition of short melodic figures
- simple form (introduction, repeated melody, and coda)

How many of the musical characteristics just heard can be identified visually (illustration 1)?

A study of the way in which music can suggest familiar scenes or sounds provides ideas for creating musical effects and accompaniments in the classroom.

Illustration 1

Compare class discoveries with the following observations about the melody: The "miniature" qualities of the music are visually identified in
- notes of high pitch
- a melodic range of only five pitches
- notes of short duration

BECOMING ACQUAINTED WITH ORCHESTRAL INSTRUMENTS

Learn to distinguish between the piccolo and the flute. In "Dance of the Mosquito" the flute plays the melody the first time, and the piccolo plays it the second time an octave higher. Compare the tone color of the two instruments. Notice that the piccolo is higher in pitch and has a more piercing quality.

Study pictures of the two instruments and compare them in size and in design. Observe that there is no mouthpiece or reed on either instrument. The tone is produced by blowing across an opening in the instrument.

COMPARING TWO ORCHESTRAL COMPOSITIONS

A comparison of two similar compositions clarifies the general and specific features of each composition and reveals a composer's ingenuity in achieving particular effects.

Liadov was a student of Nikolay Rimsky-Korsakov, who composed "The Flight of the Bumble Bee" for his opera *The Story of Tsar Saltan*.

Listen to a recording of "The Flight of the Bumble Bee" and compare it with "Dance of the Mosquito."

What are the obvious similarities between the two compositions?

What is the most obvious difference?

Listen again to discover how Rimsky-Korsakov suggests the
- swift, continuous flight of a bee
- change of direction in the flight
- humming sound

Compare the class discoveries with these observations about "The Flight of the Bumble Bee":

The continuous flight of the bee is suggested by the fast tempo, notes of short duration, and lack of pauses.

Changes in direction, such as turning and dipping, are suggested by the sudden rise and fall of the melody line.

Humming is suggested by the fast, chromatic, scale-wise movement of the melody.

SCALE   A **chromatic scale** consists of half steps, the smallest intervals in traditional Western music.

80

Listen again and follow the notation of the chromatic-scale pattern in the theme.

Illustration 2

Observe that the accidentals (♯ and ♮) form a half step between the notes in each pattern.

Notice and explain the lack of feeling for tonality in a chromatic melody.

Experiment with the chromatic scale on the piano. Many sound effects, such as the flight of a bird or plane, the wind, or the growl of an animal, can be played, even by children.

Experimentation with the piano should precede any specific keyboard training.

SONG OF THE WIND

Oo ____ Oo ____ Oo ____

On the moun - tain I hear the ___ sound of the

Oo ____

wind; Hear it blow - ing a - cross the ___ deep blue

Oo ____ Oo ____

wa - ter, Hear it blow - ing on the

Oo ____ Oo ____

moun - tain, Hear it blow - ing.

Ute mountain air

BECOMING ACQUAINTED WITH THE MUSIC

Examine the score of "Song of the Wind" to see what can be learned about the song from the

- text
- meter signature
- rhythm patterns of the melody and the two-part harmony (Are they composed largely of long, sustained notes or quickly moving notes?)
- contours of the melody and harmony parts (Do they suggest that this song should be sung vigorously or in a comparatively smooth manner?)

On the basis of responses to the above questions, determine the tempo in which "Song of the Wind" should be performed.

Now listen to the recording and compare it with the decisions made by the class.

Before attempting to play or sing a new song, develop the habit of discovering as much as possible about it from the score.

SINGING IN HARMONY

Because the two harmony parts are comparatively simple, learn to sing them before attempting the melody. Observe that each part of the harmony is composed of only two pitches. Observe, also, that these are the pitches of the G-major chord (illustration 1). Play the G-major chord on the autoharp. Then sing the two intervals that make up the harmony (illustration 2). Check accuracy by playing the intervals on a recorder or keyboard instrument.

Music chosen for beginning independent music reading should be simple, with few different pitches and easily deciphered rhythm patterns.

Illustration 1

G-major chord

Illustration 2

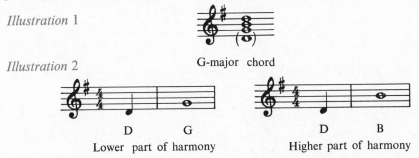

| D | G | D | B |
| Lower part of harmony | | Higher part of harmony | |

While studying the notation of "Song of the Wind," remember what has been learned about a tie. Since a whole note (𝅝) is equal to four beats and a dotted half note (𝅗𝅥.) is equal to three beats, a whole note tied to a dotted half note would be held for seven beats (🎵). A whole note tied to a whole note is held for how many beats?

Definitions and explanations of music symbols should be given only as the knowledge can be used.

SYMBOLS   A whole rest (▬) is equal in time value to a whole note. A half rest followed by a quarter rest (▬ 𝄽) is equal to a half note plus a quarter note.

Practice the rhythm pattern of the harmony, one half of the class singing the higher part and the other half the lower part. It may be helpful at this point to review the suggestions for developing good singing techniques discussed on page 27.

Why do the harmony parts sound like the wind?

Take advantage of every opportunity to develop good singing techniques. Expressive interpretation of the long phrases and sustained notes demands controlled breathing.

Prepare to play the melody of the song on recorders by observing the
- effect of the dotted rhythm
- contour of the melody (Identify the melodic figures that move on a chord line; move on a scale line; move on a repeated note.)
- repetition of melodic patterns
- form

Notice that there are only five different pitches in the melody. When the melody has been learned, sing it with the words.

PLANNING A PERFORMANCE

The wind blowing across the canyons and mesas of Colorado and Utah, sometimes gently, sometimes fiercely, played an important part in the lives and legends of the Ute Indians. "Song of the Wind" is a Ute song based on a legend that tells of a battle that took place long ago between the Cheyenne and Ute tribes. To keep them safe during the fighting, women and children were set adrift on a large raft on what is now called Grand Lake. Strong winds blowing from the mountains capsized the craft, and all aboard perished. From that day on, the Utes believed that they could hear the voices of the victims in the winds that sweep across the lake.

The class divides into three groups (melody and two harmony parts) and decides on the vocal sound, dynamics, and tempo that best interpret the song.

Practice the song, paying particular attention to the long notes (o, d., d) and the rest signs, which help produce the feeling of loneliness in the music.

Use the vocal introduction in the score and add the coda shown below.

Illustration 3

Observe that the ending pitch of the melody and the highest pitch of the final chord in the coda are the same. Notice that this pitch is the fifth (dominant) tone, not the home tone, G, in the key of G major. When performing the song, listen for the sound produced by this final note and find words to describe its effect on the music.

MELODY

Most songs end on the home tone of the key in which they are written. The few songs that end on one of the other two pitches of the home chord often suggest that the action is unresolved or "goes on forever."

Bells, recorder, autoharp, and drum provide effective accompaniments for "Song of the Wind." Yet the song is best performed *a cappella* (unaccompanied), which is probably the authentic Indian interpretation.

It is easier for the beginning music student to learn the melody of a new song on an instrument than by vocal sight-reading.

Pertinent background information on the origin of a folk song helps to recreate the music in an authentic style.

The student becomes more confident of his ability to listen sensitively to music as he begins to understand how various musical effects are created.

Instrumental accompaniments should never be added just for the sake of playing instruments. Many songs do not need instrumental tone color.

84

LESSON 19

MY LITTLE PONY

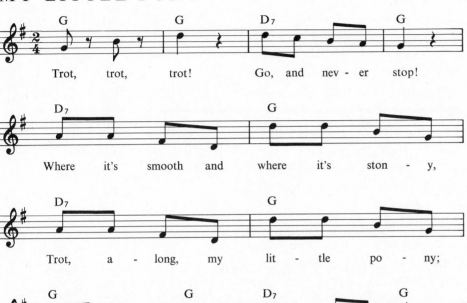

Trot, trot, trot! Go, and nev - er stop!

Where it's smooth and where it's ston - y,

Trot, a - long, my lit - tle po - ny;

Go, and nev - er stop! Trot, trot, trot, trot, trot!

Old folk song

PREPARING TO TEACH THE SONG TO GRADE TWO

Look quickly at the score of the song and, at first glance, determine
- the rhythm suggested by the words
- the mode and key, as indicated by the last note and key signature
- the form, as indicated by repeated parts
- melodic patterns moving on a scale or chord line

Compare discoveries with these observations:

The words suggest a trotting rhythm.

The key is G major.

There are three phrases; the first and the third are similar.

The melody moves on ascending and descending chord and scale lines.

Prepare to sing the song with autoharp accompaniment by
- strumming and singing the G-major chord (illustration 1) to create a feeling for the key and beginning pitch.

Develop the habit of scanning a new song. The resulting discoveries provide short cuts in learning the song.

The even rhythm patterns and scale-wise phrases in this song make it an appropriate melody for a beginning experiment in reading a score.

False starts can often be prevented by quickly establishing the sound of the tonic chord.

Illustration 1

1 3 5 3 1 5 1

85

- observing the simple rhythmic notation
- thinking of the rhythm and tempo of a trotting pony ($\frac{2}{4}$ ♪♪ ♪♪)

Let the ear help the eye in reading the score by listening carefully to the autoharp accompaniment.

Play an autoharp introduction, strumming on the first beat of each measure ($\frac{2}{4}$ ♩ 𝄽 | ♩ 𝄽 |) and sing the song with G and D₇ autoharp accompaniment. Do not be afraid of making mistakes.

Sing the song again, with more confidence.

Check and practice weak parts on the bells or piano.

Memorize the song and the autoharp accompaniment.

Select percussion instruments that imitate the sound of a trotting pony.

Plan appropriate rhythmic activities.

Carefully prepared and structured lessons free the teacher to discern each child's potential, the areas in which he is strong and the areas in which he needs help.

Plan activities to help children recognize, express with hand movements, and play the ascending and descending scale-wise figures.

Decide how the melody describes a trotting pony.

Look for an orchestral composition that will extend the singing experience into further rhythmic or listening activity. The composition may be related in title, musical similarity, or by contrast.

TEACHING THE SONG TO GRADE TWO

Invite the children to clap their hands to show various pony rhythms.

"How does a galloping pony sound [$\frac{6}{8}$ ♩ ♪♪ ♪ or $\frac{2}{4}$ ♩.♪ ♩.♪]? a trotting pony [$\frac{2}{4}$ ♪♪ ♪♪ | ♪♪ ♪♪]? a prancing pony [$\frac{2}{4}$ ♩ ♩ | ♩ ♩]?"

"Here is a new song about a pony, but instead of letting the words of the song tell you how he moves, I am going to let the melody tell you." (Sing the song on the neutral syllable "loo.")

The rhythm and contour of a good melody often suggest the text of a song. Such songs are especially appropriate for guiding children to musical understanding.

Help the children hear in the melody the rhythm they identified as trotting.

"Most of you guessed that the pony is trotting."

"Was the rhythm of the melody even, like this [Clap $\frac{2}{4}$ ♪♪ ♪♪]? or uneven, like this [$\frac{2}{4}$ ♩.♪ ♩.♪]?"

"Now listen to the words to see if you are correct."

Repeat with the children any words that might be difficult to remember.

"What words tell where the pony is trotting? Let us say the words together: 'where it's smooth and where it's stony.' "

Help the class to select percussion instruments that imitate the sound of a trotting pony. Coconut shells, gourd tone blocks, or temple blocks are effective; although paper cups, walnut-shell halves, or clicking tongues may be used as substitutes.

"While I sing the song again, Jimmy may choose a percussion instrument that sounds like a trotting pony."

Ask the children to describe the sounds of the instruments they select. Do they ring, click, or swish?

"Why is Jimmy's choice a good one?"

"While he plays the trotting rhythm, you may all sing along when you can."

Isolate scale-wise figures and help the children recognize them by playing them on the bells.

"I am going to play two parts of the song on the bells. Listen to discover which part sounds like the pony going away and which part sounds like the pony coming back home":

Illustration 2

"Show with your hand how the melody moves when the pony comes home. When he goes away."

"Draw the pattern on the chalkboard." (_ ⁻ ⁻ ⁻ ⁻ ⁻ ⁻ _)

"Sing the song again and listen to see how many times you hear the downward pattern of the pony coming home."

Encourage the children to find and play by ear on the bells or piano the ascending and descending scale patterns.

"Dennis will find and practice the downward pattern on the bells. It begins on this D."

"Dennis may play his pattern each time it is heard in the song. We will help him remember when to play."

Give children the opportunity to identify from a large chart the notation of simple patterns they have sung and played and to use these patterns in creating introductions and codas.

"Which one of these charts shows the pattern that Dennis just played?" (illustration 2)

"Which instrument should we choose to play the introduction and coda for this song?"

"Ann suggests playing the up-and-down tune of the last four measures of the song on the melody bells, and David suggests playing a trotting rhythm with the coconut shells, getting louder in the introduction and softer in the coda."

The up-and-down movement of melody is often difficult for children to distinguish. Help them recognize and hear melodic direction with the use of blank notation and hand movement.

As children in Grade Two continue to learn a song, give them turns playing percussion instruments or strumming the autoharp as a teacher presses the buttons.

Make it possible for a child to succeed at a new musical experience, thus avoiding the embarrassment of failure that may lead to a dislike for music.

Include ideas suggested by children. Musical taste and discrimination are developed as the ideas are heard and evaluated.

87

Children are intrigued with the game-like activity of making choices. Introduce new visual concepts by presenting a choice of notated patterns.

When children have sung, played, and moved to even and uneven rhythms, and discussed the difference between them, an association should be made with the notation that represents these rhythms.

Children in Grade Two may be ready to make the transfer from the large reproduction of notation on charts or chalkboard to the small notation in their songbooks.

Be sensitive to the reactions of children. Go as far as possible in teaching music but avoid over-challenging, which leads to frustration.

Simple keyboard experience in the classroom may lead to further exploration of the piano and to outside piano study.

Discuss the contribution each idea makes to the music.

"Why did you like Ann's idea?" (It was part of the song and made it easier to start singing.)

"Why did you like David's idea?" (The introduction sounded like the pony trotting closer because it got louder and louder, and the coda sounded like the pony trotting farther and farther away because it got softer.)

"Did David's introduction sound like this [$\frac{2}{4}$ ♫ ♫]? or like this [$\frac{2}{4}$ ♩.♪ ♩.♪]? Which one looks like an even rhythm?"

On another day Help children recognize the notation symbols they have experienced in singing and playing.

"Look at the song on page [appropriate number] in your songbook and find something that tells you what it is about."

"The words are a good clue. Sing the song and look for the downward melody pattern that we played on the bells. Remember, we played it two times in the song."

"Bill has a surprise for us. After playing a part of the song on the bells, he has learned to play all of it on the piano."

"Bill may be the piano teacher this week and show us how to play the last line or the whole song on the bells or piano."

"Ann is making up a piano story about circus ponies. She plays it on the black keys. Perhaps she will play it for us when it is finished."

PRESENTING A RELATED COMPOSITION TO GRADE TWO

On still another day, present a composition similar in subject, such as "The Wild Horseman" from *Album for the Young* by Robert Schumann.

Play a recording of "The Wild Horseman" for the class. Give the children an opportunity to express an immediate reaction to the music by first asking a question and then playing the music.

"Long ago a man composed a group of short musical pieces for children, describing scenes they enjoyed. What do you hear in the music that children of today might enjoy, too?"

Help children identify the sounds or contrasts in music that determine their responses.

Lead children to discover the contrasting sections.

"Listen again and find words to describe how the music changes. Tell what these changes suggest to you."

Develop an understanding of the form of this composition from the children's responses.

Children are more inclined to accept music as "their own" when they have become involved in musical performance, either through movement or by playing the appropriate instrumental sound effects.

"Betty thinks that the light music sounds like a small pony galloping and the heavy music sounds like a large horse galloping. Ben thinks that the first part sounds like a little boy riding a horse and the second part sounds like a cowboy riding a horse."

"What happened in the music that made you think of something small, then something large?"

"How many times did the music tell the small ponies to gallop? the large horses? The music we hear at the beginning of a composition is often heard again at the end."

Organize the class activity by choosing, or letting the children choose, individuals to play each of the roles.

"Betty may choose five children to be the small ponies and five to be large horses. Andy's row may find instruments that sound like the ponies and horses."

Isolate the sound of the uneven rhythm of galloping horses and associate it with uneven blank notation.

"What rhythm do you hear in the music that sounds like galloping?"
"Clap the rhythm that the wood blocks and rhythm sticks were playing with the music."
"Does the rhythm have an even sound like this [Write _ _ _ _ _ _]? or an uneven sound like this [__ _ __ _ __]?"

Associate the sound of the orchestral instruments heard most prominently on the recording with pictures of the instruments.

"Look at the pictures of these instruments and decide which one plays the melody in the light section [A]; the heavy section [B] — the galloping rhythm that is heard with the melody."

Participation may be voluntary or by invitation, but to be worthwhile it must be organized. The value of the free rhythmic movement is lost if the area in which children are moving becomes congested.

As children adapt their movements to the changes in the music, they become aware of musical form, phrases, and changes in pitch and dynamics.

Association of the appearance of orchestral instruments with the sounds they produce gives children a background for increasing their knowledge of orchestral music.

EXTENDING THE EXPERIENCE FOR INTERMEDIATE GRADES

Older children may experience further learning from hearing "The Wild Horseman." They may be asked to
- identify the change of mode from minor to major in the A and B sections
- follow the theme reproduced on a chart or chalkboard
- associate the rhythm patterns below with those played by percussion instruments in the classroom or heard in the recording

Illustration 3

Harvest Time VI

SHUCKING OF THE CORN

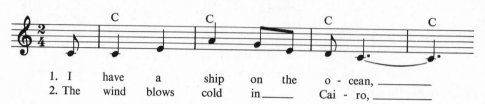

1. I have a ship on the o - cean, _____
2. The wind blows cold in_____ Cai - ro, _____

All lined with sil – ver and gold. _____
The sun re – fus – es to shine._____

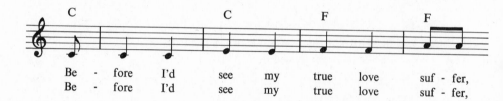

Be – fore I'd see my true love suf - fer,
Be – fore I'd see my true love suf - fer,

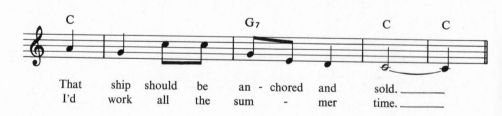

That ship should be an - chored and sold. _____
I'd work all the sum – mer time. _____

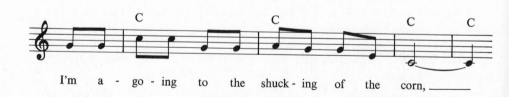

I'm a – go - ing to the shuck - ing of the corn, _____

I'm a – go - ing to the shuck - ing of the corn, _____

A - shuck - ing of the corn and a - blow - ing of the horn,

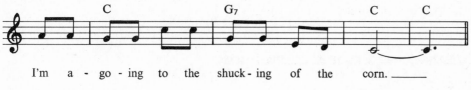

I'm a - go - ing to the shuck - ing of the corn. _____

Folk song from Tennessee
Collected by L. L. McDowell

TEACHING THE SONG TO GRADE FOUR

Lively folk tunes have special appeal for children (as they do for their teachers). "Shucking of the Corn" is a well-known folk song from Tennessee, where people used to have parties in their barns to lighten the work of shucking the corn after it had been harvested in the fall.

Introduce this song to a fourth-grade class with some pertinent information and suggestions for listening.

> "The words of a song often tell what people are doing or thinking; the music suggests how they feel about what they are doing or thinking. Listen to this folk song from Tennessee and discover what you can about the people who first sang it."

Guide the children's discussion of the song so that they become aware that the verses are about imagined or distant situations, while the refrain refers to a real and immediate one.

> "Listen to the recording and discover which part of the song tells about something that is really happening and which part is imagined."

One of a teacher's most valuable assets is the ability to discern a child's progress and potential from his responses in class discussion.

When the children have discovered this difference between the verse and the refrain, start pointing out the characteristics of the melody as they learn the song.

> "This time, hum along or sing the words you know with the recording. Listen and look to discover what important part of the music I draw on the chalkboard."

While the children hum or sing, draw a contour of the melody (illustration 1) on the chalkboard.

Take advantage of every opportunity to use appropriate visual aids to clarify musical concepts.

Illustration 1

Verse

Refrain

Because of the regular rise and fall of the melody line, it will be easy for the children to recognize it and then describe its movement with arm and hand motions.

Let children participate whenever practical.

"While you sing the song, show with hand motions the movement of the melody. Find words to describe this movement. Use the words of the song to help you, if you wish."

CREATING APPROPRIATE ACCOMPANIMENTS

Help children become involved more deeply in the spirit of the music by letting them share in developing authentic accompaniments.

Helping children to develop authentic accompaniments promotes growth in musical performance and significant understanding of musical style.

"The people who first sang this corn-shucking song often combined work with pleasure. After helping their neighbors to shuck corn, build a barn or a house, or do whatever else needed to be done, they had a party. Everyone, young and old alike, joined in the fun. 'Shucking of the Corn' is one of the songs they enjoyed at these gatherings. Musical instruments were few, so they made their own music. How do you think they kept time while they sang the song?"

After the children have sung the song, clapping hands and tapping feet on the beat, they may be ready to learn the syncopated hand-clapping accompaniment shown in illustration 2.

If children experience too much difficulty with a rhythm, never hesitate to use a simpler accompaniment at the moment and work on the more complicated rhythm at a later time.

"You have tapped and clapped the beat of the music. Now let us try an 'off-the-beat' rhythm called syncopation, which is popular with folk musicians":

Illustration 2

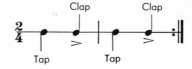

Show the children that the actual movements involved in shucking corn can develop into a colorful rhythmic accompaniment.

Experience with accompaniments that are both imaginative and appropriate will enable children to create better accompaniments on their own.

"Who can show us the hand movements used in shucking corn?"

If children do not have the information, show them how corn is shucked, or husked, and proceed to develop the rhythm pattern shown in illustration 3.

"As the husks are removed from the ear of corn, they make a swishing sound. What percussion instrument might we use to produce this sound?" (sand blocks)

"As the husks are broken from the ear of corn, there is a cracking sound. What percussion instrument will make this sound?" (rhythm sticks)

"After the corn is shucked, it is thrown into a bin or wagon. What instrument do we have to produce this sound?" (drum)

Have the children practice the "corn-shucking" accompaniment (illustration 3), standing in the order in which the instruments are played.

Give children strong and sympathetic support when they attempt a new activity.

Illustration 3

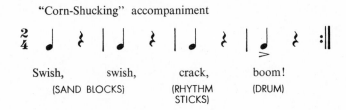

"Corn-Shucking" accompaniment

Swish,   swish,   crack,   boom!
(SAND BLOCKS)   (RHYTHM STICKS)   (DRUM)

When the players are sufficiently confident, ask them to play this rhythm pattern as an accompaniment to the singing.

Reinforce the rhythm patterns children have just experienced by showing them the notation (illustration 4) and asking them to compare the patterns.

> "Let us compare the notations of the 'keeping-time' rhythm and the 'corn-shucking' rhythm. Clap each one while looking and listening to discover how they are alike and how they are different."

To grow in independence in interpreting a score, children must understand the symbols of notation.

Illustration 4

"Keeping-Time" rhythm   "Corn-Shucking" rhythm

Make sure that the children identify the quarter note and the quarter rest and that they hear the difference in the patterns.

CREATING A DANCE

Guide the children in making up a dance that will re-create the scene and the spirit of the old social gatherings.

> "People of long ago did not have theaters, radios, and television sets, so they entertained themselves by singing and dancing."
>
> "Let us finish the study of 'Shucking of the Corn' by working out a folk dance of our own."

If the teacher or children have had much experience in folk dancing, they can choose a dance formation (circle, line, or square), decide on dance patterns ("forward and back," "swing your partner," and so on), and create their own dance.

If the teacher is inexperienced in folk dancing, however, she may want to try with her class the simple dance on the next page. (Notice that the floor pattern is based on the contour of the melody, discussed on page 91.)

Because folk dancing is a group activity and offers the security of a planned floor pattern, it encourages the participation of those children who do not freely move to music on their own.

In a music lesson the focus is always on the music itself, but no opportunity to show music in its relationship to other areas of study or activity should be ignored.

Partners should line up facing each other, boys on one side and girls on the other.

The basic step is a quick, walking shuffle, one shuffle to a beat.

Verse: Phrase 1 (A) — "I have a ship on the ocean"
Lines move forward and back.

Phrase 2 (A') — "All lined with silver and gold"
Lines move forward and back.

Phrases 3 and 4 (B and C) — "Before I'd see . . . anchored and sold"
Lines move forward; partners do-si-do and return to original positions.

Refrain: Phrase 5 (D) — "I'm a-going to the shucking of the corn"
Girls move forward a few steps, make a quick curtsy, and return to original positions.

Phrase 6 (E) — "I'm a-going to the shucking of the corn"
Boys move forward a few steps, make a quick bow, and return to original positions.

Phrases 7 and 8 (B' and C') — "A-shucking of the corn . . . to the shucking of the corn."
Lines move forward; swing partners, then return to original positions.

EXTENDING THE EXPERIENCE FOR CHILDREN

Appreciation grows as the children become more familiar with the song through repeated performances.

Learning a song is only the beginning of the enjoyment music can give.

Children especially interested in folk dancing may want to make up other dances during play periods. Encourage them to show their original dances to the class. The best of these dances can be incorporated into a performance for parents or other classes.

Children can easily learn to play the autoharp accompaniment. Point out to them that the chord pattern is the same in the verse and in the refrain.

The class may decide to use their accumulated skills to plan a performance of "Shucking of the Corn" as it might have been enjoyed at an old-fashioned corn-shucking party. Help the children choose singers who might also be able to perform the syncopated clapping accompaniment, players for percussion accompaniments, and dancers.

GOING DEEPER INTO STRUCTURE

Melody   Children will be able to see and hear the constant rise and fall of the melody. (Some children may see this as the waves of the ocean told about in the first verse.)

Rhythm   The rhythm pattern — a comparatively even, flowing rhythm pattern in $\frac{2}{4}$ meter — will be easy for the fourth-grader.

Form   Because of its comparative complexity, the form of this song is not specifically pointed out to fourth-graders. But they can sense the eight phrases of the song in the rise and fall of the melody line, in the "corn-shucking" accompaniment (one pattern on each phrase), and in the dancing. The teacher, however, will be aware that no two phrases are exactly alike, although A, A', and E are similar to each other and B and C are similar to B' and C'.

Verse: AA'BC
Refrain: DEB'C'

Harmony   The harmonic pattern is the same for the verse and the refrain. Only the primary chords (I = F; V_7 = C_7; and IV = B-flat) are used throughout the song.

What musical elements give "Shucking of the Corn" unity? What elements give it variety?

Intellectual understanding deepens appreciation of the music.

LESSON 21

BASKETS ON SHOULDERS

Baskets upon our shoulders, Garlands upon our brows,

First fruits of harvest we are bringing to Zion now.

From the vineyards, From the fertile mountain slopes,
From the valleys, We bring the first fruits of the land.

Make way and let us pass, Pilgrims each lad and lass.

Strike, drums! Cymbals clash! Dance and sing with glee,

Strike, drums! Cymbals clash! Dance and sing with glee.

Folk song from Asia Minor
Translation by Judith K. Eisenstein

BECOMING ACQUAINTED WITH THE MUSIC

When a song is sung for a particular purpose, identifying that purpose leads to a better understanding of the music.

Down through the ages, music has been a vital means of expressing gratitude and thanksgiving. All the emotions, from reverence and thoughtful appreciation to joyful exultation, are found in music. The harvest, which marks the end of a work cycle and is the fulfillment of the earth's promise, is an especially appropriate time for giving thanks.

Listen to the recording of "Baskets on Shoulders" and discover how the pageantry and gaiety of a harvest festival in Israel are revealed in the music.

In Israel, where the climate in winter is generally mild, the first harvest time of the year comes in the spring, coinciding with Shavuot, the religious holiday that commemorates the gift of the Ten Commandments to Moses on Mount Sinai. It is a time of joyful celebration. People from the country march into the cities, carrying the "first fruits" in baskets. Long ago these harvest gifts were taken to the temples; today they are given to needy families. The festival continues with singing, instrument playing, and dancing in the streets.

As the recording is played again, get into the spirit of the music by highlighting the dramatic last phrases of the song. Several students may play the drum and cymbals when they are named in the text.

Background information that puts an unfamiliar song in its original setting adds interest and meaning to the musical experience.

Playing simple instrumental passages is one of the easiest and most effective ways of becoming quickly involved in the music.

TONE COLOR ➤ The use of colorful percussion instruments is one of the simplest and most effective ways of emphasizing especially dramatic places in music.

STUDYING THE SCORE

Sing along with the recording and follow the score to discover the phrases that are repeated in the song.

In class discussion about the repetition of phrases, it will be discovered that the form of "Baskets on Shoulders" is AA′BBCDD′. Sing the song again with the recording, noting how knowledge of form helps in learning the song.

A comparatively difficult song is more easily learned when its repeated phrases are recognized.

FORM ➤ In a song, form is clearly revealed in the variety and repetition of the phrases.

Now sing the song with the recording and locate on the score the highest pitch in the music.

Compare class discoveries about this high point in the melody with these observations:

The highest pitch appears in the melody of the B phrase.

This pitch (E-flat) creates an exotic effect expected in Eastern music. E-flat is an accidental, not part of the F-major scale in which the song is written.

Learn to play the B phrase (illustration 1) on the melody bells or piano and listen to the sound the E-flat produces. Why is this phrase easy to play?

A comparatively difficult song is more easily learned when unusual melodic patterns are recognized and practiced separately.

Illustration 1

MELODY ➤ To be interesting a melody must achieve a **climax.** The climax is often provided by an upward movement of the melody, sometimes to a pitch higher than any of the others.

Sing "Baskets on Shoulders" with the recording, playing drum and cymbals on the last two phrases of the song. Notice how practicing an unusual phrase helps in singing it more accurately.

CREATING APPROPRIATE ACCOMPANIMENTS

Using the suggestions given below, write a complete percussion score based either on original rhythm patterns or on those suggested in illustration 2.

Select instruments whose sounds approximate those heard in the Near East.

Select instruments with different volumes and tone colors to emphasize the musical character of each of the phrases. Begin in phrase A and A' with an instrument with low volume. In succeeding contrasting phrases, change the instrument to build toward the colorful drum and cymbal accompaniment in the last phrases of the song (D and D').

Against the varied rhythmic ideas of the melody, play a simple $\frac{4}{4}$ ♩ ♩ ♩ ♩ or ♩ ♩ ♩ ♩ on the percussion instruments.

Illustration 2

Phrases A-A':	FINGER CYMBALS	$\frac{4}{4}$ ♩ ♩ ♩ ♩ | ♩ ♩ ♩ ♩ :‖
Phrase B:	TAMBOURINES	$\frac{4}{4}$ ♩ ♩ ♩ ♩ | ♩ ♩ ♩ ♩ :‖
Phrase C:	DRUM	$\frac{4}{4}$ ♩ ♩ ♩ ♩ | ♩ ♩ ♩ ♩ :‖
Phrases D-D':	DRUM CYMBALS TAMBOURINES	$\frac{4}{4}$ ♩ ♩ ♩ ♩ | ♩ ♩ ♩ ♩ :‖

In the percussion score, write in dynamic markings as an aid to correct and expressive playing.

SYMBOLS

p means to play or sing softly (*piano*).

The sign ⟨ means to play or sing gradually louder (*crescendo*).

ff means to play or sing loudly (*fortissimo*).

Practice the orchestration decided upon. Half the class then plays the percussion accompaniment while the other half sings the song with the recording.

Now prepare to sing "Baskets on Shoulders" without the support of the recording by learning the autoharp accompaniment given in the score.

Observe that only the three primary chords in the key of F major (F, C₇, B-flat) are used in the accompaniment.

Experiment to determine which makes the most effective accompaniment — one, two, or four strums per measure.

Sing the song with autoharp and percussion accompaniment, then experiment with adding melody bells on the B phrase (illustration 1). Decide whether this addition is effective in the orchestration.

CREATING A DANCE

Learn this simple Jewish festival dance that any number of students, even the whole class, can practice at once.

Partners stand in a large single circle, holding hands shoulder high, arms bent at elbows. (The arm position probably suggests carrying harvest baskets on shoulders).

The fundamental step is a step and bend on the same leg:

Illustration 3

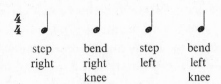

Dance pattern: Phrases A and A′ (measures 1–4)
   All circle right, using fundamental step.
  Phrase B and repeat of B (measures 5–8)
   All circle left, using fundamental step.
  Phrase C (measures 9–10)
   All move into circle (one measure) and out
   (one measure), using fundamental step.
  Phrase D (measures 11–12)
   Clap hands 4 times (one measure), then swing
   partner quickly.
  Phrase D′ (measures 13–14)
   Repeat phrase D pattern.

PLANNING A PERFORMANCE

Use the singing, instrumental, and dancing activities suggested previously in this lesson to re-create an Israeli harvest festival.

GOING DEEPER INTO STRUCTURE

As usual, the tempo and rhythm help to establish the mood of the song. The syncopated figures in the beginning measures of "Baskets on Shoulders" announce the energetic movement of the song. Sing each example in illustration 4 and compare the vitality of the first measures of the song with that of the same melody notated in even rhythm.

Illustration 4

Syncopated figures from "Baskets on Shoulders"

Same figures without syncopation

Observe that the phrases with syncopated rhythm (A,A',C) are balanced by phrases that move on even beats (B,D,D').

Observe that the melody begins with the bold leap from the tonic pitch (F) to the dominant pitch (C), two notes that immediately establish the key of F. Observe, too, that all the measures except those of the B phrase start with an interval of a third, fourth, or fifth and continue with a simple scale-wise figure. This repeated melodic idea makes the music vigorous and exciting.

Determine the effect on the listener of the repeated notes in the B phrase.

Melody determines harmony. Study illustration 5 to see that E-flat in the melody of the B phrase leads to the B-flat chord in the C phrase. For an instant the music seems to move to another key (B-flat major) but returns immediately to the key of F major.

Illustration 5

F   F₇
F major

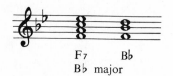
F₇   B♭
B♭ major

 HARMONY Harmonic unity is provided by the key in which a song is written. Harmonic variety is achieved when a song moves temporarily into another key, bringing a heightened sense of activity to the music.

Review the lesson and determine in how many ways the form in the song has been experienced.

LESSON 22

AMERICA, THE BEAUTIFUL

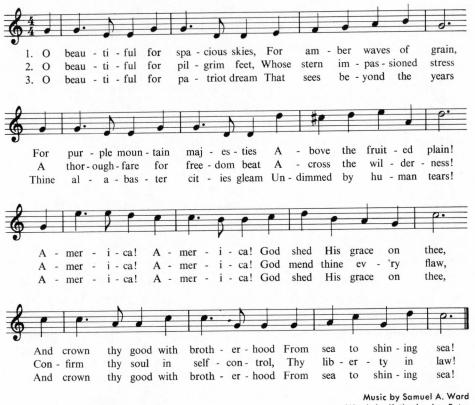

1. O beau - ti - ful for spa - cious skies, For am - ber waves of grain,
2. O beau - ti - ful for pil - grim feet, Whose stern im - pas - sioned stress
3. O beau - ti - ful for pa - triot dream That sees be - yond the years

For pur - ple moun - tain maj - es - ties A - bove the fruit - ed plain!
A thor - ough - fare for free - dom beat A - cross the wil - der - ness!
Thine al - a - bas - ter cit - ies gleam Un - dimmed by hu - man tears!

A - mer - i - ca! A - mer - i - ca! God shed His grace on thee,
A - mer - i - ca! A - mer - i - ca! God mend thine ev - 'ry flaw,
A - mer - i - ca! A - mer - i - ca! God shed His grace on thee,

And crown thy good with broth - er - hood From sea to shin - ing sea!
Con - firm thy soul in self - con - trol, Thy lib - er - ty in law!
And crown thy good with broth - er - hood From sea to shin - ing sea!

Music by Samuel A. Ward
Words by Katharine Lee Bates

BECOMING ACQUAINTED WITH THE MUSIC

Familiar, well-loved songs offer special opportunities for identifying and evaluating qualities inherent in the music.

Sing along with, or just listen to, the recording of "America, the Beautiful." Find adjectives to describe the mood created by its particular blend of poetry and melody. Decide why this old favorite is appropriate in any repertory of thanksgiving songs.

STUDYING THE MOOD

From class discussion of the mood of "America, the Beautiful," develop ideas for interpreting the music. Decide what tempo, dynamics, and attitude of the singers will help to re-create the spirit of the music. Review the singing techniques necessary to expressive performance (page 27).

In the performance of a familiar song, immediate attention can and should be given to expressive interpretation. Too often the well-known song is performed in a casual, even careless manner.

Now sing all three verses of the song either *a cappella* or with a piano accompaniment played by the teacher or by a proficient student. Evaluate the class performance.

TERM

The term **a cappella** is derived from the Italian word *cappella*, which means "chapel." Originally, *a cappella* meant music written for the choir of a chapel. The term is now used to refer to choral music sung without instrumental accompaniment.

When the melody of a song is already well-known, a harmony part can be learned with comparative speed and ease.

"America, the Beautiful" is particularly notable for the depth of feeling it conveys. One of the reasons for this is the harmony. Learn the simple harmony part (illustration 1) for the third and fourth phrases of the song. Notice that the harmony part for the third phrase is the same as the melody line of one of the phrases in the song. Locate this phrase.

After the harmony part has been learned, the class divides into two groups and sings the song, harmonizing the last two phrases.

Develop the habit of searching out with ear and eye the like and unlike phrases in the harmony as well as in the melody line.

Illustration 1

Harmony for phrase 3

Harmony for phrase 4

STUDYING THE RHYTHM

Study the characteristics of the rhythm pattern that contribute to the spirit of the song.

Prominent in establishing the strength and vigor of the song is the rhythm pattern of the melody. The recurring dotted rhythm figure ( ), which

Provide every opportunity for analyzing the tempo and rhythm of a song, for they are often the most important elements in establishing the mood or spirit of the music.

is easily identified in the rhythm pattern of the title word "A-mer-i-ca," is often found in hymns of praise and thanksgiving ("America" and "We Gather Together," for example). Observe that the dotted rhythm figures at the beginning of each phrase are followed by an even, flowing line of quarter notes, giving each phrase the same rhythm pattern.

RHYTHM

Constant repetition of a rhythmic idea gives unity and strength to music.

To understand the dramatic movement of the dotted rhythmic figure, compare it with an even rhythm by singing the phrases on quarter notes:

Illustration 2

STUDYING THE MELODY

The melody helps to create a feeling of majesty and reverence. Notice the simple chord-wise movement of the melodic figures in the beginning measures of the first and second phrases (illustration 3a) and the fourth phrase (illustration 3b).

Analyzing the characteristics of a comparatively obvious melodic idea will help build confidence in understanding new and unfamiliar melodies.

Illustration 3

The upward-flowing melody line that follows the chord-wise figures brings a majestic quality to the music.

MELODY Ascending melody lines often suggest a feeling of striving toward a goal.

Observe that the accidental, C-sharp, near the end of the second phrase prepares the way for the melodic and dramatic high point of the song, which is reached on the first "A-mer-i-ca!" Notice that after the high point, the melodic ideas, for the most part, tend to move downward.

MELODY The melodic high point — a point of great tension — is often followed by downward movement suggesting repose or resolution.

Develop the ability to discover and identify the many different ways variety and unity are used in a musical idea.

"America, the Beautiful" has four different phrases — ABCD. Sing the song to observe this form and feel the inspiring and exciting effect of the onward sweep of movement from one phrase to the next. Give special attention to performing rhythm patterns accurately and using dynamics expressively to interpret the strength and vigor of the melody.

The ultimate beauty and expressive qualities of music are further revealed in an accurate performance.

PLANNING A PERFORMANCE

"America, the Beautiful" is particularly effective in choral performance.

Use the knowledge gained about the structure and rhythm of the music to sing the melody accurately.

Use good singing techniques for better vocal quality.

Use the insights gained to decide upon the mood, dynamics, and arrangement best suited for a performance.

Decide on an arrangement that will express the slight differences in the mood of each verse. Consider singing some verses *a cappella,* others with accompaniment; some parts in unison, others in harmony.

Harmonize the song by ear or use the simple harmony suggested in the lesson for the last two phrases.

Incorporate any suggestions that will lead to an expressive, and thus impressive, class performance.

Knowledge and insight into music do not of themselves insure expressive performance, but they are valuable when they lead to sensitive and imaginative interpretation.

103

LESSON 23

FUM, FUM, FUM

1. On this joy - ful Christ - mas Day sing fum, fum, fum,
2. Thanks to God for hol - i - days, sing fum, fum, fum,

On this joy - ful Christ - mas Day sing fum, fum, fum;
Thanks to God for hol - i - days, sing fum, fum, fum;

For a bless - ed Babe was born Up - on this day at
Now we all our voic - es raise And sing a song of

break of morn, In a man - ger poor and low - ly
grate - ful praise, Cel - e - brate in song and sto - ry,

Lay the Son of God most ho - ly, Fum, fum, fum!
All the won - ders of His glo - ry, Fum, fum, fum!

Catalan carol. English words by Harry Wilson.

TEACHING THE SONG TO GRADE SIX

Play the recording of "Fum, Fum, Fum" for the class. Give the children the
opportunity to find and discuss the characteristics that identify this as a song of
festive gaiety in contrast to the more reverent carols.

"What do you hear in this carol that makes it different from most
carols?"

Lead the class to discover that the spirited tempo, running rhythm, and the change of movement suggested by the "fum, fum, fum" indicate that the song may have been danced.

"Join in on the 'fum, fum, fum' as you hear the song again and decide what in the music indicates that this carol might have been danced long ago."

To provide color and heighten interest in the song while learning it, play the "fum, fum, fum" rhythm on an appropriate percussion instrument.

The addition of a simple accompaniment that does not distract attention from the learning of the song adds stimulus by providing immediate involvement.

"This song comes from Catalan, a part of Spain. If you were dancing this song in Spain, what percussion instrument might be played to highlight the 'fum, fum, fum'?"

"Try each of your suggestions [drum and tambourine] as you sing this time and decide which sound is more appropriate."

Encourage children to learn the song with the help of the score.

"You sang along very well. Look at the score and find the characteristics that helped you learn the song."

"Which phrases are alike?"

"Which phrase is most different?"

"How is the fourth phrase like the first and second?"

"Does the melody move on notes 'close together' or 'far apart'?"

"Sing the song again and let these discoveries guide you in following the score."

Many sixth-graders will join in on the second or third hearing if they have had varied singing experiences and have been encouraged to observe the highlights of the score as they learn a new song. Other classes may need more repetition and should be invited to observe the more obvious features of the score.

CREATING APPROPRIATE ACCOMPANIMENTS

The accompaniment for this song is difficult because of its fast tempo and quick harmonic change. A sixth-grade pupil can master most accompaniments if he is permitted to take an autoharp home in the evening. In preparation, help children find by ear and eye the repetitions and patterns of harmony that facilitate learning.

Provide class members with the challenge of learning difficult accompaniments through practice.

"Who will volunteer to learn the autoharp accompaniment? Look at the chord pattern. Why will it be difficult to play?"

"The basic chords of this song are A minor, E_7, and D minor. Find these chords on the autoharp."

"Study the score again to discover in which phrases these basic chords are played. In which phrase are different chords played?"

Children can play and recognize the characteristic sound and effect of major and minor chords without knowing harmonic structure.

On another day   The sixth-graders who have practiced the autoharp at home will be ready to play the accompaniment of "Fum, Fum, Fum" for the rest of the class.

"Linda and Paul are ready to try the autoharp accompaniment for 'Fum, Fum, Fum.' They say this is the hardest accompaniment they have played."

"Recall why this is true by watching the score as you sing."

105

The resonator bells provide an effective addition to many Christmas carols. As children select and play the resonator bells, they become aware of chord structure and relationships.

Prepare the class for playing the resonator bells in three-part harmony (chords) on the repeated words "fum, fum, fum."

"In what way is the notation on the words 'fum, fum, fum' different from the rest of the song?"

"Why would the sound of the resonator bells playing these chords be appropriate for a Christmas carol?"

"How many notes are there in each chord?"

"If we had three groups, one to play the top line of the chords, one to play the middle line, and one to play the bottom line, what pitches would each group play?"

"Watch as I write on the chalkboard the bell pitches each group will need":

In an early experience of playing or singing in three parts, a large reproduction of the score on the chalkboard or chart distinguishes and clarifies the movement of each part.

Illustration 1

To hold children's interest and make economical use of time, see that a mechanical activity, such as selecting and assembling resonator bells, is an efficient, established routine.

Arrange for the distribution of the bells needed by each group and allow time for practice.

"Don may distribute the needed bells to pupils in each group. Remember that group 2 plays only one pitch, and so it will need only one bell."

"Practice the bell chords as we sing 'Fum, Fum, Fum' in rhythm."

"Now let us sing the song and add the bell accompaniment."

SINGING IN HARMONY

Teach the sixth-graders to sing the three-part harmony that they have played on the resonator bells.

An accompanying instrument, such as the bells or the autoharp, provides the support needed for first attempts in part-singing.

"Each group will look at the score and listen to the pitches your bells play."

"All three groups sing the three-part harmony with the bells."

"Now, without the bells, sing the song including the three-part harmony on the 'fum, fum, fum.' "

PLANNING A PERFORMANCE

Ideas for a performance of "Fum, Fum, Fum" may be selected from the following suggestions.

Select a tempo that will express the festive gaiety of the song.

Decide on an introduction that will establish the mood, tempo, and beginning pitch of the song — for example, by playing the "fum, fum, fum" chords on the autoharp and resonator bells.

Select a soloist or small group to sing the first part of each phrase. The remainder of the class may sing and play the three-part harmony of "Fum, Fum, Fum."

Play a coda that echoes the gaiety of the music.

GOING DEEPER INTO STRUCTURE

This song has been learned as a sixth-grade class might learn it. Now, as an adult, look at the score of the song to discover how the characteristics of the song are notated.

Mode   In previous lessons a relationship has been established between D minor and F major ("Ninna Nanna") and between G minor and B-flat major ("This Is Halloween"). Study the A-minor and C-major scales (illustration 2) and observe the same minor-major relationships.

The relationship between major and minor is best revealed in "making music." Notation and its analysis have value and interest only when the sounds represented by the notation have become familiar.

Illustration 2

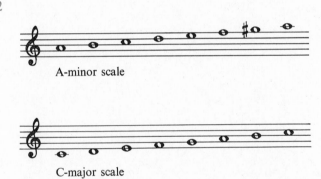

A-minor scale

C-major scale

Observe that the key signatures are the same and that the
- minor key is one and one-half steps below the major key
- pitches included in the scales are the same except that the seventh pitch of the harmonic minor is raised one-half step
- difference in the structure of a major and minor scale is the arrangement of whole and half steps

Harmony   The A-minor, E_7, and D-minor chords are the basic chords of the key of A minor. They are built on the tonic (A), the dominant (E), and the subdominant (D) of the scale.

Illustration 3

A minor   D minor   E₇

The chords played in the third phrase of the song are the familiar tonic and dominant chords in the key of C major.

Illustration 4

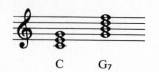

C   G₇

Rhythm   The rhythm pattern begins phrases 1, 2, and 4. The dotted eighth at the beginning of the pattern emphasizes the first note and starts each phrase with vigor.

RHYTHM   A dotted note in a series of even notes is emphasized because of its longer duration.

Notice the measure of $\frac{3}{4}$ meter made necessary by the extra number of words in the fourth phrase.

Form   The form of "Fum, Fum, Fum" is AABC. Notice that phrase C is derived from phrase A and helps to give the song its feeling of unity.

LESSON 24

VENID, PASTORES

Refrain

Ve - nid, pas - to - res, ve - nid, ¡Oh! ve - nid a Be - lén,

¡Oh! ve - nid al por - tal, ___ Yo no me voy de Be - lén

sin al Ni - ño Je - sús un mo - men - to a-do - rar. ___

Verse

1. Y la Es - tre - lla de Be - lén ___ nos guia - rá ___ con su luz ___
2. De la mon - ta - ña el pas - tor ___ de pri - sa a Be - lén va ___
3. ¿No oyes el ga - llo can - tar ___ con su po - ten - te voz? ___

has - ta el hu - mil - de por - tal ___ don - de na - ció Je - sús. ___
pa - ra a-dor - ar a Je - sús ___ que na - ció en el por - tal. ___
A - nun - ci al mun - do que ya ___ Je - su - cris - to na - ció. ___

Puerto Rican folk song

BECOMING ACQUAINTED WITH THE MUSIC

Examine the text and find the Spanish words and phrases listed below with their English translations. Look for other words commonly found in a Christmas song. Ask some member of the class acquainted with the Spanish language to assist in learning the proper pronunciation.

Some of the beauty and charm of a folk song is lost when it is not sung in its native language. Whenever possible, sing a song in the language of the people who created it.

Niño Jesús: Baby Jesus

venid, pastores: come, shepherds

Estrella de Belén: Star of Bethlehem

nos guiará con su luz: will guide us with its light

Jesucristo nació: Jesus Christ is born

| Musical growth is the result of carefully structured lessons that use past experience as a basis for learning and understanding new materials. |

Listen while "Venid, Pastores" is sung for the first time, and examine the score to compare this Puerto Rican song with "Fum, Fum, Fum." Find similarities in

- key and mode
- melody
- harmony

Observe that "Venid, Pastores" is similar to "Fum, Fum, Fum" in

- key (A minor)
- melody (scale-wise movement of melody and melodic contour)
- harmony (moves from A minor to C major in the contrasting sections)

Develop the ability to discover in the score the notation that helps produce the mood of a song.

Sing and follow the score to discover the characteristics that contribute to the reverent, pastoral mood.

Compare class discoveries with these observations about the musical characteristics of "Venid, Pastores":

The pastoral mood is created by the

- smooth, flowing rhythm of the even quarter notes in $\frac{6}{4}$ meter
- sustained notes at the end of each phrase, which give restful pauses to the melody line
- quiet scale-wise movement of the melody
- simplicity of a melodic range limited to five pitches
- repetition of melodic patterns, which gives unity and a feeling of quietness to the music.

While the song is sung again, pay particular attention to singing the simple melody and the flowing rhythm accurately. Notice how a careful performance enhances the mood of the song.

Develop the habit of expressing the mood and meaning of the text in the first attempts at singing a song.

Find adjectives to describe the change of mood between the refrain and the verse. Determine how the mood is changed in the

- words of the text
- harmony
- melody line

Examining contrasts in the structure of the music reveals deeper insight into possibilities for interpretation.

The contrast in mood from the refrain to the verse is evident in the

- words *estrella* (star) and *luz* (light) of the verse (These words demand brighter music than do the words of the refrain.)
- sudden change to the major mode and harmony, which lends brighter color to the verse.

> **MODE** A sudden key change from minor to its relative major heightens the activity in music and brings about dramatic contrast in the mood of a song.

Sing the song again, using dynamics and accents to show the change of mood between the refrain and the verse.

Listen especially to the effect created by the harmonic change from major to minor.

110

CREATING APPROPRIATE ACCOMPANIMENTS

Practice an autoharp accompaniment that imitates the sound of the Spanish guitar and use it to accompany "Venid, Pastores."

On the autoharp, locate the chords for each section:

Refrain: A minor and E_7

Verse: C, G_7, G, and D_7

Experiment with contrasting autoharp sounds for the two sections. For example, in the refrain section strum slowly across the strings so that each string sounds plucked. In the verse section, play with a more energetic strum on the first and fourth beats.

Learn to play the melody of the verse on the recorder, imitating the sound of a shepherd's pipe and add this instrument to the performance of the song.

Learn to play a bell accompaniment, imitating the sound of a church bell (illustration 1) throughout the refrain.

Illustration 1

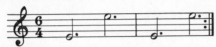

Almost any style or mood of music can be created with the autoharp. Develop the skill of playing the autoharp in the manner that best suits each song.

Take advantage of every opportunity to use melody instruments. This not only develops specific reading skills but deepens appreciation for musical sound and adds appropriate tone color to a song as well.

PLANNING A PERFORMANCE

Ideas for a performance may be selected from the following suggestions.

Plan an introduction that will establish the pastoral mood, tempo, key, and beginning pitch.

Decide on effective dynamic variations, remembering the change in mood between the two sections.

Select a soloist or a small group to sing the verses.

Begin the song with the refrain, then have at least one of the verses sung solo, as is often done in Puerto Rico.

Play a section of the song on the recorder as an interlude.

Add the bell accompaniment to one verse.

Add a coda that will echo the reverent quality of the song.

Thoughtful planning that results in expressive musical performance increases confidence and artistry in the performer.

GOING DEEPER INTO STRUCTURE

Recall the observations made in the preceding lesson ("Fum, Fum, Fum") about the relationship of A minor and C major. Study the score of "Venid, Pastores" again to discover that

- both songs begin and end on the pitch A
- the chords A minor, E_7, C, and G_7 are used in both songs
- the change from A minor to C major in each song is harmonically smooth because of the pitches common to both keys
- the interval of one and one-half steps between the sixth and seventh pitches (F to G sharp, which provides the exotic sound of the minor), is *not* heard in the melody of either song
- the two E's played in the bell accompaniment are harmonically correct because E is a pitch of each chord

When a principle of musical structure is pointed out repeatedly, the concept becomes clarified.

Illustration 2

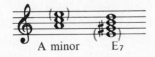

A minor E_7

LESSON 25

SUITE FROM

AMAHL AND THE NIGHT VISITORS

Knowing the story of an opera heightens the enjoyment of its orchestral music. Conversely, acquaintance with the music from an opera enhances the enjoyment of a complete performance.

Throughout the centuries the journey of the wise men and shepherds to Bethlehem has been told in story and song. Gian-Carlo Menotti retells the story in a short opera called *Amahl and the Night Visitors,* which is widely performed at Christmas.

The opera begins with an introductory scene in which Amahl, a poor, crippled shepherd boy, sits outside his hut, watching a brilliant star cross the sky. Three kings, who are traveling across the desert in their search for the Christ Child, stop for the night at Amahl's humble dwelling. Amahl's shepherd friends come to honor the kings and to dance for them.

At the end of the kings' visit, Amahl impulsively gives them his crutch to take as a gift to the Christ Child, and in so doing, he is miraculously cured of his lameness. When the three kings resume their journey to Bethlehem, Amahl goes with them.

BECOMING ACQUAINTED WITH THE MUSIC

A suite provides an effective early listening experience because of the shortness of each section and the contrasts between sections.

Three orchestral compositions from the opera have been combined into a suite.

> **FORM**   A **suite** is a group of related compositions.

Listen to a recording of the Suite from *Amahl and the Night Visitors* to
  • identify the three scenes from the opera suggested by the three compositions
  • describe the mood expressed in each section

STUDYING THE MOOD

Identification of contrasting moods in music should be followed with a study of how each mood is created.

Listen to the suite again to discover how Menotti creates the mood of each section.

Which musical characteristic is most prominent in portraying the mood of each scene?

How does the rhythm suggest the movement inherent in each scene?

Why is the tone color of the predominant instrument appropriate for each scene?

Compare class discoveries with these general observations about the suite:

First section ("Introduction"): The music suggests the tranquility of the desert night. The flowing rhythm and high, sustained pitches of the melody heard in the singing tones of the strings contribute to the serene, ethereal quality of the music.

Second section ("March of the Three Kings"): The music suggests the dignity of the three kings, though there are unexpected touches of humor (associated in the opera with Kasper, who is slightly deaf). The constantly changing range of pitch heard in the contrasting tone colors of the orchestral instruments, such as the flute and bass clarinet, adds a whimsical flavor to the majestic march music.

Third section ("Shepherds' Dance"): There are sharp contrasts within this section. The music changes from a stately, even rhythm played by the oboes, suggesting shepherds' pipes, to an uneven, rollicking rhythm played by the violins.

BECOMING ACQUAINTED WITH ORCHESTRAL INSTRUMENTS

Listen particularly to the oboe duet in the first part of the "Shepherds' Dance." Observe that the range of pitch of the oboe is similar to that of the flute.

Study a picture of an oboe and notice that the mouthpiece consists of two small reeds bound together.

The woodwind family includes three groups of instruments. One group includes the flute and piccolo whose tone is produced by blowing across an opening much as one might produce a tone by blowing across the top of a soda bottle. Another group includes the various clarinets and saxophones whose tone is produced by blowing through a mouthpiece containing a single reed. The third group includes the oboe, English horn, bassoon, and contra bassoon whose tone is produced by blowing through a double reed much as one might blow through a pinched soda straw. These double-reed instruments produce a somewhat nasal tone that can be made to sound lyrical and lovely or grotesque or humorous.

Emphasis on simple classroom instruments, important as it is in helping the student learn music, should not preclude the study of orchestral instruments and the importance of instrumental tone color in symphonic musical expression.

113

LESSON 26

LONG, LONG AGO

1. Winds through the ol - ive trees Soft - ly did blow
2. Sheep on the hill - side lay, Whit - er than snow,

Round lit - tle Beth - le - hem, Long, long a - go.
Shep - herds were watch - ing them Long, long a - go.

3. Then from the happy sky,
   Angels bent low,
   Singing their songs of joy
   Long, long ago.

4. Then from a manger bed,
   Cradled, we know,
   Christ came to Bethlehem,
   Long, long ago.

Traditional song

TEACHING THE SONG TO THE PRIMARY GRADES

"Long, Long Ago" is among the very few songs that tell the Christmas story in a way simple enough for little children to understand.

"Long, Long Ago," like "My Little Pony," may be taught in both the primary and intermediate grades. It is among the very few songs that tell the Christmas story in a way simple enough for little children to understand. In the primary grades, emphasis should be placed on the words and action of the text and on singing by imitation. In the intermediate grades, this simple tune challenges children to use their growing abilities to understand and produce more complex musical effects through a study of mood, text, melody, and harmony.

Introduce "Long, Long Ago" by singing all four verses or by playing the recording of verses 1, 3, and 4. Emphasize its quiet mood by calling attention to the story and by focusing attention on words and simple facts about the melody.

Children are eager to sing. If there is a repeated phrase they can learn quickly, they will want to join the teacher as she sings the song.

"Listen to this Christmas song and decide what the music tells about the Baby Jesus."

"As I sing the song again, join in on the last phrase, 'Long, long ago.' To make our music sound more like a lullaby, hold onto '-go' with me. Listen and learn who is told about in the song."

Discovering the story a song tells is a much more interesting and meaningful way for children to learn than by repetition of word phrases.

"Each verse of the song tells something more of the Christmas story. Let us recall the words of each verse and sing the song together."

"Now that you are more familiar with the words and the melody, let us sing the song again. Remember that to tell this Christmas story best, you must sing it softly and slowly."

114

CREATING A PANTOMIME

The four short verses of the song are like four miniatures that portray the Christmas story. Their clarity and simplicity suggest that the song would lend itself well to pantomime. Help the children plan such a performance.

> "We can make a play of the Christmas song and present it as our part of the Christmas program. What actors will we need for our performance?"
>
> "Olive trees will be on stage when our play starts. What will they be doing? Why would the sound of pompons help what is happening?"
>
> "The shepherds with their sheep come into the scene next. Will they move quickly or slowly?"
>
> "How can the angels in the third verse show by the way they stand that they are singing 'songs of joy'?"
>
> "Where shall we place Mary and Joseph in the last scene?"

Divide the class into singers and actors.

Help the children decide who shall play the different parts in the dramatization.

Help the actors practice to create the gentle swaying of the olive trees, the quiet movements of the sheep and the shepherds, the jubilant yet reverent attitude of the angels, and the entrance of Mary and Joseph.

The singers may decide to sing the verses with or without the recording.

One way to plan the dramatization is to sketch a stage arrangement on the chalkboard to show where the actors will stand in the final scene:

Illustration 1

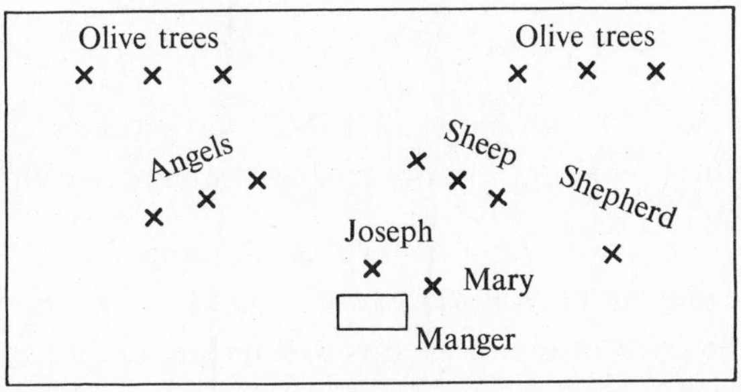

Encourage the children to create the mood of the song in their singing and in their actions.

Perfection in performance is not a goal in classroom music, but the teacher realizes that if children are to develop sensitivity to music and interest in musical performance, they must have the sense of accomplishment that results when they do their best work.

TEACHING THE SONG TO INTERMEDIATE CHILDREN

The simplicity of the melody and text makes "Long, Long Ago" an easy song for children in the intermediate grades to learn. It also affords them special opportunities to experience more mature "music-making."

Music and drama complement each other. If a song lends itself to dramatization, the musical experience is deepened by acting it out, but forced or superficial dramatization is harmful to the musical and artistic development of the child.

A collection of old draperies, curtains, bathrobes, and scarves of many colors furnishes costumes that help timid children forget themselves in their roles.

The suggestions given here are only possibilities for dramatization. Ideas created in the classroom can be fresher and more interesting than those in any textbook.

Teach the song in a straightforward manner. To emphasize the reverent mood and the quiet, rocking rhythm, sing the four verses with the recording. Encourage the children to discover in both the music and words what the song is telling and to follow the score while learning the melody.

"Follow both the score and the words of the song and join in the singing when you can. Determine why the song is easy to learn. Find words to describe its mood."

"Remember while we sing the song together that the story is best told in quiet singing."

When children understand why they are singing softly, they sing better and develop insight into the use of dynamics in music.

ADDING AN APPROPRIATE DESCANT

In beginning two-part singing, children should learn one part well before attempting a second part.

When the children have become familiar with the melody, they will be able to learn the descant shown in illustration 2.

"We can make our music more effective by adding a descant to the song. Listen while I sing the descant and follow the notes as I point to them on the chart [or chalkboard]. Determine what words in the song suggest this descant and why it will enhance the mood of the music."

Take advantage of every opportunity to associate musical sound with notation.

Illustration 2

"Sing the descant with me while I point out on the chart the notes we are singing. What do you observe in the notation that will help you remember the descant?"

Give children the opportunity to discover for themselves the meaning of musical symbols.

Practice on the descant may be varied by
• dividing the class into two groups and letting each group sing the descant while the other listens
• asking a child with sufficient keyboard experience to play the descant on the resonator bells while the class sings

Create ways to make practice both interesting and meaningful to children.

When the descant has been learned, divide the class into two groups. One group sings the descant, the other the melody, always emphasizing the song's quiet mood. The resonator bells or the teacher's voice may be necessary on the descant part.

CREATING AN APPROPRIATE ACCOMPANIMENT

Approach all learning experiences through the sound of the music. To create good accompaniments decide on an appropriate sound.

Give children the opportunity to discover that the quality of sound produced by the resonator bells is appropriate for accompanying the song.

116

"Listen to the resonator bells as I play one of the chords in the song accompaniment. Decide why this instrument will furnish a good accompaniment for 'Long, Long Ago.' "

Play the A chord on the resonator bells, all three notes at once and then one at a time (illustration 3) so that the children will be able to identify the bell sound as being appropriate for the music. Some of the pupils may suggest that the bell sound and the manner in which the instruments are played is similar to the old handbells used in worship services.

Illustration 3

In the intermediate grades, there may be some musically talented pupils who can learn to play a resonator bell accompaniment after the manner of the handbell choir.

Older children can do interesting research into the various kinds of bells and their roles in history.

"We can make the resonator bell accompaniment sound somewhat like a handbell choir by playing a special arrangement of the notes of each of the chords. This chart will help us pick out the different resonator bell pitches we will need for the accompaniment [illustration 4]."

Illustration 4

E F# A B C# D E

Ask the children to follow the accompaniment (illustration 5) on chart or chalkboard while the teacher plays the bells. Then allow time for each child to practice. If too much class time is needed for practice but interest runs high, arrange for extra sessions before or after school.

Illustration 5

When the bell accompaniment has been learned, play it through once or select a child to play it, with no singing. Encourage the class to listen for musical movement in the harmonic pattern as well as in the rhythm.

Never underestimate the perceptive abilities of children. Create situations in which they have opportunity to experience and describe the harmonic, as well as melodic and rhythmic, movement.

"We know that music moves in rhythm. Close your eyes while the bells are played and listen carefully to the way the harmonic sound of the accompaniment moves. Find words to describe the movement of the sound."

PLANNING A PERFORMANCE

The class is divided into three groups, two singing groups (melody and descant) and bell players. With the help of the teacher, the children decide on an introduction, coda, and if desired, interludes between verses. Before deciding, the class may want to experiment with the following suggestions:

Use the descant of the first phrase as the introduction, coda, and interludes.

Use the resonator bell accompaniment of the first phrase for all three purposes.

As an introduction and coda, sing the phrase "Long, long ago" twice.

As the class practices the performance, encourage them to use imagination and knowledge of the music to create the mood of the song.

In a Christmas program, "Long, Long Ago" brings a moment of reverence and quiet and may be used effectively in a manger scene or as an interlude.

LESSON 27

THE TOP AND PIZZICATO

It is not necessary to have singing in each class period. Sometimes a listening period is welcomed by both teacher and children, particularly in the middle of a crowded holiday schedule. The following lesson, like the one on "Dance of the Mosquito" and "The Flight of the Bumble Bee" (Lesson 18), gives children in the primary grades an opportunity to analyze and compare orchestral works and to hear instruments that are not readily available in the classroom.

"The Top" from *Jeux d'Enfants* by Georges Bizet and "Pizzicato" from *The Fantastic Toyshop* by Gioacchino Rossini (orchestrated by Ottorino Respighi) are two orchestral compositions appealing to children in music and subject.

PRESENTING ORCHESTRAL MUSIC TO A PRIMARY GRADE

Invite the children to listen to a recording of "The Top" without giving them background information about the music.

> "As you listen to this music, guess what it is describing."

Give the children the opportunity to show with movement what they are hearing in the music.

> "This time, instead of telling me what you think the music is about, act it out as you listen."

Ask the children to suggest titles for the composition and to give their reasons.

> "I could guess what many of you were hearing in the music as you were moving. What title would you give to this composition?"
>
> "Listen to the music again and describe the sound that suggests your titles of 'Whirlwind,' 'Top,' and 'Helicopter.'"
>
> "Some of you say the music is fast; others hear a humming sound."
>
> "Ann says, 'The music stops, then goes from low to high, like something winding or going up in the air.'"
>
> "You have good reasons for selecting your titles. I will give you a clue to the title that the composer chose. It is an old-fashioned toy that children enjoy especially at Christmas and at Hanukah."

Invite the children to act out the music, using scarves.

> "Act out again what you hear in the music. This time, select a scarf to help you show the colors of a spinning top or the speed of a whirlwind."

As the children listen again to the recording, help them follow the shape of the melody on a chart or on the chalkboard (illustration 1).

Among many approaches to listening is one in which children are invited to discover for themselves what the music expresses and to suggest a title before learning the composer's title.

A child's first response to music is usually to its rhythm.

By explaining their reasons for the choice of a title, children will be encouraged to recognize and name the obvious features heard in the music, such as tempo, pitch, or dynamics.

Give children guidance in listening to a particular part of the music and suggest a response which will give them an opportunity to reveal that they have heard it.

Children in the primary grades may be able to perceive the shape of a melody, although their understanding of specific features of notation may be limited by lack of experience and background.

"Follow the notes on the chart and show with your hand the shape of the melody that suggests the circling motion."

Illustration 1

Help children discover the variety of tone color provided by a change from woodwinds to strings.

"Name and find pictures of the instruments that played the theme the first time it is heard; the second time."

Guide class discussion so that the children will learn the following things about the music:

The music moves quickly, and the notes are staccato.

The strings, first alone and then as an accompaniment, effect the sound of the whirring, spinning top.

First the woodwinds, then the strings playing pizzicato, effect the swaying motion of the top.

 The word **pizzicato,** or its abbreviation *pizz.,* indicates that violinists and other string players are to pluck rather than bow the strings.

PRESENTING A RELATED ORCHESTRAL WORK

Play a recording of "Pizzicato." Introduce this composition by giving background information and listening instructions in as few words as possible.

"There are many old stories that tell of the magical moment at midnight when toys come to life. What toy does this music suggest to you? Listen to discover how the music tells about the toy."

Among many approaches to listening is one in which children are invited to discover the musical characteristics that describe a scene, event, or story.

Help children hear in the introduction the descriptive effect created by the slow tempo and the ascending and descending melody line. Invite them to describe what they hear.

"How does the music of the introduction describe the toy coming to life? Does the melody move up or down? Is the music fast or slow?"

"Bill says that the slow music going up sounds like the toy coming to life and lazily stretching. Jane says the music moving down sounds like the toy coming down from the shelf."

The action associated with descriptive music helps children recognize and identify musical characteristics, such as the rise and fall of melody, and changes in tempo or dynamics.

Help the children relate the fast tempo and lightness of the music to the story.

"As you hear the music again, listen especially to the fast section and decide what kind of toy is described in the music."

MOVING TO THE MUSIC

Invite the children to dramatize their ideas about the music. Plan the movement in relation to available classroom space.

> "Instead of telling me about the toy the music suggested to you, let us act out a whole toyshop. Maybe I can guess from the way you move what toy you are pretending to be. Rows 1 and 2 may start from the back, rows 3 and 4 from the front."

Children move more freely and expressively when they are identifying themselves with a particular character.

Mention class movements that were appropriate and interpretive.

> "I saw many different toys; there were mechanical toys, dolls, and animals. Some were running; others were dancing on tiptoe and whirling."

Summarize for the class some of the specific characteristics to which they responded in their dancing.

> "The introduction is smooth and slow."
>
> "The dance is fast. It changes from light to heavy, soft to loud, high to low."
>
> "There are pauses in the music that suggest that you turn and go the other way."

BECOMING ACQUAINTED WITH ORCHESTRAL INSTRUMENTS

Encourage children to identify contrasting tone colors.

> "Listen again to discover which instruments play the smooth, slow introduction and which play the light, fast dance."

Provide pictures of instruments of contrasting tone color and let the children guess which they have heard.

Children may not know the name of an instrument heard in the music, but they can often relate the sound of an instrument to a picture of it.

> "Here is a picture of brass instruments, a picture of drums, and a picture of string instruments. Which ones did you hear in the introduction? in the dance?"
>
> "Ann [who plays a violin] says that the violins were played by plucking the strings. Listen again and describe the sound the plucked strings make."

Take advantage of the repetition that a short composition of one or two minutes can provide to study and identify musical characteristics.

Let the children pluck the strings of the autoharp to produce their own pizzicato tones.

> "Pluck the strings of an autoharp to make a pizzicato sound. 'Pizzicato' is also the name of the music we have heard today."

Encourage children to learn the correct names for musical effects.

PAT-A-PAN

1. Wil - lie, take your lit - tle drum; Rob - in, bring your fife and come;

Play - ing on the fife and drum, Tu - re - lu - re - lu, pat-a-pat-a- pan,

We'll make mu - sic loud and gay, For our Christ-mas hol - i - day.

2. Shepherds glad, in ancient days,
   Gave the King of Kings their praise;
   Playing on the fife and drum,
   Tu-re-lu-re-lu, pat-a-pat-a-pan,
   They made music loud and gay,
   On the Holy Child's birthday.

3. Christian men, rejoice as one,
   Leave your work and join our fun;
   Playing on the fife and drum,
   Tu-re-lu-re-lu, pat-a-pat-a-pan,
   We'll make music loud and gay,
   For our Christmas holiday.

Early Burgundian French carol
Words translated by Janet Tobitt

From *The Ditty Bag,* copyright 1946 by Janet Tobitt.

TEACHING THE SONG TO THE INTERMEDIATE GRADES

Since children are interested in learning the customs other boys and girls enjoy during the holidays, foreign Christmas songs have special appeal.

The class listens to the recording of "Pat-a-pan." Or the teacher sings the song unaccompanied or with the autoharp, lightly and in a lively tempo to reveal its holiday spirit. Let the children discover for themselves the holiday custom described in "Pat-a-pan."

"As you listen to this French Christmas song, decide why it might be called a 'children's carol.'"

Help children discover which words contribute to the playful mood of the song.

It has been said that folk songs live only if children like them. Perhaps this is why so many old folk songs have nonsense syllables.

"Listen to the song and discover which words imitate the sound of the fife and which imitate the sound of the drum."

Encourage children to use the score as a guide in learning the song.

"Sing with me this time and discover why the 'Tu-re-lu-re-lu' will be easy to play on the bells."

Make practical use of the children's discovery of the phrase containing an ascending scale (illustration 1) by having it played on the melody instrument.

Whenever possible, follow the discovery of melodic patterns with performance activity.

Illustration 1

D E F G A

"Johnny will play the short scale-wise pattern in the melody when we sing it in the song."

Give children ideas for creating rhythm patterns.

"Let us use the rhythm of the words 'pat-a-pan' as an idea for a drum accompaniment. Clap the rhythm shown on the chart (illustration 2). Which do you think would be better for such a rhythm, a large drum or a small drum?"

Children are more secure in playing a rhythmic figure when they can associate it with a previous experience.

Follow the performance of a rhythmic figure with its notation.

Illustration 2

pat - a - pan, pat - a - pan, pat - a - pan.

"Joan has decided on the small drum. She will play the drum rhythm, and Johnny will add the bell phrase as we sing the song again."

CREATING AN APPROPRIATE ACCOMPANIMENT

Help children become aware of and identify particular musical sounds. Simulate the sound of a bagpipe by strumming the low strings of the autoharp while (1) pressing at the same time the D-minor and D₇ autoharp buttons in phrases harmonized with the D-minor chord and (2) pressing the A-minor and A₇ autoharp buttons in phrases harmonized by the A₇ chords.

"Listen to a new sound we have never heard before in our 'music making' and decide what musical instrument it imitates."

Point out the appropriateness of the bagpipe sound.

"Long ago in southern Europe the bagpipes were played to accompany some of the Christmas carols. We can imitate the bagpipe sound by pressing two buttons at once while strumming the low strings."

"As we continue to practice and learn the song, several of you may have turns playing the bagpipe sound."

The drama of hearing a "new sound" captures the attention of children. Being able to produce this sound themselves insures their interest.

Unusual sound effects should always be appropriate to the music so that their use enhances the performance and deepens musical understanding.

Planning an orchestral performance furnishes motivation for creative thinking and the development of skills. These, in turn, give children a sense of accomplishment.

Invite the children to express their ideas for creating a classroom orchestra.

"We can plan a simple accompaniment with the fife and drum sound, or we can make music 'loud and gay,' as described in the song, by adding other instruments. Which do you suggest?"

Discover with the children the contributions each class member can make to the class orchestra.

"If we plan an orchestra, more people can play. Let us list all the possibilities."

Include children's suggestions in the organization of group activity, but have a well-planned lesson in reserve to be used as needed for guidance.

After listing the instrumental possibilities, divide the class into several groups. Each group will be responsible for making a particular contribution to the music.

In organizing this type of performance it is wise to make a detailed list of what each group is going to learn and play in the class orchestra. Then review with each group the music it is to practice.

Group 1 (Autoharps) learns the chords indicated on the music or plays the bagpipe accompaniment.

For special performances, borrow an extra autoharp or set of bells from a neighboring classroom. Be sure that all instruments are tuned together.

Group 2 (Resonator bells) plays the D-minor and A_7 chords (illustration 3), as indicated on the score.

Illustration 3

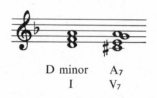

D minor A_7
I V_7

Awareness of the relationship between primary chords and their progressions is developed as children play the autoharp and resonator bell accompaniments.

Group 3 (Percussion instruments) plays the "pat-a-pan" rhythm on small, high-pitched drums to imitate the sound of children's snare drums (illustration 2).

Group 4 (Recorder or flute-like instruments) plays the "Tu-re-lu-re-lu" melody (illustration 1) and the three half notes at the end of the first and last phrases.

Children who are able to play the entire song should be encouraged to do so; others may play shorter excerpts.

Group 5 (Song bells) plays with group 4 or plays the entire melody.

Group 6 (Orchestral instruments) One child plays the melody on a flute. One or two children can pluck the open A and D strings of the violin, following the score.

A simple harmonic part for recorders, bells, or orchestral instruments is provided by playing the roots of the chords indicated in the autoharp score.

When the groups have learned their accompaniments, help the class present an artistic performance of "Pat-a-pan." There are a number of interesting vocal and instrumental combinations that the class may choose, some of which are suggested on page 125. A large simple chart showing the order in which the variations are to be played adds to the smoothness of a performance.

124

Introduction	{ Drums play four measures with gradual crescendo to give the effect of an approaching drummer.	
First playing	{ Melody:	Flute and (or) recorders
	Accompaniment:	Drums
Second playing	{ Melody:	Sing verse 1.
	Accompaniment:	Drums and autoharp
Third playing	{ Melody:	Flute and (or) recorders
	Accompaniment:	Resonator bells
Fourth playing	{ Melody:	Sing verse 2 with song bells.
	Accompaniment:	Drums and autoharp
Fifth playing	{ Melody:	Sing verse 3 with flute, recorders, and song bells.
	Accompaniment:	Autoharp, resonator bells, violin, and drums
Coda	Drums fade out.	

O HANUKAH

La la la la la la la la la la la.

O Ha - nu - kah, O Ha - nu - kah, come light the me - no - rah.

Let's have a par - ty, we'll all dance the ho - ra.

Gath - er round the ta - ble, we'll give you a treat.

Shin - ing tops to play with and pan - cakes to eat;

And while we are play - ing, The can - dles are burn - ing low,

Melody reprinted from *Gateway to Jewish Song* by Judith Eisenstein,
published by Behrman House, Inc., 1261 Broadway, N.Y. 1, N.Y.

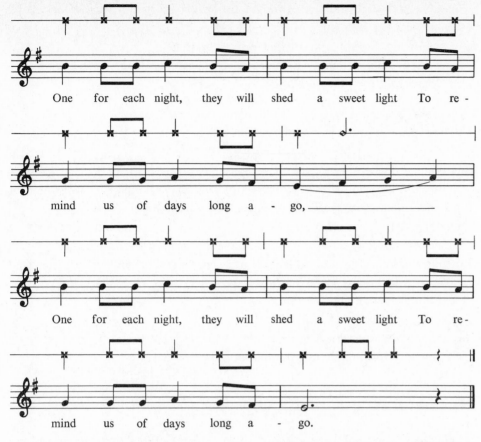

One for each night, they will shed a sweet light To re-

mind us of days long a - go, _____

One for each night, they will shed a sweet light To re-

mind us of days long a - go.

Yiddish folk song. Translated by Judith Eisenstein

BECOMING ACQUAINTED WITH THE MUSIC

Listen to the recording of "O Hanukah" and decide what combination of musical elements (melody, harmony, rhythm) and aspects of interpretation (tempo, dynamics, instrumental tone color) are especially prominent in creating the mood of the music.

The music of "O Hanukah" speaks of gaiety and festivity. The reason for the mood is revealed in the words that tell how the Jewish people celebrate Hanukah, a religious holiday decreed many hundreds of years ago in commemoration of a miracle of lights that occurred in the Temple of Jerusalem.

In 165 B.C. the Jews under the leadership of Judas Maccabaeus drove Greek invaders from their city. The invaders had defiled the temple by worshiping their many gods in the building dedicated to the one God of the Jews.

After the people had cleansed the temple, they found only one small vial of pure olive oil with which to re-light the Menorah, the sacred lights that were to burn continually as a reminder of the eternal presence of their God. Through a miracle, this one day's supply of oil lasted for eight days.

For this reason the eight-day festival of Hanukah (whose name has been transliterated into several different spellings), also called the Festival of Lights, is celebrated by the Jewish people. These eight days usually fall in December. One candle is lighted each day, and at the end of the holiday eight candles flame from the modern menorahs (candelabra) in Jewish households and temples. Although sacred in origin, Hanukah is also a time for parties, feasts, and dancing.

Exploration of the folk music of different cultures encourages study of the people, history, customs, and traditions out of which the music grew. Such knowledge, in turn, heightens sensitivity to the music itself and results in more expressive performance.

127

Follow the score while listening to the recording again and get better acquainted with the song by

- noticing the words that tell of the celebration
- discovering in the music the characteristics that identify it as having come from the Eastern world

Compare class discoveries with these observations about the music:

The melody is in the minor mode, as is much of the music of the Near East.

The recurring rhythm of quarter and eighth notes (♩ ♫♩ ♫) is characteristic of much Eastern music.

Now sing the song with the recording, listening especially for the sound of the minor mode and the effect created by the repetitions of the ♩ ♫♩ ♫ rhythmic idea.

Although the phrases of this song are regular in structure in that each phrase has four measures, the over-all form is unusual. Sing "O Hanukah" to determine which of the forms suggested below is that of the song:

1. Introduction and ABABC
2. Introduction and ABCAB
3. Introduction and ABCDD

How is this form different from that of most folk songs?

CREATING AN APPROPRIATE ACCOMPANIMENT

To bring authentic tone color to the performance, create an original tambourine accompaniment or learn the one in the score.

If the scored accompaniment is chosen, observe that there are two basic rhythm patterns for the tambourine (illustration 1). Learn these rhythms. Then study the score to locate and practice the phrases in which there are slight variations in the basic patterns.

Illustration 1

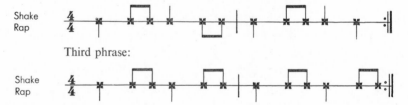

Introduction, first, second, fourth, and fifth phrases:

Shake
Rap

Third phrase:

Shake
Rap

Play the tambourine accompaniment while the song is sung with the recording.

CREATING A DANCE

To create the festive mood of "O Hanukah," learn to dance the traditional hora, a vigorous and popular dance of the Jewish people. Perhaps someone in the class knows the dance and can teach it to the group. It is usually quicker and easier to have a dance demonstrated than it is to follow written directions.

Practice the basic steps and repeat them alternately throughout the dance. Notice that the circle always moves to the right.

Formation: Closed circle, hands on neighbors' shoulders

Basic steps: First measure   Step right on right foot.

Step left foot behind right foot.

Step right again on right foot.

Swing left foot forward, hopping on right foot.

Second measure   Step on left foot in place.

Step on right foot in place.

Step on left foot in place.

Pause before beginning pattern again.

CREATING AN AUTOHARP ACCOMPANIMENT

"O Hanukah" cannot be accompanied on the autoharp in the key in which it is written. Study the score to discover clues that will help in working out *by ear* an accompaniment in a key suitable for the autoharp.

How does the score show that the song is written in the key of E minor? What major key has the same key signature of one sharp? Why do E minor and the major key have the same key signature? (If in doubt, refer to page 107.)

"O Hanukah" can be accompanied, for the most part, with only one chord. Use illustration 2 showing the primary chords of E minor to help determine the chord on which most of the song is built. This structure is especially obvious in measures 1 and 3 of the first phrase (A) and measures 1 and 2 of the third phrase (C).

Although recordings can be used to good effect in carrying on a classroom music program, students should be encouraged to develop the skills necessary to create music independently.

Illustration 2

Use the knowledge that the song can be accompanied, for the most part, on the tonic chord (I chord) to transpose (change) the song from the key of E minor to the key of D minor, a key suitable for the autoharp. Study illustration 3 to determine which chord in the new key will furnish most of the accompaniment.

Illustration 3

Because both ear and eye tell that D minor is one whole step lower than E minor, every pitch in the transposed melody will be one pitch lower. Pluck D on the autoharp. This is the beginning note of "O Hanukah" in the key of D minor.

Strum the D-minor chord on the autoharp, two strums for each measure, and sing the song. Listen carefully to discover by ear the few places that demand the V₇ (A₇) or IV (G-minor) chord. Write the chord symbols above the score.

Practice the autoharp accompaniment, add the tambourine, and use these instruments instead of the recording to accompany the singing and dancing.

Experience in playing the autoharp by ear is exciting and especially meaningful when supported by knowledge of harmonic structure.

MARCH OF THE THREE KINGS

The one a black king, and one was brown ___

Who came so far for a lit - tle Ba - by's pleas - ure.

And one was white with a gold - en crown ___

The three great kings so gal - lant and so gay.

French carol. English words
by Abbie Farwell Brown

BECOMING ACQUAINTED WITH THE MUSIC

The melody of "March of the Three Kings," a seven-hundred-year-old French carol, was used by Georges Bizet in "Prelude" in *L'Arlésienne: Suite No. 1* and in "Farandole" in *L'Arlésienne: Suite No. 2.*

Listen to the "Prelude" to discover what there is in the melody that suggests a march of kings rather than of clowns or soldiers.

Listen to the recording again. From the following list, pick *five* ways in which Bizet treats the themes.

1. Statement of the theme with almost the whole orchestra
2. Variation for string ensemble only
3. Harmonic variation for solo clarinet and woodwinds
4. Variation for trumpets and timpani
5. Variation for woodwinds and brasses, with string accompaniment
6. Variation in major mode for horns and cellos, with bassoon accompaniment
7. Processional for full orchestra

It is important to become acquainted with works of many composers and to renew acquaintance with composers whose music has been heard before.

There are two obvious advantages in studying a song as it is used in a symphonic work: The listener (1) learns the melody of the song in repeated hearings and (2) learns about the way a composer handles musical materials and orchestral instruments.

STUDYING THE SCORE

Study the score of "March of the Three Kings" and find the themes (melodic ideas) that Bizet used in his *L'Arlésienne* suites.

Prepare to sing "March of the Three Kings" by studying the words and the melody of the song.

The text tells a French version of the journey of the Magi, the three wise men who came from the East to pay homage at the feet of the Christ Child. In all stories about the Magi, one king is white, one black, and the third brown. These

Discovering in a score the themes that have been experienced aurally is an interesting and meaningful way to study music.

Study the words and notation that reveal the subject and musical structure of a song before attempting to sing it.

131

kings, following the same star, met and went on their journey together, arriving finally with their rich gifts at the manger in Bethlehem.

Observe that there are only two different melodic phrases in the song itself (AA'BB').

Observe the repeat sign at the end of the first phrase (A) and the changes in the melody at the end of the A' and B' phrases.

Now sing "March of the Three Kings" *a cappella* or with the teacher or a capable student playing a piano accompaniment. Use ears and eyes to discover the dramatic change that occurs at the second verse. How does this change dramatize the text of the song?

Make a study of the musical characteristics that deepen the understanding of a song and suggest means for expressive interpretation.

Follow the score while singing the song again, using ear and eye to discover the melodic and rhythmic characteristics that give the music vigor and strength.

Could the melody line, for the most part, be described as angular or smooth?

Could the rhythmic movement of the melody, for the most part, be described as even or uneven?

Compare class discoveries about the music with these observations on the mode, melodic contour, and rhythmic movement of the song:

The dramatic change in the music of the second verse is a change from minor mode to major mode. Perhaps the brighter color of the major mode suggests that the wise men have accomplished their mission.

Prominent in creating the dramatic and energetic mood of the song is its angular, active melody line. Large intervals dominate the first phrase, and there is a change of melodic direction in almost every measure of the music.

The desire to develop intelligent reading skills increases with the discovery that notation is a revelation of musical ideas rather than a dull sequence of hard-to-decipher notes and rests.

Prominent in establishing the feeling of vigor in the song is the dotted rhythm (uneven movement) found throughout the music.

Study the two melodic figures in illustration 1 to deepen understanding of how melody and rhythm are used to create a particular musical idea and to emphasize the importance of performing notation accurately.

Illustration 1

Observe the angular, uneven melodic idea from "March of the Three Kings" in illustration 1a and the smooth, even version in illustration 1b.

Sing these melodic fragments and compare them by finding adjectives to describe the musical effect of each.

Sing "March of the Three Kings," taking special care to perform the melodic and rhythmic patterns correctly. Decide which is more important to the mood of the song, its melody line or rhythm pattern.

132

CREATING APPROPRIATE ACCOMPANIMENTS

Select appropriate percussion instruments and create an accompaniment to dramatize the musical qualities that make this song a triumphant processional. Use class ideas or those suggested below.

The tone colors of drums and large cymbals are effective in creating the mood of a processional. Finger cymbals can be used for the contrasting color appropriate to music from the Near East.

First verse: Introduction and Phrase A and A′ — Use the large drum alone, playing a strong, stately rhythm ($\frac{4}{4}$ ♩ ♩ | ♩ ♩ :‖).

                  Phrases B and B′ — Add finger cymbals while drum continues, softer in volume ($\frac{4}{4}$ ♩♩♩♩ | ♩♩♩♩ :‖).

Second verse: Phrases A and A′ — To emphasize the change to major mode, play large cymbals at dramatic points of the melody (♩ ♩ | ♩ 𝄽 𝄽 | 𝄽 𝄽 ♩ ♩ | ♩ :‖).

                  Phrases B and B′ — Add finger cymbals as in first verse. End the song with a crash of big cymbals.

Use dynamics to suggest the approach of the procession.

Practice the percussion accompaniment decided upon and add it to the performance of the song.

If a piano is not available, the resonator bells will probably make the best possible accompaniment the class can play on a pitched instrument.

Study illustration 2 to recall how the primary chords in a key are determined and how chords are built.

Observe that the V₇ (D₇) chord is the same in both the G-minor and G-major keys.

Observe that the change of mode, G minor to G major, is effected by simply changing one pitch in each of the G and C chords: to make the G-minor chord a major chord, the B-flat becomes B-natural; to make the C-minor a C-major chord, the E-flat becomes E-natural.

Learn to be discriminating in choosing from the pitched instruments available. Use the one that produces the accompaniment most appropriate for the song.

HARMONY   Pitches in a triad are called **root, third,** and **fifth.** The root and fifth are called **basic tones.** The third is called the **color tone.**

Illustration 2

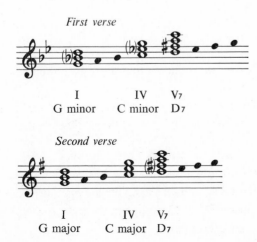

First verse

I   IV   V₇
G minor   C minor   D₇

Second verse

I   IV   V₇
G major   C major   D₇

Illustration 3 shows chord positions (inversions) that are pleasing in effect.

Observe in illustration 3 that some notes are common to two different chords: D in both the G chord and the D₇ chord; C in both the C chord and the D₇ chord. Persons playing pitches common to two chords must play them each time they occur in the chord pattern.

As noted in the study of illustration 2, the change from minor to major chords is simple. Those playing the B-flat and the E-flat pitches of the G-minor and C-minor chords can also play the B-natural and E-natural pitches of the G-major and C-major chords of the major mode in the second verse.

Illustration 3

G minor C minor D₇   G major C major D₇

Each individual selects one pitch from the set of resonator bells and plays his pitch whenever it occurs in any chord. Practice the accompaniment under the direction of the teacher or a capable student, then create an effective bell introduction.

Sing "March of the Three Kings" with instrumental accompaniment.

PLANNING A PERFORMANCE

Songs that tell a story and have a particularly descriptive rhythm are especially appropriate for rhythmic dramatization. Such a dramatization must be performed in the spirit and mood of the music if it is to enhance the musical experience.

Re-create the drama inherent in the words and music by re-enacting the journey of the Magi. These suggestions may help in planning such a dramatization:

Three members of the class are chosen to be kings. The rest of the class divides into singers, percussionists, and resonator bell players.

Select a place in the room, probably the front, as the manger scene. Three kings take their places at three different points of the room, as far as possible from the manger scene.

While the singers and accompanists perform the music, the kings dramatize the story, perhaps in the following manner.

Introduction: Kings stand silently and proudly in their respective "countries."

First verse: Phrase A — First king starts his journey, moving in the stately rhythm played throughout by the drum

(4/4 ♩ ♩ | ♩ ♩ :‖).

Phrase A′ — Second king begins his journey.

Phrase B — Third king begins his journey.

Phrase B — The kings meet and proceed together toward the manger scene.

Second verse: Phrase A — The kings are at the manger, kneeling at the feet of the Christ Child.

Phrase A' — The kings rise and start the journey back to the East. At the end of the phrase, the first king leaves the other two and starts in the direction of his "country."

Phrase B — At the end of the phrase, the second king turns in the direction of his "country."

Phrase B' — The three kings, each now moving in a different direction, continue their journey and reach "home" at the end of the performance.

The "pulling together" of the various performance media into a final presentation provides a sense of accomplishment and encourages creative thinking and development of skills.

If a more complete performance is desired, experiment with the following suggestions.

As an introduction, sing phrases A and A' as a two-part round. Observe in the score of the song that the second part enters on the third note of the melody. (Phrases B and B' cannot be sung effectively in round form.)

As a coda, sing the same two-part round used in the introduction.

Use dynamics to create the illusion of distance in the music. The kings come from afar, reach the manger, and return to their distant countries.

EXTENDING INDIVIDUAL EXPERIENCE

This old French carol has endured for more than seven hundred years and must be classified as a "good" melody. Look for the principles of melodic composition used in the song.

Students of composition know that a good song has balance in melodic idea for example, a high point and a low point, usually found only once in a melody line. Check "March of the Three Kings" to discover whether this balance is evident.

A good melody must also have balance in rhythmic idea. Check "March of the Three Kings" to discover how the uneven rhythmic movement of the first two measures of each phrase are balanced by the even rhythmic movement of the last two measures of each phrase.

Listen to a recording of the Suite from *Amahl and the Night Visitors,* paying particular attention to the section called "March of the Three Kings." Compare the two marches and decide in what ways they are similar and in what ways they are different.

LESSON 31

OH, SUSANNA

1. I__ came from Al - a - ba - ma With my ban-jo on my knee,
2. I__ had a dream the oth-er night, When ev-'ry-thing was still.

I'm__ going to Loui - si - an - a, My____ true love for to see;
I__ thought I saw Su - san - na A - com - ing down the hill.

It__ rained all night the day I left, The weath-er it was dry;
The__ buck-wheat cake was in her mouth, The tear was in her eye.

The__ sun so hot I froze to death; Su - san - na, don't you cry.
Says__ I, "I'm com - ing from the South, Su - san - na, don't you cry."

Refrain

Oh, Su - san - na, Oh, don't you cry for me,

I've__ come from Al - a - ba - ma With my ban-jo on my knee.

Words and music by Stephen Foster

CREATING APPROPRIATE ACCOMPANIMENTS

The autoharp accompaniment to a familiar song will be learned quickly when the ear helps the eye.

On the autoharp, locate the chords needed to accompany this song — F, C₇, and B-flat.

Observe that there is a chord change on the strong beat at the beginning of each phrase and one or more changes near the end of each phrase.

Experiment with an imitation of the sound of a banjo.

Practice an "oom-pah" accompaniment (illustration 1) by strumming a few low strings on the first beat of the measure, then a few high strings on the second beat.

Illustration 1

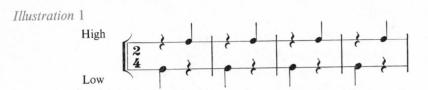

Play a two-measure introduction on the F chord in the tempo of the song:

Illustration 2

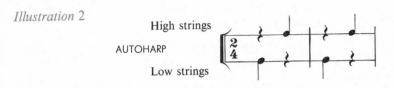

Sing and play the song in the spirit of a minstrel show. Observe that the lively mood is created partially by the rhythmic pattern of the melody above the steady, underlying beat played on the autoharp.

Illustration 3

Create another sound effect of a minstrel show by adding several tambourines to the accompaniment. Raise the left hand in front of the body, crooking the elbow. Hold the tambourine in the right and tap the pattern shown below.

Musical discrimination is developed as the appropriateness of an accompaniment is determined.

Illustration 4

Play this rhythm throughout the refrain.

Vary the accompaniment by changing the tambourine to the left hand and reversing the pattern.

On the melody bells, play the pattern shown in illustration 5 each time it occurs in the song and add it to the accompaniment as a part of the minstrel band.

Take advantage of every opportunity to identify melodic figures with their notation.

Illustration 5

SINGING A PARODY

On their way to California, in the middle 1800's, the gold seekers made song texts of their experiences and sang them to the popular tunes of the day.

Learn these words and sing them with autoharp accompaniment:

Verse: I come from Salem City With my wash bowl on my knee,

               I'm going to California, The gold dust for to see;

               I soon shall be in 'Frisco, And then I'll look around;

               And when I see the gold lumps there; I'll pick them off the ground.

Refrain: Oh, California, That's the land for me,

               I'm bound for Sacramento With my wash bowl on my knee.

CREATING A DANCE

Creating or learning a dance in the style of the period from which the music evolved is one of the basic ways of becoming personally involved in the music and bringing it to life.

Everyone took part in singing and dancing, which was the main recreation of the pioneers. Plan a dance the Forty-niners might have enjoyed, using familiar dance patterns or selected patterns from the following suggestions.

Circle right.

Circle left.

Girls take four steps into center and back.

Boys take four steps into center and back.

Grand right and left (Partners give each other right hands, pass on to the next dancer, giving left hands, and so forth, until dancers have returned to original positions.)

Promenade (Girls take partner's right arm and walk around in a circle.)

Observe that the ending of each phrase provides an effective place to change the dance step.

The form of music is sensed and clarified through movement.

Those standing on the sidelines tapped their feet and clapped their hands in rhythm. Practice the pattern in illustration 6 and add it to the accompaniment.

Illustration 6

Use unusual or bold percussion sounds with reservation. Such color is often effective at the end or climax of a song.

Since the covered wagons provided space for only small musical instruments, such as the fiddle, banjo, or harmonica, domestic articles were often used to provide rhythmic accompaniments.

Experiment with rhythm patterns played on a small washboard or cowbell and add their effects sparingly to the singing and dancing. (A notched gourd tone block may be substituted for a washboard.)

On the chart below, identify the rhythm pattern played by each accompanying instrument.

Illustration 7

Give students an opportunity to see in notation the rhythm pattern they are playing. Several patterns on a chart reveal the relative duration of note values.

PLANNING A PERFORMANCE

Plan a performance of the parody, "Oh, California," as it might have evolved within the circle of covered wagons camped for the night.

The class divides into groups of singers, dancers, and instrumentalists.

Plan an introduction that will include the autoharp and a percussion instrument.

Decide on a sequence of singing, dancing, and playing.

Invite class members who play instruments, such as the violin or the harmonica, to join in the "music-making."

Take advantage of the contribution that may be made to a performance by class members who play orchestral instruments.

GOING DEEPER INTO STRUCTURE

Form   Which phrases are similar, giving unity to the music? What is the form of the song?

Melody   Are the notes "close together" (moving scale-wise) or "far apart"?

Rhythm   Are the notes, for the most part, of long or short duration? How does the rhythm give unity and variety to the song?

Harmony   Determine why the three primary chords (illustration 8) played in the autoharp accompaniment are called I, V_7, IV.

Studying the score of a familiar song is an effective way of relating a specific musical idea to its notation.

Illustration 8

Compare the sound of the phrases ending on the V_7 (C_7) chord with the sound of the phrases ending on the I (C) chord. Which phrase endings are comparable to a question (unresolved)? to an answer (resolved)?

 A cadence that ends on the V_7 (dominant seventh) chord provides an unresolved effect. A cadence that ends on the I (tonic) chord provides a resolved effect.

139

Death Valley Suite by Ferde Grofé was written in commemoration of the one hundredth anniversary of the discovery of the bleak, hostile desert country, later appropriately named Death Valley, which many pioneers crossed on their way to seek gold in southern California in 1849.

Listen to a recording of "Desert Water Hole" from *Death Valley Suite* to discover

- which sounds and movements of pioneers crossing the desert are suggested in the music
- at what point in the composition the mode changes from minor to major
- in what ways the music suggests that the search for water is over
- what three Stephen Foster songs are included or suggested in the music
- which two of these songs are played simultaneously

When the program of a composition has been determined, discover the musical devices the composer chose to provide the musical description.

Compare class discoveries with these observations about "Desert Water Hole":

The thin, high tones of the violins at the very beginning of the movement suggest the relentless heat and loneliness of the barren desert.

The slow tempo and even rhythm of the music suggest the steady plodding of the oxen.

A rising and falling pattern in the accompaniment suggests the turning of the wagon wheels.

The sudden change from the minor mode to the major mode suggests that there is reason for optimism.

The chorale-like melody and the tone of the chimes suggest a moment of prayerful gratitude when the water hole is discovered.

In contrast to the struggle for survival described in the first section, the fiddle introduces the section of dancing and gaiety.

Sections of "Old Folks at Home" and "Old Black Joe" are heard in the dance music.

"Oh, Susanna" and the chorus of "Old Black Joe" are played together.

LESSON 32

BATTLE HYMN OF THE REPUBLIC

1. Mine eyes have seen the glo - ry of the
2. I have seen Him in the watch - fires of a

com - ing of the Lord; He is tram - pling out the
hun - dred cir - cling camps, They have build - ed Him an

vin - tage where the grapes of wrath are stored;
al - tar in the eve - ning dews and damps;

He hath loosed the fate - ful light - ning of His
I can read His right - eous sen - tence by the

ter - ri - ble swift sword; His truth is march - ing on.
dim and flar - ing lamps; His day is march - ing on.

Refrain

Glo - ry, glo - ry, hal - le - lu - jah! Glo - ry, glo - ry, hal - le - lu - jah!

Glo - ry, glo - ry, hal - le - lu - jah! His truth is march - ing on.

3. He has sounded forth the trumpet
That shall never call retreat;
He is sifting out the hearts of men
Before the judgment seat.
Oh, be swift, my soul, to answer Him!
Be jubilant, my feet!
Our God is marching on.

4. In the beauty of the lilies
Christ was born across the sea,
With a glory in His bosom
That transfigures you and me;
As He died to make men holy,
Let us die to make men free,
While God is marching on.

Music by William Steffe
Words by Julia Ward Howe

141

BECOMING ACQUAINTED WITH THE MUSIC

Listen to a recording of "Battle Hymn of the Republic" by a well-known singing group like the Mormon Tabernacle Choir and find adjectives to describe the spirit it conveys and the emotions it excites. Determine what is heard in the music that creates the mood of the song.

Familiar songs afford a special opportunity for creating an expressive performance at the first singing.

On the basis of class discussion of the spirit of the song and the musical features that produce its particular mood, decide on the tempo, dynamics, and expressive qualities necessary for an effective performance of the song. Sing "Battle Hymn of the Republic" unaccompanied or with the teacher or a capable student playing the piano. Evaluate the performance.

When the spirit of a song is dependent largely on a particular musical characteristic, that feature should be studied and learned before further performance is attempted.

The musical element most prominent in establishing the vigorous, martial spirit of the music is the rhythm. To learn the energetic, dotted rhythm pattern correctly and to discover the importance of performing it precisely, try the following experiment.

Sing "Battle Hymn of the Republic" in the even rhythm pattern shown in illustration 1 and describe the change in the spirit of the music.

Sing the song with its original dotted rhythm pattern, shown in illustration 2. Describe the effect this pattern creates in the music.

When students experience and recognize the effect that a particular rhythmic figure has in the music, they are encouraged to develop skills necessary to interpret rhythmic notation accurately.

Illustration 1

Illustration 2

Sing "Battle Hymn of the Republic" in tempo and with the dynamics decided most effective, giving special attention to performing the dotted rhythm precisely. Observe that the dotted rhythm patterns break up the even rhythmic flow of the melody and create points of rhythmic tension in the music.

SINGING IN HARMONY

Singing in harmony demands attentive listening and concentration on the part of the performer.

The blend of martial spirit and religious mood in "Battle Hymn of the Republic" makes it a stirring and inspiring song. To enhance the emotional depth of the music in class performance, learn the simple descant shown in illustration 3 and sing it with the refrain. Listen carefully and find adjectives to describe the effect of the harmony.

  Harmony lends richness, color, and weight to a melody line and adds depth to the music.

Illustration 3

Glo - ry, glo - ry, hal - le - lu - jah!

Glo - ry, glo - ry, His truth is march - ing on.

CREATING APPROPRIATE ACCOMPANIMENTS

Percussion instruments are especially appropriate for emphasizing the vigor inherent in march tunes. Listen while the teacher uses a drum to play one of the rhythm patterns shown in illustration 4 and determine which pattern is being played.

Only those percussion instruments appropriate to the style and spirit of the music should be used in accompaniments.

Illustration 4

Practice the rhythm pattern chosen from illustration 4 and sing "Battle Hymn of the Republic" with drum accompaniment. Discover how the rhythm of the drum enhances the spirit of the music.

The deep sound of a large drum played in stately rhythm adds a feeling of dignity to music.

Use dynamics to make the class performance more dramatic. Begin by playing the large drum softly, as if heard from a distance, and gradually increase the volume.

Sing the song again with drum accompaniment. After the singing has concluded, continue the drum as a coda, gradually decreasing the volume until the sound seems to fade into the distance.

In a performance, take advantage of every opportunity to enhance the drama inherent in the music.

Now listen while the teacher plays several chords on the resonator bells and determine why the quality of the sound makes it an appropriate accompanying instrument for "Battle Hymn of the Republic."

Prepare to play a resonator bell accompaniment by studying illustration 5 to determine the pitches of each chord used in the song.

Observe that the key of B-flat in which the song is sung has two flats — B-flat and E-flat.

In choosing from the pitched instruments available, be discriminating and select the one whose sound is most appropriate for the music.

Observe that all three of the primary chords in the key of B-flat shown in illustration 5 are used in the accompaniment and that the chord pattern of the verse is repeated in the refrain.

Observe and describe the structure of the chords as seen in the notation:

Illustration 5

Understanding of chord structure and the part harmony plays in musical expression develops with the experience of playing chords, hearing them, and seeing them on the score simultaneously.

Study illustration 6 to discover which position of each chord will sound best in the resonator bell accompaniment. Observe that the I and V₇ chords do not appear in root position. The process of changing a chord from its root position is called **inversion.**

Three persons select the pitches of the I (B-flat) chord and play the three pitches at once so that the class may hear the sound of the tonic chord.

Observe that B-flat is found in both the B-flat and E-flat chords. Two more persons select the remaining pitches of the E-flat chord and play them with the B-flat pitch so that the class may hear the sound of the E-flat chord.

Observe that the E-flat and F pitches of the F₇ chord are already held by persons playing the E-flat and B-flat chords.

These two persons will play with the two others who select the remaining pitches of the F₇ chord.

Illustration 6

The elements of music (melody, rhythm, harmony) become vital and expressive only as they are given appropriate interpretation through tempo and dynamics by the imaginative performer.

The easiest way to play these chords on the resonator bells is for the players to stand in chord groups (the persons with the pitches common to two chords must remember to play in both) and to follow a conductor, who will point to each group when its chord occurs in the harmonic accompaniment. Practice following the conductor's cues.

Sing all four verses of "Battle Hymn of the Republic," using the resonator bell and drum accompaniments and singing the descant (illustration 3) in the refrain. Listen carefully to the music created by the entire group and evaluate the performance.

GOING DEEPER INTO STRUCTURE

The outstanding rhythmic quality of the song — the dotted rhythm pattern — was studied at the beginning of the lesson.

However, also important in establishing the vigor and strength of "Battle Hymn of the Republic" is the structure of the melody line, which is built, for the most part, on the notes of the B-flat and E-flat chords. To discover how prevalent the chord notes are in the melody, review illustrations 5 and 6 to recall the pitches of the accompanying chords and to identify the chord structure in the melody. For example, all but two of the notes in the first measure belong to the B-flat chord.

Other well-known songs built on chord lines are "The Star-Spangled Banner," "Reveille," and "Taps." Determine what qualities all of these songs have in common.

The feeling of majestic reverence is established in the music both by the structure of the melody and by the harmonic (chord) pattern.

On the resonator bells or piano, play the two cadences shown in illustration 7. Which of the two cadences is the one heard on the "amen" at the end of hymns?

Learning the characteristics of the harmonic movement in a familiar song helps the student to listen with more sensitivity to harmony and to gain knowledge of harmonic structure.

Illustration 7

Examine the score to determine that the IV (E-flat) chord is used in only one measure of the verse and the refrain.

After the feeling of reverence has been established by the use of the I (B-flat) and IV (E-flat) chords, both verse and refrain are brought to resolute conclusions by the use of the V_7 (F_7) chord.

While "Battle Hymn of the Republic" is sung again, listen for the spirit and mood produced in the melody and harmony as well as in the more obvious rhythm and text of the song.

WHEN JOHNNY COMES MARCHING HOME

1. When John - ny comes march-ing home a - gain, Hur-rah!_ Hur-rah!_
2. Get read - y for the ju - bi - lee Hur-rah!_ Hur-rah!_

We'll give him a heart - y wel - come then, Hur-rah!_ Hur-rah!_
We'll give ___ the he - roes three times three, Hur-rah!_ Hur-rah!_

The_ men will cheer,_ the boys will shout, The la - dies they_ will all turn out,
The_ lau - rel wreath_ is read - y now To place up - on_ his loy - al brow,

And we'll all feel gay When John - ny comes march - ing home!_
And we'll all feel gay When John - ny comes march - ing home!_

Words and music by Louis Lambert

BECOMING ACQUAINTED WITH THE MUSIC

This old favorite was written during the War Between the States. It became popular during the Spanish-American War and has retained its popularity since that time.

Sing the song with autoharp or piano accompaniment played by the teacher. Decide which would be more effective to accompany the exuberant "hurrahs," a drum or large cymbals.

Adding a simple sound effect appropriate to one idea in the music lends further meaning and interest to the learning stages of a song.

TONE COLOR Instruments with bright and dramatic tone color, such as large cymbals, are effective when used sparingly to highlight strong rhythmic points of the music.

Adding a simple accompaniment appropriate to the mood enhances interest and adds meaning to the learning of the song.

While the players are preparing to add the chosen percussion instrument to the "hurrahs," practice a simple autoharp accompaniment that will lend vigor to the performance and enhance the music.

Press at the same time the G-minor and the G-major buttons on the autoharp and strum the low strings of the instrument.

146

Listen to the sound that will be recognized as similar to that of a bagpipe.

This sound is appropriate as an accompaniment for "When Johnny Comes Marching Home" because some historians believe that this melody originally came from Ireland, where the bagpipe is played. Notice that the song is not unlike "Paddy Works on the Railroad" (Lesson 40).

Sing "When Johnny Comes Marching Home," using the autoharp to play an introduction and accompaniment in bagpipe style. Play the percussion instrument on the "hurrahs."

Take turns playing the new sound in the autoharp accompaniment in order to give everyone in the class an opportunity to become familiar with the melody.

CREATING AN ORCHESTRATION

Begin an orchestration by creating a special sound effect in the music.

On the second verse of the song, play the pattern shown in illustration 1 on the melody bells to simulate the sound of church bells.

While playing the pattern as an accompaniment, discover why alternating the low D and the D an octave higher is more effective than sounding D always on the same pitch level.

Illustration 1

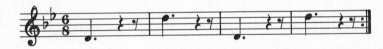

| TERM | The term **octave** literally means "eight." It is the name of the musical phenomenon of two pitches, eight diatonic notes apart, duplicating each other in sound. The octave is the only interval common to almost every scale evolved and is called the "basic miracle of music." |

| TERM | The term **diatonic** is used to refer to any scale, melody, or harmony based on a natural scale (five whole steps and two half steps) without chromatic alterations or accidentals. |

Add the sound of the glockenspiel to the last two phrases of the song by playing the melody bells in the pattern shown below.

Illustration 2

Observe that the notes of the first four measures in illustration 2 occur on the first beat of each measure in the same rhythm as that of the "church bells" and "bagpipe."

Observe that the notes of the last four measures in illustration 2 move two notes to the measure.

Observe that the melodic figures in each of the four-measure phrases are in descending, scale-wise movement.

Practice the whole two-phrase melody.

Sing "When Johnny Comes Marching Home" and play the glockenspiel pattern on the last two phrases.

Complete the orchestration by playing drums in a rhythm often heard in marching band music.

Listen and try to identify on the chart in illustration 3 the rhythm patterns the teacher chooses to play.

Listen again. Determine which rhythm pattern is most appropriate for bass drum (large drum) and which is most appropriate for snare drums (small drums).

Rhythmic notation has greater meaning for the student when he becomes aware of the effect created by various rhythm patterns and learns to recognize these effects in note values of long and short duration.

Illustration 3   Typical Drum Rhythms in **6/8** Meter

Visual aids, such as charts, are especially effective in focusing class attention on specific symbols of notation and in showing the relationship between these symbols and musical performance.

Practice the two patterns chosen, one for large drum, one for small drums, and add them to the orchestration.

PLANNING A PERFORMANCE

Beginning with the Spanish-American War, "When Johnny Comes Marching Home" was sung in gala parades that sent the soldiers off to battle and welcomed them home again.

Re-create a parade scene with soldiers, a marching band, and cheering spectators. The following suggestions will help in planning the performance.

The class divides into groups of singers and players of autoharps, melody bells, drums, and cymbals.

As an introduction, create the illusion of soldiers and a band coming from a distance. Start the rhythm of the large drum softly and continue to increase the volume as the small drums and "bagpipe" are added.

Start the parade of the soldiers and the drum and cymbal players at the beginning of the first verse.

Decide on changes in dynamics that will best interpret the different sections of the music and the texts of the three verses.

Use cymbals and the two patterns of melody bells that simulate church bells and glockenspiel, as suggested previously in the lesson.

Use drum and autoharp interludes between the verses if the class decides they would be effective in the performance.

Rhythmic dramatization of realistic situations holds more meaning and interest for the beginning music student than creating rhythmic movement on abstract musical ideas.

Take advantage of every opportunity to use dynamics to enhance the dramatic qualities inherent in the music.

Listen for, and become sensitive to, the over-all effect heard in a musical performance. Learn how these effects are created and develop the individual skills necessary to the class performance. This sequence of development and variety of musical experiences are possible only in classroom situations.

When the song is finished, play a coda that will give the illusion of the soldiers and band marching away into the distance. Gradually decrease the volume of drums and autoharp and continue to play the large drum, even more softly, after the autoharp and small drums have stopped.

Listen and observe, even as the class is involved in performance, and decide on ways to make the sound and movement more expressive and effective.

GOING DEEPER INTO STRUCTURE

"When Johnny Comes Marching Home" is a good example of the effect that a quick tempo and lively rhythm can produce in a melody. In a slow tempo and languorous rhythm, this song would be melancholy in mood. Even in the brisk tempo of the song, the sound of the melody adds a wistful note.

To determine why this mood is inherent in the melody, compare the sound of the natural form of the G-minor scale on which it is built to that of the corresponding G-major scale.

Listen while the teacher plays the G-major scale shown in illustration 4.

Now listen while the teacher plays the natural minor scale shown in illustration 4.

Describe the difference between the sounds of these two scales:

Illustration 4

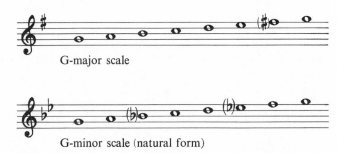

G-major scale

G-minor scale (natural form)

The discovery of the mood inherent in music and the growing knowledge and understanding of tempo, dynamics, rhythm, and mode encourage independence in determining the musical content of a song.

It is of primary importance to recognize the effect of the *sound* of the melody built on a minor scale. Comparing the minor with the major scale is an aid to understanding the difference between the two modes and is helpful in studying new scores.

To discover why the two scales are different in sound, study the structure of the natural minor scale by comparing it with the structure of the major scale.

Observe in illustration 5 that both scales are made up of whole and half steps.

Observe that there are two half steps in both scales.

Observe that the half steps occur in different places in the scale. It is this difference in the position of the half steps that makes the sound of the natural minor scale different from the major.

Observe in the natural minor scale that the first half step is created by the flatted third, and that the second half step is created by the flatted sixth.

 It is the third pitch of the scale that determines its major or minor quality, the flatted third producing the minor mode. The flatting of the sixth pitch is typical of many minor scales.

Observe that the impetus given to the major scale by the half step between the seventh and eighth pitches is *not* found in the natural minor, where there is a whole step between these two pitches.

MODE The natural minor scale sounds foreign to Western ears because of the whole step between the seventh and eighth pitches.

Illustration 5

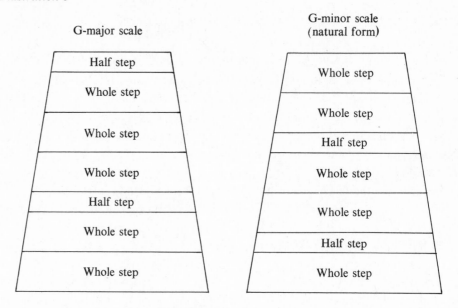

As learned in Lesson 6 on "Ninna Nanna," every minor scale has a relative major scale. The relationship of the minor and its relative major is apparent in both the melodic and harmonic structure of "When Johnny Comes Marching Home."

Study illustration 6 to determine the relative major key of G minor.

Compare the harmonic chord pattern of "When Johnny Comes Marching Home" with the two primary chords shown for B-flat major and G minor in illustration 6 to discover that both major and minor keys are found in the song.

On the autoharp, learn to play the harmonic chord accompaniment as well as the "bagpipe" accompaniment.

Learning how simple melodic patterns are created encourages the student to study and experiment with such patterns on his own.

Study illustration 6 to discover that the pitch D is found in every chord of the accompaniment except one. This makes it possible to play the "church bell" pattern (illustration 1) without too much dissonance.

Illustration 6

150

Study illustration 7 to discover why the sound of a bagpipe can be simulated on the autoharp by pressing the G-major and G-minor chord buttons simultaneously.

Observe that the pitches of the G-major and G-minor chords are the same except for the middle pitch — B in G major; B-flat in G minor.

Pressing the G-major chord button dampens out the B-flat of the minor chord; pressing the G-minor button dampens out the B of the major chord, and only the G and D strings sound.

The G and D strings played simultaneously produce the sound of the open fifth (see last figure in illustration 7), which simulates the drones of the bagpipe.

Illustration 7

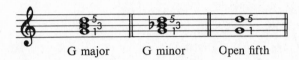

G major   G minor   Open fifth

 The term **open fifth** is commonly applied when two notes a perfect fifth apart are sounded simultaneously, with the third of the chord omitted.

LISTENING TO ORCHESTRAL MUSIC

Study briefly the following questions and guides, then listen to a recording of Morton Gould's "American Salute."

Listen for the familiar melody in the colorful and rather lengthy introduction.

What orchestral instrument first plays the well-known tune?

The melody is heard in its entirety three times before the variations occur — twice softly, once loudly.

What two musical effects, previously experienced in the class performance of "When Johnny Comes Marching Home," are produced in the orchestration the first two times the melody is heard?

Describe each of the three variations.

After the variations, the theme recurs in its original form and is followed by the coda. Does the music end with dramatic movement and tone color or does it fade away into the distance?

After a class discussion of first responses to the music, use the following as a guide while listening to the recording again.

How does the composer highlight and dramatize the spirited rhythmic figure in the introduction?

What melodic fragments are heard in the interludes?

How does the composer sustain the dramatic movement and suggest "something is about to happen" in the interludes?

Describe the orchestral ornamentations in the music.

How does the composer change instrumentation, tempo, dynamics, and rhythm to create the variations?

What is the predominant musical characteristic of each variation?

The dramatic impact of the lively rhythms and the colorful orchestration of a well-known tune tend to insure interest and attention. General suggestions for listening are a help in becoming better acquainted with the over-all content and structure of music on the first hearing.

When the general content has been identified, more detailed aspects of the music may be studied.

151

Describe the contrasting sound in the music that concludes the dirgelike third variation.

How is the dramatic ending effected in the music?

IDENTIFYING PROMINENT VARIATIONS IN THE SCORE

Experience with the score helps to associate sounds and rhythms with notation. Such experience also clarifies the characteristics that produce various effects in the music.

Recall the musical characteristics of the three obvious variations. Study the notation of a few measures of these variations shown, *out of order,* in illustration 8 and identify each by its notation. Determine the visual clues on the score that make identification possible.

Locate the first variation, which might be described as lively in rhythm, high in pitch, with an over-all effect of "busyness."

Locate the second variation, which might be described as syncopated in rhythm, and loud in dynamics, with an over-all effect of jazzlike music and humor.

Locate the third variation, which might be described as slow in movement, dirgelike in melody, with an over-all effect of solemnity.

Illustration 8

Compare the results of class discussion with these observations on the three variations:

The most obvious contrasts in the meters and tempos of the three variations are

First variation: quick tempo
    Meter: $\frac{12}{8}$
    Underlying pulse: ♩.
    Dominating rhythmic figure:

Second variation: quick tempo
    Meter: ₵ (or $\frac{2}{2}$)
    Underlying pulse:
    Dominating rhythmic figure:

Third variation: slow tempo
    Meter: $\frac{4}{4}$
    Underlying pulse:
    Dominating rhythmic figure:

The most obvious contrasts in the melodies are

First variation: high pitch
Second variation: angular contour
Third variation: smooth contour

The identification on the score of various meters and melodic patterns already experienced aurally deepens intellectual understanding of musical structure and increases knowledge of the written symbols of music.

IDENTIFYING DRAMATIC CONTRASTS IN THE MUSIC

Contrasts in dynamics provide one of the most important aspects of dramatic effect in music.

Listen to the recording as many times as necessary and write down the contrasts found in the music. On a sheet of paper, write the following headings: Dynamics, Tempo, Tone Color, Pitch, and Instruments. Select appropriate descriptive terms from these lists:

Discovery of the important role that the interpretive devices (dynamics, tempo, tone color) play in musical expression will encourage the development of the ability to use these devices.

Dynamics

fff — very, very loud
ff — very loud
f — loud
mf — moderately loud
mp — moderately soft
p — soft
pp — very soft
ppp — very, very soft

Pitch

High
Medium
Low

Tempo

Fast
Medium
Slow

Tone Color

Bright
Medium
Somber

Instruments

Brass
Woodwinds
Strings
Percussion

THE LONESOME DOVE

Oh, don't you see that lone-some dove That flies from vine to vine,

It's mourn-ing for its own true love, Just like I mourn for mine.

Just like I mourn for mine, my_ love,___ Be - lieve me what I say;

You are the dar-ling of my heart, Un - til my dy - ing day.

From *The Singin' Gatherin'* by Jean Thomas, the "Traipsin' Woman," and Joseph A. Leeder, © 1939, Silver Burdett Company.

Kentucky folk song

BECOMING ACQUAINTED WITH THE MUSIC

Personal reaction is always a part of the immediate response to music. Songs with strong emotional appeal are especially appropriate for inviting students to describe their personal reactions.

Listen to the recording of "The Lonesome Dove" and describe the emotional effect of the music.

"The Lonesome Dove" is one of many "lonesome" love songs, including "On Top of Old Smokey" and "Down in the Valley," which were found in the southern Appalachian Mountains. "Lonesome" tunes flourished in the isolated and solitary communities of the Appalachians, where "singin' " was an important part of life.

Pertinent notes on the historical background of a song often heighten appreciation and deepen understanding of the music.

Early twentieth-century folk-song collectors discovered that the people of these communities had preserved the speech and folk-song traditions of the original English settlers, who came to the region in the eighteenth century. Elizabethan expressions and melodies are so evident in these love songs that the southern mountaineers have been called "contemporary Elizabethans."

In 1933, Jean Thomas, called the "Traipsin' Woman" by the mountaineers, was introduced to this song by Mrs. Alice Williams, who said, "Canas, my man, usen to court me with this song-ballet; he'd sing as he come over the mountain. I can hear him yit as he usen to sing 'The Lonesome Dove' as he rid away from our house when the moon were high."

Discover how the dynamics, tempo, and meter fit the love-song text and lonesome mood of the song.

MOOD — Music that is soft in dynamics suggests a quiet, contemplative mood. In slow tempo, $\frac{3}{4}$ meter often suggests a sentimental mood.

STUDYING MELODIC AND RHYTHMIC PATTERNS

The impression that the song is easy to learn, because of its brief and seemingly repetitious phrases, may be deceptive.

Sing the song with the recording, following the score carefully, and reconstruct mentally the general contour of the melody.

Reconstruct visually the general contour of a melody when such an experience will help in learning the song.

Compare the notation of the first and second phrases with the general contour, shown in illustration 1. Observe the

- comparatively long, upward movement of the first melodic figure and its repetition in the second phrase
- dipping movement of the second figure of the first phrase
- downward movement of the final figure of the second phrase

Illustration 1

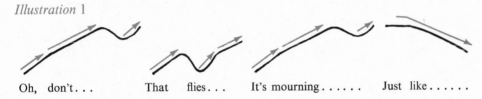

Oh, don't...   That flies...   It's mourning......   Just like......

Sing the song again with the recording, following with the ear and the eye the contour of the entire melody.

Study the rhythmic figures in the score that add a quiet, lilting movement to the constant rise and fall of the melody.

A practical and meaningful study of music and its notation includes the discovery of similarities and contrasts within the structure of a composition.

Observe that the rhythm patterns of phrases A and B are almost identical. On the score, locate the rhythmic difference between the two.

SYMBOLS — This music symbol $\frown$ is a **fermata.** It indicates that the note or chord below it is to be prolonged to satisfy the expressive demands of the music.

Study and practice the two characteristic rhythm patterns shown below.

Illustration 2

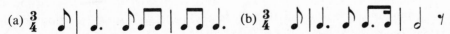

Observe how the second rhythm pattern differs from the first. Describe the effect of the figure.

RHYTHM — Uneven rhythmic figures, even in slow tempo, lend vitality and interest to music.

Sing the song with the recording, then describe how the rhythm pattern of the melody enhances the mood of the song.

155

CREATING AN APPROPRIATE ACCOMPANIMENT

An autoharp accompaniment is especially effective when it simulates the sound of the instrument used by the people who created the song.

The autoharp can be used to simulate the sound of the guitar or three-stringed dulcimer, which the mountain people probably used to accompany the song.

From visual clues (last note, key signature), determine the key in which the song is written.

On the autoharp, locate the five chords used in the accompaniment.

To make the chord buttons easier to reach, place the middle finger on the tonic chord, F major. The index finger is then free to press the A-minor chord button, the ring finger is in position for the D-minor and C₇ chords, the little finger is in position for the G-minor chord.

Study the score to determine where the chord changes occur and practice the pattern on the autoharp.

Play a simple introduction (F C₇ C₇ F), then sing the song with autoharp accompaniment. Strum one long stroke on the first beat of each measure except the seventh, where a second chord (C₇) is played on the third beat.

Describe the effect the minor chords of the accompaniment create in the music.

When the chord changes can be performed on the autoharp, create a more interesting accompaniment by changing the rhythm pattern. Study and practice the swinging movement of the pattern shown in illustration 3 and use it to accompany the song.

Illustration 3

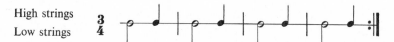

ADDING AN APPROPRIATE DESCANT

Vocal sound effects, such as those created by a simple descant, should be used only when they enhance the mood of the music.

The plaintive cooing of the turtledove is one of the most lonesome sounds in the world. To simulate the sound of the dove, learn the simple descant shown in illustration 4.

Observe that the rhythmic figure ♩ | ♩ is repeated throughout the descant.

Observe that, with the exception of the seventh measure, the interval of a third is sung throughout the song.

Locate the pitches of the descant on a pitched instrument. Practice the descant:

Illustration 4

When the descant is well learned, the class divides into two groups and sings the melody and descant with autoharp accompaniment. Describe the effect created by the descant.

GOING DEEPER INTO STRUCTURE

The unusual scale on which the song is constructed is one of the reasons for the haunting quality of the music.

Study illustration 5 to determine this scale.

Observe that the seventh pitch of the scale is not found in the song.

Observe that the fourth pitch is found only a few times on very weak pulses of the music.

The absence of the seventh pitch (E) and the infrequent use of the fourth (B-flat) make "The Lonesome Dove" almost pentatonic in mode. (Refer to the five-tone scales studied in lessons on Oriental songs.)

Play the scale shown in illustration 5, excluding the fourth and seventh (B-flat and E), to hear the sound that enhances the melancholy mood of "The Lonesome Dove."

Illustration 5

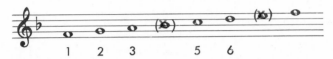

Study illustration 6 to learn the structure and the nature of the chords used in accompanying the song.

Observe the sparing use of the three primary chords (I, IV, and V_7 — F, B-flat, and C_7). The I chord is used in only six measures, the V_7 in two measures, and the IV chord not at all.

Observe that the chords that give the song its prevailing emotional color are minor chords.

HARMONY Chords built on the second, third, and sixth pitches of the scale are **secondary chords.** They give the music harmonic color.

Illustration 6

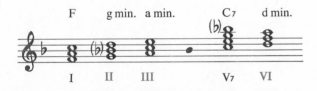

PRESENTING ORCHESTRAL MUSIC TO THE INTERMEDIATE GRADES

"Conversations of Beauty and the Beast" from *Mother Goose Suite* by Maurice Ravel could be presented to an intermediate grade after a St. Valentine's Day lesson on "The Lonesome Dove."

Prepare the class for the listening lesson by asking the children to recall fairy tales with which they are familiar.

"Name some fairy tales that would be appropriate for St. Valentine's Day."

"Composers have often been inspired by the fairy tales learned in their childhood. Parts of several fairy tales are described in *Mother Goose Suite*. One of these tells of conversations between Beauty and the Beast."

An awareness that certain moods can be enhanced by the use of unusual scales adds meaning and interest to the study of scales.

An awareness that the mood of music can be enhanced by its harmonic structure adds interest and meaning to the study of chords.

Among the many approaches to listening is one in which the children are introduced to the story and to the main themes before hearing the music.

Greater musical growth will result in the limited classroom time available for musical experiences if attention is focused on the music itself. Further study of the composer and his music may be encouraged by providing books on music written for children.

Ask the children to recall the story of "Beauty and the Beast," then identify the part of the story described in the music.

"Gentle, frightened Beauty, realizing that the ugly Beast is actually kind, promises to marry him. In that magic instant, the evil spell is broken, and the Beast is transformed into a handsome prince."

Ask the children to consider the musical characteristics that can contribute to a description of contrasting characters.

"How do you expect the music to identify each of the two characters — the one, ugly and clumsy; the other, lovely and gentle?"

Relate aural experiences to visual experiences by using the score during lessons.

Introduce the charted themes and lead the children to discover the difference in pitch indicated by the bass staff and the treble staff (illustration 1).

"Look at the two charted themes for a clue that will help you identify the theme representing the Beast."

Illustration 1

Reprint permission granted by Durand et Cie., Paris, France, and Elkan-Vogel Co., Inc., Philadelphia, Pennsylvania.

Play the themes on the piano or bells and ask the class to compare their particular effects.

"Describe the effect of each theme. Which theme is characteristic of Beauty? What effect does the large, descending interval contribute to the Beast's theme? What do the long, sustained notes in each theme suggest to you?"

BECOMING ACQUAINTED WITH ORCHESTRAL INSTRUMENTS

Ask the class to consider the possibilities of tone color in musical description.

"What instrument would you select to portray the ugly Beast? the graceful Beauty? Give reasons for your selection."

Focus attention on one of the obvious features of the music — the contrasting instrumental tone color. The class discovers that the clarinet is used for Beauty, the contra bassoon for the Beast, the cymbals for the breaking of the evil spell, and the harp for the instant of magic.

"You will recognize the characters of Beauty and the Beast by their individual themes. Discover which instrument plays the theme that represents [1] Beauty, [2] the Beast, [3] the breaking of the evil spell, and [4] the instant of magic."

Provide pictures of the tuba, bass viol, bass clarinet, and contra bassoon. Ask the children to identify the one they heard portraying the Beast.

To identify a less familiar instrument, relate it to others of comparable pitch or of the same family.

"Study these pictures. Which instrument do you think played the Beast's theme?"

"This is one of the few opportunities we have to hear the contra bassoon play a theme."

Help the children discover that the Beast's theme is played by the violin five octaves higher to portray the handsome prince, following the moment of magic.

"As you listen again, determine which theme the violin plays to represent the prince after the moment of magic created by the harp. Follow the score of each theme as it is heard."

After the entire composition has become familiar, parts of the music may be replayed to assist in studying specific details.

Play the recording again and ask the class to listen for the various ways the themes are used to suggest the conversations between Beauty and the Beast — (1) alternately, (2) in part, (3) as question and answer, and (4) together.

"Recall the various ways the two themes are presented in the composition to suggest conversation."

Give the children an opportunity to describe their personal reactions to the way Ravel tells the story.

"There are several ways that music can suggest a story. Which do you think was the most important in telling this story — rhythm, harmony, form, tone color, dynamics, or tempo?"

EVERY NIGHT WHEN THE SUN GOES IN

1. Ev - 'ry night_____ when the sun goes in,_____
2. How I wish_____ that__ train would come,_____

Ev - 'ry night_____ when the sun goes in,_____
How I wish_____ that__ train would come,_____

Ev - 'ry night_____ when the sun goes in,_____
How I wish_____ that__ train would come,_____

I hang down my head_____ and mourn - ful cry._____
and take___ me back_____ where I come from._____

Refrain

True love, don't weep,_____ true love, don't mourn,_____

True love, don't weep,_____ true love, don't mourn,_____

True love, don't weep,_____ nor mourn for me;_____

I'm go - ing a - way_____ to Mar - ble - town._____

From *English Folk Songs of the Southern Appalachians*
by Cecil Sharp, copyright by Oxford University Press,
London.

BECOMING ACQUAINTED WITH THE MUSIC

Expressing the mood created by long, sustained notes and phrases requires deep, controlled breathing.

Sing along with, or listen to, "Every Night When the Sun Goes In" and decide what style of music it represents.

Now sing the song and follow the score to determine the musical characteristics of the

- melody (Listen for one unusual tone.)
- rhythm
- harmony

Compare class discoveries with these observations about the music:

The lonesome or Appalachian folk mood of this song is created by the use of the B-flat in the melody. This note (B-flat) is the flatted seventh of the C-major scale:

Try to discover with the ear and the eye the characteristics that identify a distinctive musical style.

Illustration 1

MOOD The mood of a composition is often changed when the structure of a scale is varied. The flatted seventh may result in a lonesome or "blues" effect.

The notes of longer duration and the repeated rhythm pattern of the first three phrases contribute to the suggestion of melancholy and loneliness.

The figure ♩♩♩, which appears in the last phrase of the verse and of the refrain, is a triplet.

RHYTHM The **triplet** is a rhythmic device in which three notes are performed in the time normally allotted to two of the same value (♩♩♩ = ♩♩).

The melody is based on the tonic (C) chord, resulting in a sameness in harmony that also contributes to the mood.

CREATING AN AUTOHARP ACCOMPANIMENT

Experiment with the autoharp to create the style of accompaniment that might have been played on a guitar in the southern Appalachian Mountains, where the song is said to have originated. Vary the accompaniment from verse to refrain.

In the accompaniment, include only the sounds inherent in or appropriate to the music.

GOING DEEPER INTO STRUCTURE

Although the "lonesome" songs of the southern Appalachian Mountains are separated in time and in origin from the modern "blues" music called jazz, there are similarities between the two styles. One similarity is mood; another is the use of "blue notes." The flatted seventh is used in "Every Night When the Sun Goes In." This note as well as the flatted third and the flatted sixth are "blue notes," which appear frequently in modern jazz.

161

Make up a blues tune, using the flatted seventh or the flatted third and including a syncopated rhythm pattern.

Experiment with the harmony pattern on which some blues songs are based by playing the chords on the autoharp (illustration 2a) or piano (illustration 2b), and improvising melodies that fit the chord pattern.

Illustration 2

Listen to the sounds of jazz emerge!

LESSON 36

LA NOCHE 'STA SERENA (*The Night Is Serene*)

La no - che 'sta se - re - na, Tran - qui - lo el a - qui - lón ___
So fair and still the night is, The winds are all a - sleep. ___

Tu dul - ce cen - ti - ne - la Te guar - da el co - ra - zón, ___
Thy guard - ian stands and watch - es To guard thy slum - ber deep. ___

Y en a - las de los ze - fi - ros, Que va - gan por do - quier ___
And on the wings of zeph - yrs soft, He sends his one re - quest. ___

Vo - lan - do van mis sú - pli - cas A tí, be - lla mu - jer, ___
He sends his love through - out the night To bring thee peace and rest, ___

Vo - lan - do van mis sú - pli - cas A tí, be - lla mu - jer. ___
He sends his love through - out the night To bring thee peace and rest. ___

English translation by Roberta McLaughlin

Tune from *Spanish Songs of Old California* collected and
translated by C. F. Lummis and A. Farwell. Copyright
1923, 1951 by G. Schirmer, Inc. Used by permission.

BECOMING ACQUAINTED WITH THE MUSIC

The romance of early California days is relived in the songs of the Spanish
caballeros, whose guitars and singing were part of a colorful era.

Take advantage of the knowledge gained in previous musical experiences to
perform this song independently.

163

Make a habit of finding clues in the text that will suggest ideas for expressive interpretation.

Find words in the text that will reveal the mood of the song.

Describe, in general, the tempo, rhythm, harmony, and melody that might best express this mood.

Discover from the notation how the song is similar to "Barcarolle" in

- meter
- rhythm
- melody
- harmony

Determine the form as revealed by the succession of phrases.

Now locate the chords of the accompaniment on the autoharp. Decide on a tempo and style of autoharp accompaniment appropriate to the mood. On a pitched instrument, locate the beginning tone and sing the song with autoharp accompaniment.

Guided class discussion should follow, not precede, opportunity for individual and class discovery.

Compare class discoveries about the song with these observations:

The words *serena* and *tranquilo* reveal the mood of the song.

The text implies a moderate tempo, flowing rhythm, smooth melody, and simple harmony.

Observe that both this song and "Barcarolle" use

- $\frac{6}{8}$ meter
- the rocking rhythm
- scale-wise melodic movement
- the chord pattern I V$_7$, V$_7$ I in the first four measures

The form is ABCAB.

CREATING AN APPROPRIATE ACCOMPANIMENT

Develop the skill of mentally determining the tempo and rhythmic flow of a song. Establish them in the introduction and continue them throughout the performance.

Decide on an accompaniment style that imitates a Spanish guitar and is appropriate for a love song.

Experiment with one and two strums to a measure and decide which is more effective.

Select a harmonic sequence, such as the one below, for an introduction.

The sound of the primary chords in an introduction establishes a definite feeling for key.

Illustration 1

An introduction should be long enough to indicate the mood and style of the song.

Pluck the autoharp string that sounds the beginning pitch.

Play the introduction with a rhythmic precision that permits the class to sing on cue.

Musical leadership is developed through practice in accompanying and leading songs.

Take turns practicing this sequence to develop skill in playing autoharp introductions and accompaniments: (1) "think" the tempo, (2) pluck the beginning pitch, (3) play the introduction, and (4) maintain strict rhythm while playing the accompaniment so that the singers will be kept together.

PLANNING A PERFORMANCE

Expressive interpretation of the song demands smooth, continuous phrasing. Recall the suggestion made about posture and breathing, page 27.

Maintain the quiet serenity of this love song by making the performance simple.

Plan an introduction that will establish the mood.

Learn to play the melody on the recorder and bells and use them in the accompaniment or as an interlude between repetitions of the song.

Harmonize the song by ear with the assistance of the teacher and other students.

Use a subtle change of dynamics to emphasize the contrasting third phrase.

Experiment with interpretive ideas about tempo and dynamics to express the text of the song effectively.

GOING DEEPER INTO STRUCTURE

Harmony   The harmonic accompaniment of the repeated phrases (ABAB) includes the primary chords C, G_7, and F. The harmony of the third phrase (C) provides contrast in the song with the chords A minor and D_7:

Illustration 2

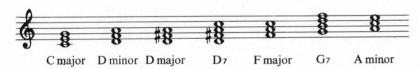

C major   D minor   D major   D₇   F major   G₇   A minor

Observe that the D-minor chord is changed to D major by raising the middle pitch of the chord and to D_7 by adding the interval of a seventh from the root of the chord.

The middle pitch of a triad (chord of three pitches in root position) determines the major or minor sound.

Melody   Observe that the climax of the melody in the third phrase occurs on the highest pitch, which is emphasized by an approach through a large interval — a sixth:

Illustration 3

165

OLD WOMAN AND THE PIG

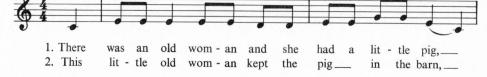

1. There was an old wom-an and she had a lit-tle pig,—
2. This lit-tle old wom-an kept the pig— in the barn,—

Oink, oink, oink. There was an old wom-an and she had a lit-tle pig,
Oink, oink, oink. This lit-tle old wom-an kept the pig— in the barn,

He did-n't cost much 'cause he was-n't ver-y big,— Oink, oink, oink.
The pret-ti-est thing she — had — on the farm,— Oink, oink, oink.

American folk song

Humorous and nonsense songs, found throughout folk literature, are important in a child's repertory, not only for the enjoyment they bring, but because they are a part of folk heritage.

TEACHING THE SONG TO THE PRIMARY GRADES

Introduce "Old Woman and the Pig" by singing both verses in the simple, straightforward manner of a folk song.

> "This folk song is very old. It was sung during the time of George Washington. There is a part you can sing with me. Join the singing when you find out what it is."

Songs with repeated words are learned quickly and easily.

Help the children to learn the text by beginning the words of a phrase and letting them finish it:

> "There was an old woman and . . .   There was an old woman and . . .   He didn't cost much 'cause . . ."
> "Now let us sing the first verse together."

Teachers learn quickly which child needs an opportunity to play a "leading role." It may be the quiet, timid child or the insecure show-off.

Teach the text of the second verse in the same manner and encourage the children to join in the singing.

CREATING AN APPROPRIATE ACCOMPANIMENT

Before the class session, let a child decide which instrument is appropriate for the "oink" of the pig, the finger cymbals, the drum, or the notched tone gourd.

"I asked Charles to help me plan a surprise for you. He has decided on an instrument that he thinks sounds like the 'oink' of the pig. Let us sing the entire song, except the 'Oink, oink, oink,' and listen to the sound of the instrument that Charles has chosen for that effect."

Let the children discover how Charles made his choice by permitting them to hear the finger cymbals and the drum as well.

"Charles will play other percussion instruments so you can discover why he chose the notched tone gourd for the sound of the pig."

Give several children the experience of playing the notched tone gourd. This affords the class an opportunity to sing the song many times and to become increasingly familiar with the words and the melody.

"Charles will choose someone to play the notched tone gourd, then we will sing the song."

Display three charts (illustration 1) that show the three melodic ideas of the song. Ask the class to identify the melodic figure being studied (chart 2).

"While we sing the song, observe these charts, and locate the one that shows the notes of the 'Oink, oink, oink' phrase."

Illustration 1

Chart 1

Chart 2

Chart 3

When the children have discovered the notation for "Oink, oink, oink," help a child locate and play the notes on the melody bells.

"Mary will bring the melody bells to the front of the room, and I will help her find and play the notes of the 'Oink, oink, oink' phrase. We will use the melody bells instead of the tone gourd to accompany our singing."

Children respond immediately and often with delight on hearing the raucous sound of the tone gourd. At the same time, they are learning that it is very important to choose the instrument that best simulates a particular sound.

Playing the notched tone gourd affords children the experience of playing a particular rhythm pattern at a particular time and helps sustain interest through many repetitions of the song.

Charts are used in the primary grades to show children what the music they sing looks like and to familiarize them with the visual appearance of the score.

Whenever possible, relate discoveries made about notation to the actual performance.

Give several children an opportunity to play the melody bells, then provide the opportunity for every child to learn the pattern.

> "As Johnny played the melody bells, he discovered that the names of the notes are D, D, C. I will put the names of the notes on the chart so that all of you can learn the melody pattern on the bells during your free time."

Now help the children to identify on the charts the notation of the two other short phrases they have been singing.

> "We have two other phrases to locate on the charts. On which of the two charts are the notes higher?" (chart 3)
>
> "While we sing the first verse of the song, raise your hand on the part where the highest notes are sung."

When the children have determined the part of the song that matches the chart with the highest notes (chart 3), follow with the hand the melodic contour of the phrase while the class sings it from the chart.

Now ask the class to identify the last chart (chart 1). With the hand follow the contour of this phrase while the class sings it from the chart.

Now ask the class to sing both verses of the song.

> "I will point out to you the notation of the song while you sing it. Jimmy will point out on the chart the notes sung on the 'Oink, oink, oink' phrase."

When the class has identified the phrases in notation and is familiar with their sequence in the song, have three children stand in front of class, each holding one of the charts. Each child will step forward when his phrase is sung in the song. The children holding chart 1 and chart 2 will step forward twice, the child with chart 3 only once.

Help the children review what has been learned from the class activities.

> "Why did you agree with Charles that the tone gourd was better for the sound of the pig than either the finger cymbals or the drum?"
>
> "Why were you able to locate the 'Oink, oink, oink' phrase in the music charts so quickly?"
>
> "Why were you able to locate on the charts the highest notes you sang in the song?"

168

LESSON 38

POP! GOES THE WEASEL

1. A penny for a spool — of thread, A
   penny for a nee - dle, That's the way the
   mon - ey goes, Pop! goes the wea - sel.
   All a - round the cob - bler's bench The
   mon - key chased the wea - sel, The mon - key thought 'twas
   all in fun, } Pop! goes the wea - sel.

2. Po - ta - toes for an I - rish-man's taste, A
   doc - tor for the mea - sles, A fid - dler al - ways
   for — a dance, or Pop! goes the wea - sel. Blood
   pud - ding for a Dutch - man's meal, A
   work - man for a chis - el, The tune that ev - 'ry
   bod - y sings is } Pop! goes the wea - sel.

American Square Dance Tune

BECOMING ACQUAINTED WITH THE MUSIC

Sing "Pop! Goes the Weasel" with the recording. Reflect the jiglike rhythm and humorous words in the manner of singing the song.

Before singing the song again, select several different percussion instruments to play, one at a time, instead of singing the word "Pop!" Decide which instruments are most effective.

Highlight dramatic rhythmic or melodic points of a song with appropriate sound effects.

169

"Pop! Goes the Weasel" was sung in England as early as the seventeenth century. Brought to America by the early colonists, it quickly caught on in the New World and became one of the favorite "fiddlin'" tunes of the pioneers.

Some historians believe that the first verse is one of the original versions and that it tells about the difficulties of a tailor who spent the few pennies he had on thread and needle and was forced to pawn (pop) his pressing iron (weasel) to buy other necessities of life. The "monkey" in the song was, perhaps, one of the tools used by the tailor in his trade.

CREATING A DANCE

"Fiddlin' music" is, by and large, music for dancing. Learn this simple dance for "Pop! Goes the Weasel" or create a new one in square-dance style.

The dance formation is made up of four couples in a square. The first couple is called the "head couple." The couple to the right is called the "second couple," and so forth. The basic step is a walk or a skip.

head couple
o ×

second ×   o fourth
couple o   × couple

× o
third couple

Introduction: Dancers honor (bow to) partner, honor corner.

First verse: First phrase — Head couple steps out, joins hands with second couple, and all four persons move in a small circle to the right.

Second phrase — These two couples continue circling to the right until the word "Pop!" Head couple then "pops" under the raised arms of second couple toward the center of the square and moves on to third couple.

Third phrase — Head couple and third couple join hands and move in a small circle to the right.

Fourth phrase — These two couples continue circling right until the word "Pop!" Head couple then "pops" under the raised arms of third couple toward center of square and moves on to fourth couple.

Second verse: First phrase — Head couple and fourth couple join hands and move in a small circle to the right.

Second phrase — These two couples continue circling until the word "Pop!" Head couple then "pops" under the raised arms of fourth couple toward center of square and returns to original position in the square formation.

Third phrase — All four couples promenade around the square.

Fourth phrase — Four couples continue the promenade back to their original positions. They swing partners.

This whole pattern may be repeated, the second couple becoming the head couple and moving to the right in the figure of the dance, and so on.

170

Relating a song to the historical period in which it originated and explaining certain words no longer in general use deepens interest in the music and contributes to knowledge of the customs of the people at that time.

A dance, true to the style and spirit of the music, has much greater educational value than mere superficial rhythmic movement.

Both rhythm and form are experienced in the traditional movement and pattern of the square dance.

Prepare to listen to a recording of "Variations on the Theme — Pop! Goes the Weasel" by Lucien Cailliet.

Study the names Cailliet gave to his variations and decide what rhythms, sounds, and musical styles he might have chosen for each. Before listening to the recording, write a brief description of the style that might be expected for each of the following variations: "Introduction," "Theme," "Fugue," "Minuet," "In Jerusalem," "Music Box," and "In Jazz."

The word **fugue** is from the Latin word *fuga,* which means "flight" and suggests the flight of a melody from one voice or instrument to another. The fugue is somewhat like a round in that voices enter one after another with the same melodic idea.

Have seven persons hold charts on which the names of the sections of the music are printed:

Illustration 1

Introduction	Theme	Fugue

Minuet

In Jerusalem	Music Box	In Jazz

Now listen to the recording. As each section is identified by the class, the person holding the chart for that section will place it in the front of the room (on the tray of a chalkboard if no other facilities are available) and return to his seat.

When the variations of the composition have been identified from the recording, study briefly the following questions and try to find answers while the recording is played again.

"Introduction": What short, melodic figure from the melody is heard many times?

"Theme": What sound does Cailliet use on the word "Pop!"?

"Fugue": What four different sound effects are heard on the word "Pop!"?
What instruments can be heard in the main theme?

"Minuet": What kind of instrument plays the tune "Pop! Goes the Weasel" after the violins introduce the new minuet melody?

"In Jerusalem": What is the effect of the melody in this variation? What changes in tempo, rhythm, and mode occur in this variation? What instrument plays the "laugh" at the end?

"Music Box": What words would describe the sounds and rhythm of this variation?

"In Jazz": What makes this variation easy to recognize as a jazzlike style?

After a general introduction to a composition, the student gains increased knowledge of the music when he is given specific suggestions for succeeding hearings.

171

Every opportunity should be taken to relate aural experiences and consequent understandings with visual experiences and musical knowledge.

Before the recording is played a third time, study the notation of the *last* four variations shown in illustration 2. Identify each by such visual clues as rhythm patterns, pitch levels, and interpretive markings.

Illustration 2

As the recording is played again, follow these four variations as they occur in the composition.

LESSON 39

JOHNNY HAS GONE FOR A SOLDIER

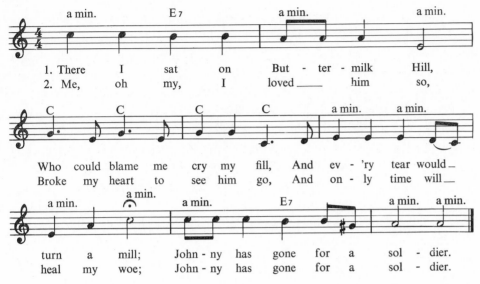

1. There I sat on But-ter-milk Hill,
2. Me, oh my, I loved____ him so,

Who could blame me cry my fill, And ev-'ry tear would___
Broke my heart to see him go, And on-ly time will___

turn a mill; John-ny has gone for a sol-dier.
heal my woe; John-ny has gone for a sol-dier.

Song of the American Revolution

BECOMING ACQUAINTED WITH THE MUSIC

Prepare to sight-read "Johnny Has Gone for a Soldier." Examine the score to find visual clues that suggest the mood of the song and for notation patterns that appear to be new or difficult.

Observe the comparatively even movement of the rhythm patterns in $\frac{4}{4}$ meter.

Observe the downward movement of the melody line in the first phrase and in the last part of the second phrase.

Observe the mode of the song as revealed in the chord symbols of the accompaniment.

Observe the *fermata* (⌒) in the sixth measure of the song.

Study the chord pattern of the autoharp accompaniment and find the chords on the autoharp. Practice the accompaniment pattern, strumming two long, slow strokes per measure.

Observe that the rhythm pattern of the melody is made up of even beats (♩♩♩♩ and ♩ ♩) or evenly divided beats (♫) except in the third and fourth measures (♩. ♪♩. ♪). Study and practice this dotted rhythmic figure.

On a pitched instrument, locate the beginning note of the song. Strum a simple, A-minor introduction on the autoharp, then sing "Johnny Has Gone for a Soldier" with autoharp accompaniment.

Listen carefully to the autoharp accompaniment so that the ear can help the eye read the pitches of the melody accurately.

Before attempting to sight-read, develop the habit of examining the score to determine the general characteristics of the music.

When sight-reading a new score, learn to use the harmony pattern to guide the ears as well as the eyes.

Learn to decipher the dotted rhythms that lend rhythmic interest to the music.

173

Never lose sight of the expressive qualities of music, even while learning the song from the score.

After sight-reading the song, decide on the difficult parts of the melody to be practiced and on the tempo and dynamics most appropriate for the music.

Sing the song again and find adjectives to describe its mood as revealed in the sound of the music as well as in the words of the text.

CREATING AN APPROPRIATE DESCANT

Putting a song in its historical setting deepens intellectual appreciation.

"Johnny Has Gone for a Soldier" is an American adaptation of the old Irish air "Shule Agra" or "Shule Aroon," which can be traced back to the late seventeenth or early eighteenth century. Although there are many verses to this song, the best known are laments voiced by Irish women whose sweethearts left home to become "Wild Geese" — Irish Jacobites who fled their country (1691–1745) to serve in the French army after the defeat of James II.

During the American Revolution, parts of the melody and text were changed to apply to Colonial America (Buttermilk Hill, for instance), and the result was the song known today as "Johnny Has Gone for a Soldier."

Singing a simple harmonic part that enhances the mood of the music is a particularly satisfying aural experience.

A few high voices may sing the simple descant shown in illustration 1 while the rest of the class sings the melody.

Listen and determine how the sound of the two-part harmony enhances the plaintive quality of the music.

Illustration 1

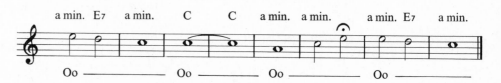

CREATING APPROPRIATE ACCOMPANIMENTS

Experimenting with the many and varied musical effects that can be created with the autoharp encourages exploration of the instrument and the development of original accompaniments.

Create a different kind of autoharp accompaniment (illustration 2) by using the instrument in a new way:

Observe in illustration 2 that the pitches of the accompaniment are in the bass staff (𝄢).

For ease in playing, place the autoharp so that the strings are perpendicular to the body and the low strings on the left. Locate the pitches of the accompaniment among the low, heavy strings of the instrument.

Observe the slow movement of the repeated rhythmic figure ($\frac{4}{4}$ ♩ ♩ | o).

Practice this simple accompaniment by plucking each pitch in rhythm and use it to accompany the song.

Determine the qualities of this autoharp accompaniment that make it appropriate to the music.

Illustration 2

GOING DEEPER INTO STRUCTURE

Observe the structure of the scale on which the song is built (illustration 3) and determine from experience in previous lessons what mode is used. Determine the name of this scale and its mode. Observe that the next to the last pitch of the melody is altered.

Experiences based on previous learning are especially meaningful to students.

Illustration 3

$$1 \quad \frac{1}{2} \quad 1 \quad 1 \quad \frac{1}{2} \quad 1\frac{1}{2} \quad 1\frac{1}{2}$$

Study the harmonic (chord) structures of the song to determine
* why this altered pitch gives the ending of the song a strong feeling of finality
* how the autoharp accompaniment and descant evolved from the chord structure.

Discovering the structure of the simple descants and accompaniments strengthens the student's performance skill with musical knowledge and understanding.

The G-sharp of the melody is also found in the chord built on the pitch E, making it a major chord, E_7. Recall from previous study that the major V_7 chord (E_7) creates a strong harmonic effect and leads to the final tonic chord (A minor).

Compare the pitches of the descant (illustration 1) with the pitches in the chords of the accompaniment (illustration 4) to discover that every pitch sung is found in the chords.

Notice that the single-string autoharp accompaniment (illustration 2) uses only three notes (A, E, G), all of which are contained in the chords of the song:

Illustration 4

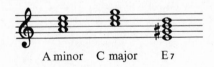

A minor   C major   E 7

EXTENDING INDIVIDUAL EXPERIENCE

On the recorder, learn the melody of "Johnny Has Gone for a Soldier."

PADDY WORKS ON THE RAILROAD

3. In eighteen hundred and forty-three,
   'Twas then I met sweet Biddy Magee,
   And an illygant wife she's been to me
   While workin' on the railroad.

4. In eighteen hundred and forty-six,
   They pelted me with stones and bricks,
   Oh, I was in an awful fix
   While workin' on the railroad.

American railroad song

TEACHING THE SONG TO GRADE SIX

Sing the song to the class without revealing the title or the source.

"Listen to the first verse of this song and tell why it is appropriate for St. Patrick's Day."

Relate the lively rhythm and minor mode to the background of the song.

"This time, sing all four verses along with me. Decide what musical characteristic suggests the rollicking good humor of the Irishman. Then discover the musical characteristic that suggests the hardships expressed in the words."

Lead the class to discover similarities in mode, rhythm, and melody between "Paddy Works on the Railroad" and "When Johnny Comes Marching Home."

"In what ways is this song similar to 'When Johnny Comes Marching Home'?"

Help the class to discover the harmonic pattern in "Paddy Works on the Railroad."

"Bill has discovered that there are only two chords in the accompaniment, so he may play the autoharp as we sing this time. Listen for and describe the effect of an accompaniment limited to A-minor and C-major chords."

MOVING TO MUSIC

Organize two groups on opposite sides of an imaginary railroad track and re-enact the work of driving railroad spikes.

"There was rhythm in the work of building railroads. Men who drove spikes in laying the rails worked in teams — one team standing on either side of the track. They moved in rhythm to avoid being hit by the other hammers."

"Let us act out the driving of spikes to discover the rhythmic movement in the music. To sense this slow work rhythm, it is necessary to feel the weight of the heavy sledge hammer with every blow."

Relate the movement of men driving spikes to a rhythm pattern of $\frac{6}{8}$ meter. Ask the class to find on the chart (illustration 1) the rhythm pattern
- created by the movement of the team as they alternate in driving the spikes
- created by the movement of each worker
- of the melody

Illustration 1

Take advantage of the opportunity provided by a song with several verses to acquaint the children quickly with the general characteristics of the music.

Encourage children to use understandings and skills developed in previous musical experiences to develop independence in learning new songs.

As the song is practiced and performed, give other children a chance to play the autoharp and learn the accompaniment.

A song is performed with more vitality when it is related to appropriate movements.

The ability to sense and recognize various rhythmic movements and to identify these rhythms in notation is developed through the experiences of hearing, playing, moving, singing, and creating rhythms. Rhythm patterns played and practiced out of context become nothing but a mathematical drill.

177

Invite the children to select an instrument that imitates the ring of the hammer on the railroad spike.

"Your suggestion of playing the resonator bells to imitate the ring of the hammer is a good one because bells provide harmony as well as an appropriate sound effect."

Let the children build the chords on a staff on the chalkboard. Piano students can often lead the way in first attempts at writing notation.

"Who can write on the staff the notes of the C-major chord? of the A-minor chord?"

"Ann and Jack have placed the chords in root position, which means that the note that gives the chord its name is the lowest on the staff."

Provide opportunities for children who have had private instrumental study to make specific contributions to the lesson.

Children learn quickly the names of lines and spaces when the information is needed for the successful performance of music. Until the notes are actually used in "music-making," memorization of the names of lines and spaces is meaningless and wastes time.

Illustration 2

A minor   C major

"Playing the chords in root position on the resonator bells will provide an appropriate clanging sound of a hammer. What pitches do we need for the A-minor chord? the C-major chord?"

Invite the children to play the resonator bells and organize them into chord groups.

Take advantage of every opportunity to invite children who do not volunteer often to play instrumental accompaniments.

"Those playing the A-minor chord stand together, and those playing the C-major chord stand together."

"Follow the harmonic pattern written on the chalkboard as I point to the chord to be played [illustration 3]."

Illustration 3

| A minor | A minor | C major | C major |
| A minor | A minor | C major | A minor |

Each child must be given the opportunity to play with confidence and freedom the part of the performance for which he is responsible.

"When we have practiced the chord pattern, we will sing the song with resonator bell accompaniment."

If resonator bells are not available, a high and low E (octave) may be played on the song bells to imitate the ring of the hammer:

Illustration 4

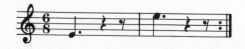

PLANNING A PERFORMANCE

Help the children plan a performance of the song, selecting ideas from the following suggestions.

Plan an instrumental introduction — on the resonator bells, for example — that will establish the tempo and feeling for key.

Select a soloist or small group to sing each verse, with the remainder of the class joining in on the chorus.

Decide whether the bagpipe sound used in "When Johnny Comes Marching Home" would make an appropriate accompaniment. Pressing the A$_7$ and A-minor chord buttons at the same time will produce this sound for "Paddy Works on the Railroad."

Select one group to sing, one to play an accompaniment, and another to be the men who drive the spikes.

GOING DEEPER INTO STRUCTURE

This song has been learned as a sixth-grade class might learn it. Now, as an adult, look at the score to discover in the setting of this song some of the musical characteristics observed in previous songs.

Mode   The song is written in the natural form of the A-minor scale.

Harmony   The use of the A-minor and C-major chords emphasizes the characteristic sound of the natural minor.

Rhythm   Observe the effect of the fast tempo of "Paddy Works on the Railroad" and contrast it with the tempo of "La Noche 'Sta Serena."

In a slow tempo, the rhythm of $\frac{6}{8}$ meter provides a swaying, unaccented movement appropriate for a quiet nighttime song.

In a fast tempo, the rhythm of $\frac{6}{8}$ meter provides a rollicking, active movement appropriate for a song with a lively text.

RHYTHM   In a fast tempo, the characteristic ♩ ♪♪ ♪ of $\frac{6}{8}$ meter has a unique rhythmic vitality not common in music of slower tempo.

Form   Observe that, except for a slight variation, the two phrases of the verse are similar to the two phrases of the refrain.

Reinforce understanding of the specific musical characteristics studied in previous lessons by reviewing them when they occur in new experiences.

The tempo of a song is one of the most important aspects of interpretation. Develop the habit of experimenting with and establishing the tempo appropriate to the expression of the song.

179

LONDONDERRY AIR

Irish folk song

BECOMING ACQUAINTED WITH THE MUSIC

"Londonderry Air" is a folk melody from County Derry in Ireland.

It is difficult to define the characteristics of a good melody or to explain why some melodies have endured for centuries and why others have not. Good melodies, however, seem to have certain qualities in common, and these qualities can be described.

A composition may be listened to purely for enjoyment, but musical growth results from a study of the characteristics that give the music its enjoyable qualities.

Recall observations made about melodic structure in previous lessons and listen to a recording of "Londonderry Air." An orchestral version by Percy Grainger, who has arranged many folk songs of the British Isles, is especially well known.

Describe the melodic characteristics that may account for the popularity of the melody.

COMPARING MUSIC AND DRAMA

Consider that a successful melody has some of the same features that exist in the text of a good drama. Look for

Structural principles of one art form are clarified by relating them to similar principles in another art form.

- unity and variety
- tension and release
- form and design
- high point or climax
- conclusion

180

Listen to the recording of "Londonderry Air" again to determine which of these features are expressed by the music. Which are inherent in the melody? Which are emphasized by the accompaniment?

Compare class discoveries with these observations about the music:

Unity is achieved by repeated rhythmic and melodic patterns.

Variety is achieved by the wide range of pitch and the contrast in duration of notes.

Tension is suggested by the upward movement of the melody.

Release is suggested by the downward movement of the melody and by cadences.

Form is inherent in the succession of the like and unlike phrases.

The climax of the melody appears in the fourth phrase and is anticipated by the high pitches in the third phrase. This high point is further emphasized by being reached from a large interval and by a gradual increase in volume (crescendo).

 A particular tone in a melody is emphasized when approached through a large interval.

The conclusion is achieved by the (1) gradually descending melody line, (2) decrescendo, and (3) ritardando.

STUDYING THE SCORE

To discover features of the notation, study the score of "Londonderry Air" while listening again to the recording. Find the
- climax of the melody
- repeated melodic and rhythmic patterns

STUDYING THE TECHNIQUES OF INTERPRETATION

Consider the responsibility of a conductor or performer who must interpret the musical score.

Every musical composition requires sensitive interpretation, and the notes on a score are sometimes incomplete representations of the composer's idea. If music is to be more than a mechanical reproduction of sounds of various pitches and duration, the conductor or performer must understand what the notes are meant to express and must adjust dynamics, tempos, and rhythms to achieve the desired effect in an artistic way.

A musical composition generates its own interpretation. Although faulty interpretation results if the same rigid rules are applied to all compositions, guiding principles are needed:

To express repose, notes of longer duration are held their full time value.

To express activity, shorter notes move along in strict tempo. A **ritardando** (gradual slackening of tempo) at the end of each phrase or on each descending melody line destroys the rhythmic movement of the music.

To accentuate the contrast between activity and repose, a series of shorter notes is sometimes played **accelerando** (accelerated). The time gained as a result of the accelerando is "paid back," generally within the phrase, by lengthening the longer notes. This temporary "borrowing" is called **rubato**.

A dedicated musician — a conductor, performer, teacher, or student — never stops studying more effective ways of interpreting music artistically and honestly.

181

STREETS OF LAREDO

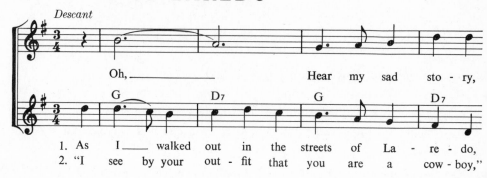

Descant

Oh, _____ Hear my sad sto - ry,

1. As I ___ walked out in the streets of La - re - do,
2. "I see by your out - fit that you are a cow - boy,"

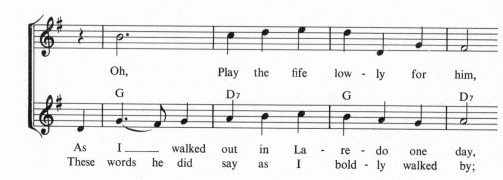

Oh, Play the fife low - ly for him,

As I ___ walked out in La - re - do one day,
These words he did say as I bold - ly walked by;

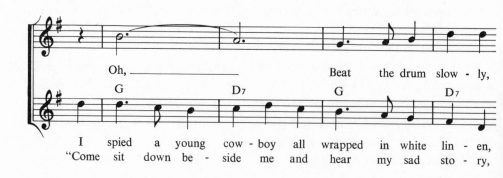

Oh, _____ Beat the drum slow - ly,

I spied a young cow - boy all wrapped in white lin - en,
"Come sit down be - side me and hear my sad sto - ry,

Oh, _____ As the sun grows dim.

All wrapped in white lin - en and cold as the clay.
I'm shot in the breast and I know I must die."

3. "Get six jolly cowboys to carry my coffin,
   Get six purty maidens to sing me a song,
   Take me to the valley and lay the sod o'er me,
   For I'm a young cowboy and know I've done wrong."

4. "Oh, beat the drum slowly and play the fife lowly,
   Play the dead march as you carry me along;
   Put bunches of roses all over my coffin,
   Roses to deaden the clods as they fall."

American cowboy song

BECOMING ACQUAINTED WITH THE MUSIC

Listen to the recording of "Streets of Laredo." Notice the effect of the descant. Determine whether the rhythm of the melody expresses the story in the text or the rhythmic movement of a cowboy riding easily on his horse.

Study the score to discover repeated patterns that will make it easier to learn and perform this song. Look for patterns in the

- rhythm
- melodic contour
- harmony
- form

Recognizing the patterns in which the materials of music are organized is of the utmost importance in learning to interpret a score.

Use these discoveries to help in singing the first verse. An autoharp accompaniment will help to keep the tempo steady. Then sing the three remaining verses, using the discoveries of the patterns in the score to assist in singing the song accurately and expressively.

Compare class discoveries with these observations:

A two-measure rhythm pattern, consisting of one measure of uneven rhythm and one of even rhythm, begins each phrase.

The rhythmic swing of the $\frac{3}{4}$ meter suggests the slow swaying of the cowboy in the saddle.

The rise and fall of the melody contribute to the suggestion of swaying heard in the rhythm.

The change from the G chord to the D₇ chord provides a pattern of harmony alternating between a passive chord (I) and an active chord (V₇). This also contributes to the swaying movement of the music.

The form of the song is ABAC.

Leadership is needed in first attempts at reading a score. Success motivates further music study.

CREATING APPROPRIATE ACCOMPANIMENTS

Play the autoharp to imitate a guitar. Practice an "oom-pah-pah" guitar rhythm by strumming a few low strings on the first beat of the measure and then a few higher strings on the second and third beats.

Emphasize the swaying rhythm by playing the low strings with more pressure and accent on the first beat and by playing the high strings lightly on the second and third beats.

Let the ear help the eye in playing the alternating chord pattern. (The D_7 chord may be substituted for the A-minor chord in the last phrase.)

To best interpret each verse, vary the autoharp accompaniment. Strum the "oom-pah-pah" rhythm or strum only on the first beat of each measure.

Play the last phrase as an introduction to the song.

Play a percussion instrument to imitate the "clip, clop, clop" sound often associated with cowboy songs. Select from the various clicking sounds produced by coconut shells, gourd tone block, wood block, temple blocks, rhythm sticks, or paper cups. Explore the different pitches that can be produced on the same instrument to provide a high pitch for the "clip" (first beat) and a lower pitch for the "clop, clop" (second and third beats).

Add a bass viol accompaniment by plucking the open G, D, and A strings (the roots of the G, D_7, and A-minor chords) in the same pattern as the auto-harp chords.

On the last verse, create a dramatic effect by playing a drum with a soft beater to produce a muffled tone.

Study the chart in illustration 1 to relate the notation to the various rhythm patterns played in the accompaniment. Identify the
- rhythm pattern of the "oom-pah-pah" accompaniment played on the autoharp
- rhythm pattern of the melody
- strong beat played by the bass viol and drum
- underlying beat played with the "clip, clop, clop" sound

Illustration 1

SINGING IN HARMONY

The class divides into two groups. The first group sings the melody and provides the autoharp accompaniment. The second group sings the descant by following the score, relying on a conductor if necessary.

Isolate and practice those sections that prove to be a problem — particularly the measures with the dotted half notes, which provide contrast to the moving melody, and the seventh measure with the octave interval.

Learn the descant (or the melody) on the recorder to provide the sound of the fife mentioned in the fourth verse.

Observe that the sound of the descant contributes to the mournful mood of the text.

Create accompaniments that are as authentic or appropriate as possible within the limitations of available instruments.

Those whose singing ability seems to be limited can gain satisfaction from making other contributions to musical activities. In this way they may develop the confidence that overcomes difficulties in singing.

The goal of first attempts at part-singing is to progress through the song from beginning to end. Perfection is not to be expected, and failure must be avoided.

For correct performance, difficult patterns in rhythm and melody should first be recognized, then isolated, studied in terms of their notation, and finally returned to the song context.

Create a "bunkhouse" music session.

The class divides into three groups. One group plays the instruments, one sings the melody, and the third sings the descant.

Add appropriate instruments, such as the fiddle, banjo, guitar, or harmonica.

Decide on an introduction, using autoharp, bass viol, and the "clip, clop, clop" rhythm instrument. The chords of the last phrase may be used as a basis for the introduction.

Vary each verse with different instrumentation or sound effects.

Play a verse with the recorder (imitating the fife) and drum as an interlude before the fourth verse or as a coda to end the performance.

Observe that although the scale-wise melody and the alternating chords of the harmony could easily be played on bells or piano these instruments are not appropriate for the performance because their tone colors have no relation to the source, text, or activity of the song.

If the bass viol is not used in the performance, the song may be transposed to the key of F for a more comfortable singing range.

> Singing a harmony part is often considered a special privilege. Everyone in the class should be given a chance to sing the harmony part.

GOING DEEPER INTO STRUCTURE

Study the chords in illustration 2 and discover why the A-minor chord could be substituted for the D_7 chord.

Illustration 2

D7   A minor

The primary chords, I, V_7, and IV are major chords. Notice that the II, III, VI, and VII chords provide substitutes for the primary chords to give variety in harmonic color:

Illustration 3

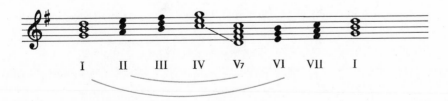

I   II   III   IV   V7   VI   VII   I

Observe that the dotted quarter note (♩.) adds variety to the otherwise steady beat of the rhythm and, as the result of its longer duration, gives emphasis to the strong beat of the measure.

The wealth of melodic material found in a rich environment of folk music has inspired many great composers to use these simple tunes in their orchestral works. Listen to a recording of "Cattle" from *The Plow That Broke the Plains* by Virgil Thomson to hear a symphonic setting of cowboy songs.

Listen to discover the

A characteristic of folk music is the constant change resulting from personal interpretation and stylization.

- three tunes included in the composition
- order in which the tunes occur and are repeated
- rhythmic characteristic common to all three of the tunes

The transformation of a folk song from its original version to a symphonic setting requires deliberately planned musical refinement.

Listen to "Cattle" a second time to discover how

- Virgil Thomson refines the cowboy song through organization and tone color
- he retains some of the original flavor and color of cowboy music
- the "oom-pah-pah" rhythm, played by the autoharp in "Streets of Laredo," is provided in the orchestral music

Compare class discoveries with these observations:

The three songs represented are "I Ride an Old Paint," "My Home's In Montana," and "Laredo." (Observe that this song is different from the "Streets of Laredo" used in this lesson.)

The identification of a new form is less difficult when the composition is based on familiar themes.

The three tunes occur in an order known as rondo form (ABACABA coda). This formal organization is part of the refinement of the cowboy tunes.

FORM Rondo form is a musical design in which the main theme alternates with other themes or returns (comes around) after each new theme — for example, ABABA or ABACABA.

All three songs are performed in a waltz-like rhythm.

An "oom-pah-pah" rhythm is played by the guitar or the bass viol and guitar.

The repeated rhythm pattern found in "Streets of Laredo" and heard slightly varied in each of the three tunes of the composition gives unity to the music ( ).

Discoveries made about instrumental tone color can suggest appropriate sounds and contrasts for songs performed in the classroom.

The flavor of cowboy music is retained by the tone color of the guitar and cowbell.

The first section (ABA), performed by solo woodwinds, suggests quiet, lonely spaces.

In the first ABA sections, solo woodwinds introduce the themes.

The repetition of the ABA section provides a variation in dynamics and a contrast in color with the sounds of strings and brasses.

The coda, based on the C section and featuring woodwind solos, ends the composition in the quiet mood in which it began.

Observe that the artistically produced tones of the orchestral instruments contribute to the refinement of the folk-song setting.

In previous lessons, simple instruments of contrasting tone colors have been used in interesting and musical sequence to give unity and variety to music performed in the classroom.

Study the orchestral instruments in "Cattle" and the way Virgil Thomson has used them to provide contrast in the music.

Compare the tone colors of the English horn and the clarinet heard in the first section.

Observe that the use of solo woodwinds throughout the composition provides unity in the music.

Compare the tone color of the strings and French horns heard in the second ABA section.

Describe the effect of the contrast between the tone color of the flute and that of the strings and brasses.

Determine how many of the four orchestral families are included in the music and what each family contributes to unit and variety.

THE BLACKSMITH

1. Oh, the black - smith's a fine stur - dy fel - low!
2. Blow the fire, stir the coals, heap - ing more on,
3. Let the blows, strong and sure, quick - ly fall - ing,

Hard his hand, but his heart's true and mel - low.
Till the iron's all a - glow, let it roar on!
Haste the work, for the iron fast is cool - ing.

See him stand there, his huge bel - lows blow - ing,
While the smith high his ham - mer's a swing - ing,
Oh, the smith he's a fine stur - y fel - low!

With his strong, brawn - y arms free and bare.
Fier - y sparks fall in showers all a - round,
Brave - ly work - ing from morn - ing till night.

See the fire in the fur - nace a glow - ing,
And the sledge on the an - vil is ring - ing,
Hard his hand, but his heart's true and mel - low,

Bright its spar - kle and flash, loud its roar.
Fills the air with its loud clang - ing sound.
Like his an - vil, he stands for the right.

Music by Wolfgang Amadeus Mozart

BECOMING ACQUAINTED WITH THE MUSIC

The ringing anvils of the blacksmith's shop added musical sounds to the chorus of a working and singing America. This text, set to a Mozart melody, captures the rhythm and the spirit of the blacksmith's work.

Prepare to learn "The Blacksmith." Study the score and decide

- whether the melody line is angular or smooth
- whether the melody moves scale-wise or on a chord line
- what two pitches of the melody are not included in the C chord
- how many four-measure phrases are included
- which phrase includes a melodic sequence
- whether the rhythm is even or uneven
- how many times the rhythm pattern of the first two measures is found in the song

Strum the C chord on the autoharp and sing the pitches of the C chord included in the melody:

Illustration 1

C

Learn the rhythm pattern of the melody (illustration 2) and compare it with the rhythm studied in "Battle Hymn of the Republic" (illustration 3).

Illustration 2

Illustration 3

Sing the song with help from the score, a conductor, and the autoharp accompaniment.

Sing the song again and determine how this melody from Mozart's opera *The Marriage of Figaro* expresses the vigor and strength of a blacksmith.

Compare class discoveries about the music with these observations:

The large intervals and the constant change of direction create an active, angular melody that contributes to the vigor of the song.

The repeated use of the chord line (C major) in the melody suggests a quality of militant strength.

The sequence within the first phrase and the repetition of the second phrase in the ABB form contribute unity to this vigorous melody.

The uneven dotted rhythm and the repetition of the two-measure rhythm pattern throughout the melody contribute to the forceful vitality of the song.

 Mathematically and visually, the short note of this dotted rhythm (♩. ♪) is linked to the preceding note; musically, it acts as an impulse to the beat that follows, giving it strength and emphasis.

The tonic (C) and dominant (G₇) chords in the melody and accompaniment contribute to the sturdy simplicity of the music.

Experimentation with the tone color and pitch of percussion instruments increases awareness of contrasts in the tone color and pitch of melodic orchestral instruments.

As an accompaniment to the song, add ringing sounds that might be heard in the blacksmith's shop.

Experiment with percussion instruments, such as the gong, cymbals, triangles, or finger cymbals, and select those that are appropriate.

Decide on rhythm patterns that imitate the rhythmic movement of the black-smith. Select the percussion instrument most appropriate for each pattern:

Collect metal objects that provide a clear, ringing tone to substitute for, or supplement, available percussion instruments.

Illustration 4

Sing "The Blacksmith" with percussion accompaniment.

Students should be encouraged to experiment with appropriate rhythm patterns and to explain the choices they make.

Now add the ringing harmonic accompaniment of the resonator bells. Determine the pitches needed for the C and G_7 chords:

Illustration 5

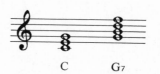

C   G₇

Learning proceeds best when students have an active part in the learning process.

Re-arrange the pitches of the chords from root position to an inversion in order to provide smoother harmonic movement (the D of the G_7 chord may be omitted):

Illustration 6

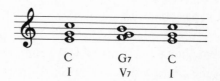

C   G₇   C
I   V₇   I

To make economical use of time, any mechanical activity, such as selecting resonator bells and players, should be an efficient, established routine.

Practice playing the chords and create a simple introduction.

Sing the song with resonator bell accompaniment, following the chord symbols shown above the score, playing on the first and third beat of the measure.

On the piano, locate the C and G_7 chords shown in illustration 7. Play them with the song, following the chord symbols shown above the score.

Illustration 7

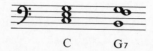

C   G₇

LESSON 44

SAKURA

1. Sa - ku - ra.   Sa - ku - ra,   Cher - ry blos - soms ev - 'ry - where.
2. Sa - ku - ra,   Sa - ku - ra,   Blos - soms wav - ing in the breeze.
   Sa - ku - ra,   *Sa - ku - ra,*   *Yo - yo - gi no so - ra wa,*

Clouds of glo - ry   fill the sky,   Mist of beau - ty
Yo - shi - no, the   cher - ry - land,   Tat - su - ta, the
Mi - wa - ta su   ka - gi - ri,   Ka - su - mi ka

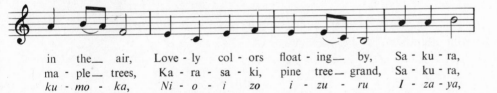

in the air, Love - ly col - ors float - ing by, Sa - ku - ra,
ma - ple - trees, Ka - ra - sa - ki, pine tree - grand, Sa - ku - ra,
ku - mo - ka, Ni - o - i zo i - zu - ru I - za - ya,

Sa - ku - ra,   Let all come sing - ing.
Sa - ku - ra,   Let all come sing - ing.
i - za - ya   mi ni yu - kan.

Japanese folk song
Translation by Lorene Hoyt

BECOMING ACQUAINTED WITH THE MUSIC

A people's attitude toward nature and life itself is expressed in their music.
Listen to the recording of "Sakura" to discover
- what sounds in the music identify the people who created this song
- what characteristics of the music express a serenity of mood
- how the music reveals an appreciation for the ethereal beauty of the
cherry blossoms

Compare the discoveries made by the class with these general observations:

The combination of a Japanese flute (*shakuhachi*) and the stringed instrument (*koto*) is a typical Japanese accompaniment.

The mood of serenity is established by the slow tempo, the even-flowing rhythm and melody, and the absence of strong contrasts in dynamics.

The pentatonic scale, in which Japanese music is often written, gives the song its exotic sound.

Now sing along with the recording, following the score, to find the repetitions in the melody that help to establish the calm, serene mood.

Sing the song with the recording again, following the score, to find the simple rhythm patterns that contribute to the quiet beauty of the melody. Determine how the last three measures are different from the rest of the song. What is the musical effect of these last three measures?

Look for the spirit or mood of a piece of music in the *combination* of its particular musical characteristics — not in any *one* of its characteristics.

CREATING APPROPRIATE ACCOMPANIMENTS

When re-creating the music of another culture, use those instruments and rhythmic and harmonic ideas that most nearly approximate the accompaniments authentic to that particular music.

Create an accompaniment that will imitate the Oriental sounds and express the mood of the song. Use the autoharp to simulate the koto, plucking the lowest E and A strings together on the first beat of each measure:

Illustration 1

Use the finger cymbals or triangle to provide the contrasting tone color and pitch often heard in Japanese music:

Illustration 2

Use the gong, striking it once at the beginning and once at the end of the song. To create the attitude of reverence the Japanese feel toward the beauties of nature, allow the tone to die away each time the gong is struck.

PLANNING A PERFORMANCE

Strike the gong and wait until the sound dies away.

Play a four-measure introduction, using the autoharp and finger cymbals as shown in illustration 2. Continue this instrumental accompaniment throughout the song.

Sing the first verse.

Play four measures of the instrumental accompaniment as an interlude.

Sing the second verse.

Play another four measures of the instrumental accompaniment as a coda.

Strike the gong and wait until the sound dies away.

192

When the class has learned "Sakura" well enough that the performance moves smoothly, add the reading of *haiku*, short Japanese poems. Read the first poem before the gong is struck and the song has begun and the second when the song has ended and the sound of the gong has died away.

Cherry blossoms at night!
Just like angels
Come down from heaven.

The temple bell dies away,
The scent of flowers in the evening
Is still tolling the bell.

From *Haiku*, Vol. I, "Spring," by R. H. Blyth, © 1950.
The Hokuseido Press, Tokyo. By permission of the publishers.

Carefully selected poetry can enhance the drama and heighten the aesthetic quality of a musical experience.

GOING DEEPER INTO STRUCTURE

As stated at the beginning of this lesson, "Sakura" is written in a pentatonic scale. Play the pitches of this pentatonic scale (illustration 3) on a keyboard instrument and sing the scale on the neutral syllable "loo." Recall what has been learned about pentatonic scales in general (Lesson 8).

Illustration 3

Compare this pentatonic scale with the natural form of the minor scale in illustration 4. (To hear the musical effect of this scale, review "Paddy Works on the Railroad," Lesson 40.)

Illustration 4

A - minor scale (natural form)

Compare class discoveries with these observations:

The important difference between this pentatonic scale and the natural form of the minor scale is that the fourth and seventh tones of the minor scale are omitted in the pentatonic. It is the omission of these two pitches that is responsible for the absence of a feeling for key and of the various chords and harmonic progressions associated with Western music.

A melodic figure that includes the descending interval of a fourth is often heard in Oriental music. Observe this descending interval in "Sakura":

Illustration 5

JAPANESE RAIN SONG

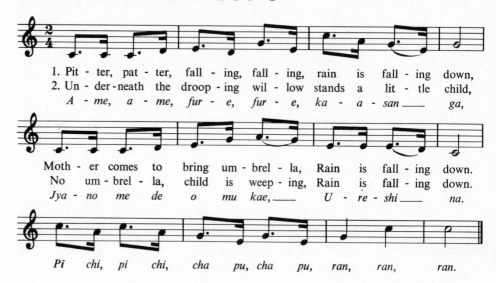

1. Pit - ter, pat - ter, fall - ing, fall - ing, rain is fall - ing down,
2. Un - der - neath the droop - ing wil - low stands a lit - tle child,
A - me, a - me, fur - e, fur - e, ka - a - san ga,

Moth - er comes to bring um - brel - la, Rain is fall - ing down.
No um - brel - la, child is weep - ing, Rain is fall - ing down.
Jya - no me de o mu kae, U - re - shi na.

Pi chi, pi chi, cha pu, cha pu, ran, ran, ran.

Japanese folk song contributed by
Elizabeth Clure and Helen Rumsey.
English words by Roberta McLaughlin

From *Sing a Song* by Roberta McLaughlin and Lucille
Wood, © 1960, Prentice-Hall, Inc. By permission of the
publishers.

BECOMING ACQUAINTED WITH THE MUSIC

Musical characteristics are more quickly identified by ear, more easily recognized by the eye, and more intelligently discussed when two contrasting songs are compared.

"Japanese Rain Song" is a children's play song that contrasts sharply in mood with "Sakura." Listen as "Japanese Rain Song" is sung for the first time and compare it with "Sakura" in

- mood
- text
- melody
- mode

Sing the song again and observe how the rhythm pattern of the melody suggests the childlike character of the song.

Sing a folk song in the language of the people who created it. Take advantage of the help that class members or other persons in the school may be able to give in pronouncing the words.

RHYTHM In a lively tempo, uneven rhythm ($\frac{2}{4}$ ♩♫ ♩♫ | ♩♫ ♩♫) expresses the sprightly, skipping motion of a child.

Learn the Japanese words of the song by reading them together and by studying the pronunciation of each word carefully. "Pi chi, pi chi, cha pu, cha pu, ran, ran, ran" are nonsense syllables to which Japanese children splash and stomp in the water.

PLAYING AN APPROPRIATE ACCOMPANIMENT

"Japanese Rain Song," like "Sakura," is written on a pentatonic scale, as shown in illustration 1. Play the notes of the scale on the bells.

Illustration 1

Sing this scale on "loo" and describe the sound this sequence of pitches produces.

Create an Oriental accompaniment by making up counter melodies on the bells, using only the pitches of the pentatonic scale. The melody patterns may be simple or complex:

The performance of a pentatonic accompaniment provides an opportunity for quick success because there are no "wrong" notes in the harmony provided by the five-tone scale.

Illustration 2

 In the pentatonic scale the absence of a "leading tone," a tone one-half step below the tonic, removes the strong feeling of tonality and the demand for particular harmonies.

Sing the song while several students play simultaneously their original pentatonic patterns on the bells as an accompaniment. If these patterns are different from each other and if they are played with the lightness of raindrops, the effect will suggest the sound of Japanese wind chimes.

Four measures of the bell patterns may be used as an introduction and coda.

GOING DEEPER INTO STRUCTURE

With ear and eye, compare the pentatonic scale with the major scale built on the same pitch, C, by singing the two scales and studying their structure.

Illustration 3

Pentatonic scale   Major scale

The pentatonic scale, like the major and minor scales, can be constructed from any pitch.

The pentatonic scale includes five pitches; the major scale, seven.

The fourth and seventh pitches of the major scale are not found in the pentatonic. The absence of these "active tones" gives the pentatonic its unusual effect.

Review the concept of tonal magnetism (Lesson 8) and note that the leading tone is one of the "active tones."

195

LESSON 46

LAIDERONETTE, EMPRESS OF THE PAGODAS

Composers find inspiration in the sounds of music from other cultures. The story of the orchestral composition "Laideronette, Empress of the Pagodas" from *Mother Goose Suite* by Maurice Ravel is taken from a French fairy tale. This musical episode portrays a scene in which porcelain Oriental figures (the Pagodas) serenade their beautiful empress, Laideronette, with music played on miniature musical instruments made of walnut and almond shells.

Listen to a recording to discover the
- section of the music representing the tiny Oriental musicians
- section representing the empress
- contrasts between the two sections
- form of the music (Is it ABB, ABA, or AAB?)

The background and maturity of the group should be the guide in determining how much can be discovered in each hearing.

IDENTIFYING MUSICAL CHARACTERISTICS IN NOTATION

Follow the notation of the two themes in illustration 1 to observe the
- contrasts in rhythm and duration
- contrasts in pitch
- characteristics that permit these themes to be played on the black keys of the piano

Illustration 1

Listen again to identify the characteristics discussed in lessons devoted to other Oriental songs. Notice the unusual sounds provided by certain orchestral instruments.

Compare class discoveries with these observations:

The sounds of Oriental music are suggested by percussion instruments, woodwinds, and pizzicato (plucked) strings.

The sound of the gong suggests a feeling of reverence for the empress.

Notes of short duration portray the music of the tiny musicians

The ability to read a score develops from a growing awareness of relationships in music as they are expressed in each new setting.

Notes of longer duration portray the majestic empress.

196

The high pitches played by the piccolo, celesta, xylophone, glockenspiel, and harp represent the tiny musicians. The lower pitches represent the majestic empress.

The scale is pentatonic because the pitches 1, 2, 3, 5, and 6 of the major scale predominate. The pentatonic scale based on F-sharp can be played on the black keys of a keyboard instrument:

Illustration 2

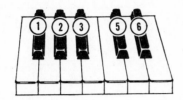

COMPOSING AN ORIENTAL COMPOSITION

Create an original composition with an Oriental flavor.

Select a pentatonic scale.

Use the song bells or piano to make up a tune that asks a musical question and states a musical answer.

 Two phrases in the relation of question and answer are called a **period**.

Establish the meter by deciding whether the rhythm of the melody moves in groups of two or in groups of three.

Make up a second tune that differs from the first in pitch and in rhythm pattern but retains the same key and meter.

Decide on the form, determining which tune will be repeated (ABA, AAB, ABB, or AABA).

Record the two melodies in notation or use simplified symbols such as numbers or blank notation.

Add Oriental percussion instruments, such as wood block, drums, finger cymbals, triangle, gong, and temple blocks.

Select percussion instruments that provide contrasts in mood, pitch, and dynamics.

Experiment with temple blocks. If tuned to a pentatonic scale, they can sometimes provide all or part of the melody.

Select a title for the new composition and plan a performance.

Original musical ideas will be expressed more freely in a classroom atmosphere where friendly, constructive criticism is appreciated and discouraging criticism is avoided.

Interest in notation is stimulated when students discover that it serves their own purposes.

Creative experience implies that there are choices to be made but that guidance will be given when needed. Bewilderment, frustration, and failure do not lead to musical growth.

HARU GA KITA *(Spring Has Come!)*

1. Ha - ru ga ki - ta, Ha - ru ga ki - ta!
1. Spring has___ come, Oh, spring has___ come! Oh,

Do - ko ni ki - ta? Ya - ma ni ki - ta,
Where___ has it come? To the___ hills and

Sa - to ni ki - ta, No ni mo ki - ta.
To the___ vil - lage Mea - dow it has come!

2. Hana ga saku,
Hana ga saku!
Doko ni saku?
Yama ni saku,
Sato ni saku,
No ni mo saku.

2. Flowers are blooming,
Flowers are blooming!
Where do they bloom?
On the hills and
On the village
Meadow see them bloom!

Japanese folk song
Translation by San-ichi Kesen

BECOMING ACQUAINTED WITH THE MUSIC

"Haru Ga Kita" is a favorite spring song of Japanese children.

Learn and sing the Japanese text, keeping in mind the English translation of each of the following words:

haru — spring

kita — come

doko — where

yama — hills or mountain

sato — village

no — meadow or plain

Play an autoharp accompaniment or sing the song unaccompanied in a simple, childlike style.

MOVING TO MUSIC

Interpret the words of the song with a Japanese fan (or a fan made of paper).

Use wide arm movements, moving the arms from left to right in a straight line or circle.

With these movements, express the contour of the mountain and the plain.

Place the fan above the eyes and turn as though searching the horizon for spring.

Always follow the movement of the fan with the eyes and body.

Moving the body rhythmically is a vivid way of sensing the phrases of a song. Such movement, however, should always be appropriate to the idea and style of the music — never superficially imposed on the song for the sake of teaching a musical concept.

GOING DEEPER INTO STRUCTURE

Observe that although most of the pitches of the song are from the pentatonic scale a feeling for the key of C major is provided by the
- inclusion of the fourth pitch of the scale (F)
- melodic intervals suggesting harmony of the primary chords (C, G_7, F)
- tonic chord line in the melody

LESSON 48

ALLELUIA

All crea-tures of our God and King,

Lift up your voice and with us sing, Al-le-lu-ia! Al-le-lu-ia!

Thou burn-ing sun with gold-en beam,

Thou sil-ver moon with soft-er gleam! Al-le-lu-ia! Al-le-lu-ia!

Al-le-lu-ia! Al-le-lu-ia! Al-le-lu-ia!

17th-century German melody
Words from St. Francis of Assisi

Translation from *Curwen Edition No. 80649*,
by permission of J. Curwen & Sons Ltd.

BECOMING ACQUAINTED WITH THE MUSIC

Sometimes poetry be-comes more memorable when set to a melody. In effective song, music has qualities appropriate to the text.

The words of "Alleluia" are taken from the writings of Francis of Assisi, the saint who spoke of various natural phenomena and of all nature's creatures as his "brothers" and "sisters." Listen to the recording of the song, also known as "Hymn to St. Francis," and decide why this seventeenth-century German melody is especially appropriate for the text.

Before singing the song in two parts as it is heard in the recording, learn the simple melody on page 200. With the teacher's help, sing the song unaccompanied. Recall the meaning of the *fermata* ($\frown$) and observe it in performance.

The class divides into two groups. One group sings the first part of the phrases, and the other responds with the "Alleluias."

When students have heard a comparatively simple melody, they should familiarize themselves with it through singing so they will have a general idea of its content before progressing to a deeper study of the score.

STUDYING THE SCORE

To become more secure in singing the song, study the rhythmic design of the melody.

Observe that there are only two different rhythmic figures in the whole song (♩ | ♩♩♩♩♩♩| o and ♩♩| ♩ ♩). Locate these figures where they occur in the score.

Observe that the last rhythmic figure of the song (♩♩ | o. | o) is a variation on the ♩♩| ♩ ♩ figure. Decide why this variation is effective at the end of the song.

Studying a musical score reveals the association between sound and notation, helps develop music reading skills, and deepens intellectual understanding of musical structure.

TERM The device of increasing the time value of notes, usually to twice their original length, is called **augmentation.**

Recall what has been learned about the meter signature.

SYMBOLS The $\frac{3}{2}$ meter signature tells that there are three beats to the measure and that a half note receives one beat.

SYMBOLS The relationship among the time values of notes remains the same whatever the meter signature.

$$♩ ♩ = ♩$$
$$♩ ♩ = o$$
$$♩ ♩ ♩ = o.$$

To develop rhythmic accuracy, practice reading the text together in the rhythmic pattern of the music.

Study the melodic design in the music to discover and locate the four different motives that make up the sixteen measures of the music.

The study of melodic design reveals to the student the more subtle as well as the more obvious characteristics of melody and gives him insight and knowledge with which to explore music on his own.

MELODY A **motive,** or motif, is the smallest meaningful fragment in music. It is the germ idea of many musical compositions.

Observe that the motives in the first and seventh measures are repeated immediately after they are first presented. Compare these two motives.

Locate the remaining motives and determine how many times they are repeated.

Determine how both unity and variety are created in the melody line of the song.

201

A study of melodic design should enhance interpretive and expressive performance.

Practice the four different motives and then decide on the interpretation that will best reflect the spirit of the music.

Locate the melodic high points of the song and use dynamics to express these parts of the music.

Experiment with echo effects on the repeated "Alleluia" patterns.

Make final decisions on dynamics and tempo and sing the song with sensitivity to its meaning.

SINGING IN HARMONY

Knowledge of notation can guide students in following a score intelligently before they have developed the skill of independent music reading.

Study the score on the opposite page to discover that the second part is created by using two kinds of harmonic writing.

On the score, locate the parts of the music to be sung in the imitative style of a round or canon.

Observe that the two lines, though shown on different staves, are written on the treble staff and that the harmony in the last line is often an interval of a third below the melody.

In beginning two-part harmony experiences, one part, usually the melody, should be well learned before the second part is attempted.

Observe that the melody line of the top staff is exactly like the melody just learned except for the rests ( ) at the beginning of the second phrase.

SYMBOLS Rest symbols designate silences in music. The half rest (➖) is equal in time value to the half note ($\downarrow$). In $\frac{3}{2}$ meter the half rest means silence for one pulse in the rhythmic movement.

The ease with which part-singing can be developed depends on the degree to which accuracy of intonation and rhythmic precision have been developed in previous singing experiences.

Sing the top staff of the score, observing the half rests in the music.

Study the bottom staff of the score.

Observe the rest signs that show the second part enters on the third beat of the first measure of the music.

Observe that the melody line changes to a harmony part on the last beat of the fourth measure.

Observe the natural-sign (♮) in the sixth measure and learn the first six measures of this harmony part.

SYMBOLS The natural-sign (♮) is one of the accidentals that lends color to a melodic line or harmonic progression by temporarily canceling a sharp or flat in a key signature. In this instance, the fourth note of the scale.

In part-singing, students should be encouraged to listen attentively to all parts, letting the ear help the eye read the score.

Observe the simplicity of the movement of the harmony part in the last seven measures of the song and learn this part.

When the second part has been learned, review the decisions made on tempo and dynamics. The class is now ready to divide into two sections and, under the direction of a conductor, sing the two-part arrangement of the song.

CREATING AN APPROPRIATE ACCOMPANIMENT

First considerations when deciding on appropriate instrumental accompaniments are: Does the tone color enhance the music? Is the style of the accompaniment appropriate to the music?

Prepare to play a simple resonator bell accompaniment with the melody of the song. The resonator bells of the E-flat scale (illustration 1) are distributed to eight members of the class.

Illustration 1

On the score, locate a descending scale line of
- all eight pitches (8, 7, 6, 5, 4, 3, 2, 1)
- the four highest pitches (8, 7, 6, 5)
- the four lowest pitches (4, 3, 2, 1)

An important reason for using instruments in classroom music is that advantage can be taken of the tone color and interest they bring to a musical performance. A second reason is that they give students first-hand experience in interpreting a score.

Practice these motives in the rhythm of the melody, then play them on the "Alleluias" while the class sings the song.

Persons playing pitches 1, 3, 5 (E-flat chord) practice playing the chord (illustration 2) on every beat of the first four measures. Then, in "tremolo" style (striking the chord rapidly and repeatedly like this ), practice playing the E-flat chord throughout the four measures beginning with the words "Thou burning sun."

Illustration 2

Sing the melody of "Alleluia," using the resonator bell accompaniments (scale line, chord, and "tremolo") at the proper times and describe the effect of the accompaniment. Determine why this effect is an appropriate accompaniment.

Observe that three flatted pitches (E-flat, B-flat, and A-flat) were played in the scale line and that they correspond to the three flats in the key signature.

THE LARK SONG AND LITTLE BIRD

Make up a story about a bird or a family of birds, telling of its adventures, realistic or imaginary. (The class may be divided into small groups, each group creating a story.)

Experiment with sounds produced on the piano to help tell the story. These sounds may include contrasts in

- pitch — high or low
- dynamics — soft or loud
- tempo — fast or slow
- duration — long or short
- rhythm — even or uneven
- texture — single tone or clusters of tone
- direction — ascending or descending

Consider the use of trills (studied in Lesson 10) and glissandos in the sound effects.

TERM   **Glissando** is the term for the effect produced by sliding the finger quickly along the keys of the piano or a string.

BECOMING ACQUAINTED WITH THE MUSIC

Listen to recordings of "The Lark Song" by Tchaikovsky and "Little Bird" by Grieg, orchestrated by Herbert Donaldson. Discover how the musical characteristics chosen by the composers compare with those selected by the class.

Listen again and decide to what extent the tone color of the orchestral instruments reflects the descriptive qualities of the compositions, which were originally composed for piano.

Listen once more and compare the two compositions by following the themes in illustrations 1 and 2.

Illustration 1

Illustration 2

Among the many approaches to a listening experience is one in which the class expresses its own musical ideas relating to a particular subject and compares their ideas with those of the composer.

The piano provides another means of "making music" and clarifying contrasts in music.

A comparison of two similar or contrasting compositions stimulates ideas for discussion of the music materials used by the composers.

Determine
- how the songs of the birds differ
- what orchestral instruments play the birds' songs
- what "miniature" musical qualities appropriate for the description of little birds can be identified by ear and eye
- how an element of drama is introduced into one of the compositions

Compare class discoveries with these observations about the music:

The tone color and high pitch of the piccolo, flute, and violin provide a quality that is an appropriate and realistic description of a bird's song.

The trill-like ornament in the melody of "The Lark Song" (illustration 1) is different from the short trill in the melody of "Little Bird" (illustration 2).

The low tones in "Little Bird" suggest a brief dramatic incident in contrast to the general mood.

The "miniature" effect is created by the high pitches and by notes of short duration.

RHYTHM The triplet (illustration 1) is a rhythmic device in which three notes are performed in the time normally allotted to two of the same value ( ).

RHYTHM An important aspect of rhythm is the relationship among notes of different duration. The eighth note (♪) is four times as long as the thirty-second note (♬).

FOUR CORNFIELDS

From my ranch house I looked toward the corn - fields,___
From the corn - fields I looked toward the ranch house,___

Where the corn was reach - ing toward the sky.___
Stand - ing bright - ly in the set - ting sun.___

I wel - comed the hoe - ing that kept corn
That ranch was my treas - ure, it gave me

a - grow - ing Till it grew sky high.___
the pleas - ure Of life's work well done.___

I'll re - mem - ber the ranch all the days of my
I'll re - mem - ber the ranch all the days of my

life, And the corn-fields that I loved to hoe,___
life, As the home that I real - ly a - dore,___

In the eve - 'ning I walked in be - tween rows of
But a - round me the white doves are coo - ing and

gi - ants, Then list - ened and heard the corn grow.___
sigh - ing, That I won't go there an - y more.___

Mexican folk song
Words by Eleanor Graham Vance

207

BECOMING ACQUAINTED WITH THE MUSIC

An interesting way to study a song is to identify it with the musical tradition of the country in which it was created.

Listen to the recording of "Four Cornfields" and describe the characteristics of the melody, rhythm, and instrumental accompaniment that reveal the song is from Mexico.

Listen to, or sing along with, the recording. Determine the two contrasting moods — the one suggested by the tempo and rhythm, the other by the words and melody line.

Further study will reveal the musical characteristics associated with that country and how they contribute to the distinctive effect of its music.

Note the repetition of the A and B phrases, the C and D phrases.

STUDYING THE RHYTHM

Follow the score carefully and sing with the recording. Observe that the melody is easy to sing, although the rhythmic pattern includes comparatively difficult figures. With ear and eye, locate these figures and describe the effect they have in the music.

Compare class discoveries about the rhythmic figures in the melody with these observations:

The values of studying and learning particular rhythmic figures are (1) accuracy in performance, (2) easier learning in future musical experiences, and (3) increased knowledge of rhythmic notation.

The most obvious difference between the rhythm pattern of this song and that of songs studied before is the exceptionally long, sustained notes at the ends of the phrases.

Song phrases are often four or eight measures long. On the score, locate the phrases whose lengths are extended by tied half notes.

Practice each of these sustained note patterns, counting three beats for each of the tied dotted half notes.

Observe the dotted rhythmic figure (♩ ♩. ♪) found throughout the music. Remember that dotted rhythms are uneven rhythms and give variety to music. Review the time value of the dotted quarter and eighth note and practice the figure.

Even while rhythmic ideas are analyzed, the teacher and the student should never lose sight of the effect they produce in the music.

Observe the syncopated figures in the first part of the song (♩ ♩ ♩ ♩ ♩) and (♩ ♩ ♩ | ♩.). In these figures, the accent on the third beat in the first measure would more naturally fall on the first beat in the following measure. This syncopation adds interest to the rhythmic movement.

Observe the points in the music where the rhythm consists of these simple patterns in $\frac{3}{4}$ meter: ♩ ♩ and ♩ ♩ ♩ .

Allow enough time to study and practice a difficult rhythm pattern.

Note that the song begins on the second beat of the measure. Practice and learn the rhythm pattern of the melody by reading the words of the song in rhythm.

Practice sessions lose effectiveness unless they are followed immediately by opportunities to realize results in performance.

Sing "Four Cornfields" with the recording, paying particular attention to the rhythm pattern of the melody. Determine how the spirit and mood of the music is revealed in the different rhythmic figures.

CREATING AN APPROPRIATE ACCOMPANIMENT

The autoharp simulates the sound of the guitar and is especially effective with songs that call for guitar accompaniment.

Play the autoharp to simulate the sound of the guitar, an instrument popular in Mexico and widely used to accompany folk songs.

Determine the key of the song by
- noting the final chord of the music
- observing that there are no sharps or flats in the key signature

On the autoharp, locate the three primary chords of the key (I = C; IV = F; V_7 = G_7).

Play an introduction, such as the one shown in illustration 1, and sing the song with autoharp accompaniment, strumming only on the first beat of each measure.

Illustration 1

$\frac{3}{4}$ C   F G_7 C

One   *two*   *ready*   *sing*   From   my

Continue to develop the skill of creating and playing effective introductions. They are important to the music in setting key and tempo and suggesting the style and mood of songs.

When the autoharp chord pattern has become familiar, experiment with more interesting rhythmic accompaniments on the instrument.

Play a light, fast rhythmic pattern on every beat of the music. On the strong beat of each measure, strum a short stroke on the low strings. On the last two beats of each measure, strum on the high strings:

Once the student is familiar with the autoharp, he should be encouraged to explore the instrument and to discover the variety of musical effects that can be created to enhance the style and mood of the songs in his repertory.

Illustration 2

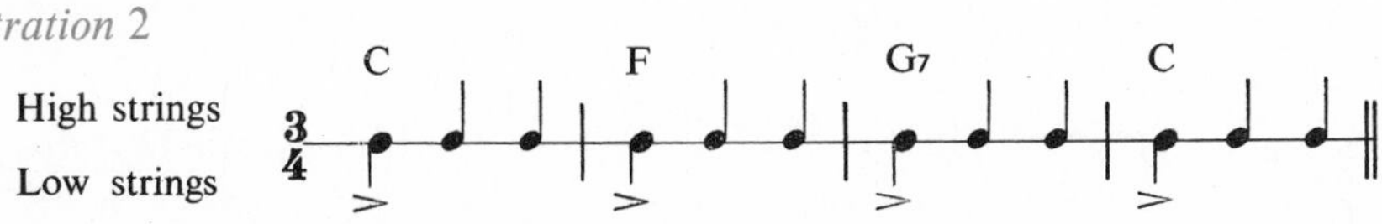

High strings
Low strings
$\frac{3}{4}$ C   F G_7 C

Play the pattern shown in illustration 3. On the first beat of each measure, strum a short stroke on the low strings. On the third beat, strum a short stroke on the high strings.

Illustration 3

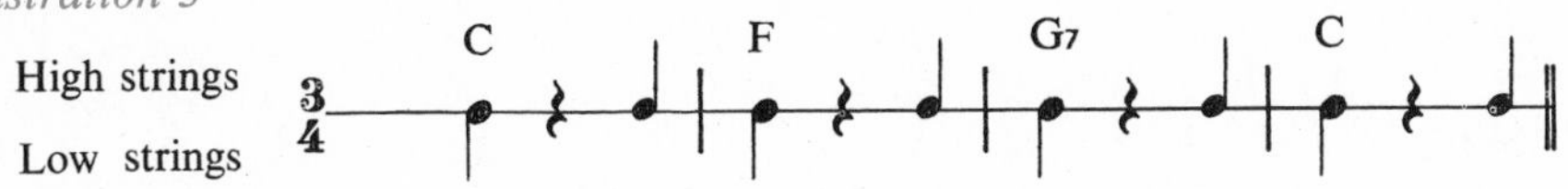

High strings
Low strings
$\frac{3}{4}$ C   F G_7 C

Determine which of the two accompaniments (illustration 2 or 3) is more effective for the song.

SINGING IN HARMONY

Harmony parts can be created for many Mexican folk songs by singing in intervals of thirds and sixths with the melody.

Study the score of "Four Cornfields" to observe the interval that creates the harmony.

Observe that the contour and rhythm pattern of the harmony part is exactly like that of the melody.

On a pitched instrument, find the beginning pitch of the harmony line. Practice the harmony part by singing it in unison with autoharp accompaniment.

Inherent in the text, melody, and harmony is the nostalgic quality of the song. This mood can be re-created by the imaginative interpretation of the performers. The lively tempo and varied rhythmic figures that suggest the contrasting mood must be carefully considered to give the song its special charm in performance.

Decide on the most effective autoharp accompaniment and sing the song in two-part harmony.

Evaluate the performance and describe the effect of the music.

Creating harmony — even simple two-part harmony — is a satisfying and enriching experience, especially when the harmonization is characteristic of music such as spirituals and Mexican folk songs.

Good part-singing grows out of good unison singing. Students should be encouraged to listen to both parts during performance and to use the ear to achieve good tonal blend.

FARMYARD SONG

1. The barn door is o-pen, Come out, gen-tle cow,
2. When win-ter's first snow-storm Sweeps o-ver the land,

Come, Puss, with your kit-ten, The sun's shin-ing now.
All hud-dled at barn door, The farm crea-tures stand.

Come, Dob-bin, old fel-low, Come, duck-lings so yel-low,
Come, pi-geons, a-coo-ing, Come, cow, gen-tly moo-ing,

The door's o-pen wide, So hur-ry out-side.
The door's o-pen wide, So hur-ry in-side.

Come, pi-geons, a-fly-ing, Stop coo-ing and sigh-ing.
Now, Dob-bin, come pranc-ing, Come new colt, a-danc-ing.

Come out ev-'ry one, Come feel the warm sun.
Here's warm co-zy stall And good feed for all.

For sum-mer days have come to the farm-yard,
Now win-ter days have come to the farm-yard,

So come, so come to my call - - ing.
So come, so come to my call - - ing.

Music by Edvard Grieg
English translation by Louise Kessler

BECOMING ACQUAINTED WITH THE MUSIC

Edvard Grieg is known as one of "music's voices of the North." In his works are found tone pictures of his native Norway, including its natural phenomena, everyday life, Norse legends, and fantasies about fairies and gnomes. In his music are heard the contrasting moods of melancholy and gaiety typical of Scandinavian cultures. To become familiar with the descriptive qualities of Grieg's music, listen to two contrasting selections from *Peer Gynt: Suite No. 1* and discover how the music portrays the subject suggested by the title.

Listen to the recording of "Farmyard Song" and determine the musical characteristics that create its mood. Decide why the mood of the music is appropriate to the text, which tells about farm life in Grieg's far northern country.

When a musical composition is strongly influenced by the composer's life and native country, pertinent information on the composer and his country lends interest and meaning to the listening experience.

STUDYING INTERPRETIVE MARKINGS

Folk songs were often Grieg's inspiration, and he sometimes used open fifths in the bass to suggest peasants' bagpipes. Listen to the recording of "Farmyard Song" again to identify the phrases in which the sound of the bagpipe is heard in the accompaniment.

On the score, locate the interpretive markings shown below. Follow the score while listening to the recording, using the ear to help determine what each marking suggests in dynamics or tempo. Write a definition for each of the following.

1. *p*
2. *rit.*
3. ⌢
4. *a tempo*
5. >

Musical expression of the art song is revealed, too, in the composer's accompaniment. Study of the accompaniment aids understanding and appreciation.

How do these interpretive markings suggest that the song is one of tender, thoughtful happiness rather than one of unrestrained gaiety?

Sing the song with the recording, observing the interpretive markings carefully.

The art song should be interpreted as nearly as possible in the way the composer intended. A study of interpretive markings is necessary for authentic and artistic performance.

GOING DEEPER INTO STRUCTURE

Form Prepare to determine the form by singing the song and locating its eight-measure phrases. Notice that the last phrase is lengthened to nine measures. Discover the two phrases that are similar.

From class discussion, determine which of the forms suggested below is that of "Farmyard Song:"

1. AAAA
2. AABB
3. ABA'C
4. AABC

Rhythm   Although there is musical variety in the song, Grieg is consistent in his use of rhythm patterns.

Observe that the melodic figure of each short phrase begins on the last beat of the measure. This rhythmic arrangement (illustration 1) gives impetus to the first pulse of the following measure.

Illustration 1

Observe that, for the most part, the rhythm pattern of the song consists of eighth notes (♪) and a few sixteenth (♬) and quarter notes (♩).

Observe the rhythmic variation provided by the tied notes at the end of the

song (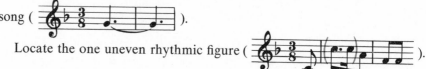).

Locate the one uneven rhythmic figure ( ).

Sing the song with the recording and describe the
- over-all effect of the rhythm pattern of the melody
- effect created by the uneven figure
- effect of the tied note at the end of the last phrase

Melody   To discover the three-note melodic figure most used in the music, follow the score while humming the melody softly. Is this figure built on a chord line or on a scale line? Identify the chord or scale.

Locate other melodic figures that are stated, then repeated at least once.

Sing the song with the recording, observing how Grieg created the song out of the repetitions of a few melodic ideas.

Harmony   Strum the accompanying chords on the autoharp so that the harmonic pattern of the music can be heard more clearly.

Observe the simplicity of the tonic harmony in the first four measures and the change in harmonic progression and heightened contrast of the D-minor, G_7, and C chords in the last measures of the first phrase (A).

HARMONY   The VI (D-minor) chord is a secondary chord and is used to give variety to the harmony. The G_7 chord is actually the V_7 chord in the key of C major to which the music goes briefly before returning to the original key. Modulations of this kind also give variety to the music.

Observe the straightforward sturdiness of the V_7 (C_7) chord throughout most of the second phrase (B) and the color that the ending chord sequence (G minor, C_7, F) gives the music.

The G-minor chord is a secondary chord in the key of F major and lends harmonic color to the music.

Grieg uses the I_7 (F_7) chord (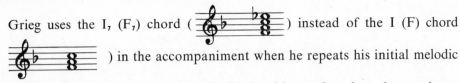) instead of the I (F) chord

(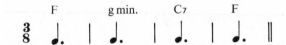) in the accompaniment when he repeats his initial melodic idea in the third phrase (A'). Since the F_7 chord is not found on the autoharp, play it on the piano to hear the difference between the two (F and F_7). Observe the repetition of the G-minor and F-major chords at the end of the phrase.

Observe the simplicity of the C and F chords at the beginning of the last phrase and the long cadence that ends the song: F, B-flat, G minor, C_7, F.

Learn the autoharp accompaniment; play the simple introduction shown in illustration 2; and sing "Farmyard Song" with the autoharp, strumming on the first beat of each measure.

Illustration 2

Evaluate the performance.

Was the tempo appropriate to the mood of the song?

Were the melodic and rhythmic figures performed accurately?

Were the interpretive markings performed expressively?

Did the performance re-create the mood of the song as it is revealed in the text and music?

Only when an imaginative interpretation is substantiated by knowledge of the music can an expressive and artistic musical performance be achieved.

RAISINS AND ALMONDS

Bei mein kind - e - le's vi - ge - le.
To my lit - tle one's cra - dle in the night,

Shtait a klor vise tsi - ge - le;
Comes a new little goat snow - y white;

Dos si - ge - le iz ge - for - en hand - len.
The goat will trot to the mar - ket.

Dos vet zein dein ba - ruf, Ro - zhin - kes mit
While moth-er, her watch will keep, To bring you back rais - ins and

mand - len; Shlof, mein kind - e - le, shlof.
al - monds; Sleep, my lit - tle one, sleep.

Jewish folk song
Translated by Sylvia and John Kolb

When a song is artistically interpreted in its initial presentation, students will be interested in creating their own musical interpretations.

BECOMING ACQUAINTED WITH THE MUSIC

Listen while "Raisins and Almonds" is sung and determine why it is called a lullaby-fantasy.

Follow the score and sing along. Decide how the mood of a lullaby is expressed in the

- swaying rhythm of $\frac{6}{8}$ meter in slow tempo
- notes of long duration at the end of each two-measure phrase
- repetition of two phrases
- return to the D-minor chord at the end of each two-measure phrase

CREATING APPROPRIATE ACCOMPANIMENTS

Prepare to play an autoharp accompaniment by locating the primary chords in the key of D minor (D minor, A$_7$, and G minor).

Play the autoharp with long, sustained strokes to produce a harp-like sound.

Experiment with one and two strums in each measure to determine the most appropriate accompaniment for a lullaby.

Learn to play the lower notes of the staff on the recorder or bells and add these instruments to the autoharp accompaniment.

GOING DEEPER INTO STRUCTURE

With ear and eye, compare the sound and structure of the *natural minor mode* (as studied in "Paddy Works on the Railroad," Lesson 40) with the *harmonic minor mode* of "Raisins and Almonds." On the piano or bells, play the D-minor scale (natural form) and the D harmonic minor scale (illustration 1).

Recall that the natural form of the minor scale includes the same pitches as its relative major. (In this case, D minor is the relative of F major).

Listen particularly to the last three pitches of each minor scale.

Locate the altered pitch in the harmonic minor scale first by ear, then on the score.

On the keyboard, observe the distance between a half step, a whole step, and one and one-half steps.

Musical growth is the result of carefully structured lessons that use past experience as a basis for learning and understanding new material.

Analysis of notation should be related to immediate musical activity.

Illustration 1

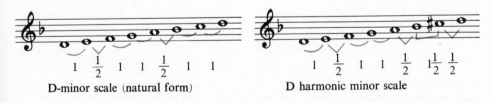

D-minor scale (natural form)   D harmonic minor scale

After class discussion of the difference between the harmonic and natural minor, compare class discoveries with these observations:

The interval of one and one-half steps between the sixth and seventh pitches of the harmonic minor scale, compared to the interval of a whole step between the sixth and seventh pitches of the natural minor, identifies the harmonic minor and gives the scale its distinctive sound.

215

Observe that the altered pitch of the harmonic minor scale is the seventh (C-sharp in the D-minor scale). Because of this altered pitch, the chord built on the fifth (dominant) becomes a major chord:

Illustration 2

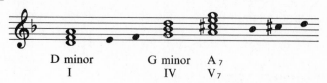

D minor   G minor   A $_7$
I   IV   V $_7$

Notice on the score of "Raisins and Almonds" that the first three pitches of the melody, the notes of the D-minor (I) chord, quickly establish the feeling for the minor key.

LESSON 53

BYE'M BYE

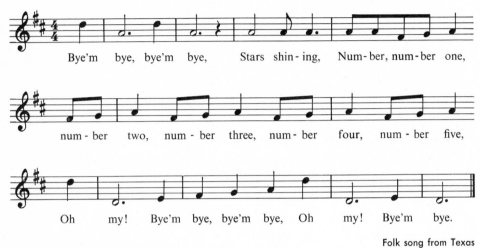

Bye'm bye, bye'm bye, Stars shin-ing, Num-ber, num-ber one,

num-ber two, num-ber three, num-ber four, num-ber five,

Oh my! Bye'm bye, bye'm bye, Oh my! Bye'm bye.

Folk song from Texas

TEACHING THE SONG TO THE PRIMARY GRADES

Besides the pleasure of just sitting and counting stars in the sky, this little folk song offers an infinite promise — not now, but "Bye'm bye." For the most effective musical experience, choose an appropriate time and introduce the song in an atmosphere of quiet wonder.

> "When this song was first sung in Texas, the singers had no idea that rocket ships would someday explore outer space. Listen to 'Bye'm Bye' and discover what Texan children did as they watched the stars at night."

Sing the song quietly for the class, unaccompanied or with autoharp, increasing the tempo in the third measure.

After the children have discovered that this is a "counting" song, invite them to join in on the first "Bye'm bye."

> "There is a part of the song that is like an echo. I'll sing the first two words, 'Bye'm bye,' and you repeat them softly, like an echo."

Invite the children to join in on the repetition of the "counting" phrase.

> "Count the stars with me this time."

If necessary, have the children listen once more to the last phrase before they sing the whole song.

> "You already know the first part of the song. Listen to the last part once more, then sing it with me."

Each song should be introduced and performed in an atmosphere appropriate to its mood. Quiet songs must be presented with sensitivity and skill if children are to enjoy the aesthetic experience inherent in the music.

Children delight in "counting" songs and take pleasure in producing interesting vocal sounds.

ADDING APPROPRIATE SOUND EFFECTS

When children are guided into the realization that well-chosen instruments enhance their music, they will take pride in performance, grow in knowledge and appreciation of music, and develop skill in "making music."

Give the children an opportunity to decide on sounds most appropriate to the music.

"We know that stars make no sound at all, so we will select the instrument that most reminds us of stars."
"Will the sound of this instrument be heavy or light?"
"Will it be a booming sound or a tinkling sound?"
"Will we play the instrument loudly or softly?"

Ask the children to select instruments with which they have had experience.

Use tact and patience when guiding children to decisions involving appropriate instrumental effects.

"What instrument do we have that best suits a song about the stars?"
"Mary has chosen the finger cymbals. She will give one set of cymbals to each of three persons, who will play them softly, one at a time, as we count the stars in the song. Listen and decide how the cymbals help us make music."

CREATING AN APPROPRIATE ACCOMPANIMENT

Make a practice of identifying on charts the melodic patterns that are effective and easily played on a pitched instrument.

Give the children an opportunity to associate the melodic phrases they are singing with pitched instruments and with musical notation. Show a musical notation chart of the two measures (illustration 1).

"Here is the music-writing for one part of the song. Decide which part of the song it shows."

Children can focus attention on and understand the notation on a chart long before they can focus on and understand the score in a songbook.

Illustration 1

Let the children tell how they made their decisions, then help them play the phrase on the melody bells.

Keep ears and mind open when asking children's reasons for their decisions. Dismissing wrong answers inhibits children's thinking and their progress in musical understanding.

"The letter names of the notes on the chart help us locate the notes on the melody bells. I will help Tommy find these pitches on the instrument so that he can play them as we sing the song. Listen, and decide whether he plays softly enough."

Encourage the children to take turns playing instruments and help them to create song introductions.

"Those who have the finger cymbals give them to three different persons while Tommy teaches Alice the melody bell part. When we sing, she will play the pattern as an introduction to the song."

218

Encourage all of the children to play the melody bells and to make discoveries about notation by themselves.

"I will place the music chart we worked with today [illustration 1] above our music table so that each of you can practice the melody bells in your free time."

"Here is the music-writing for another part of the song that we will play on the melody bells when we sing 'Bye'm Bye' again [illustration 2]. It will be above the music table, too. Use your eyes and your ears while playing the melody bells in order to discover which part of the song is shown on the chart."

Time prevents giving every child an opportunity to develop skill in playing instruments. Take advantage of the child's natural curiosity and desire to perform by setting up situations in which he can learn on his own initiative.

Illustration 2

A A F# G A F# G A F# G A

TUTÚ MARAMBA

Tu - tú Ma - ram - ba,____ stop scratch - ing at my door.____

The mas - ter is home, He will fright - en you a - way.____

Tu - tú Ma - ram - ba,____ don't come here an - y more;____

My child must be safe in his sleep, in his play.____

Loud - ly ring - ing bells will drive a - way all e - vil things,

Things that lurk in dusk - y holes or dart on cru - el wings.__

A - ran - ha Ta - tan - ha, A - ran - ha Ta - tan - ha,

If Tu - tú should come back, he must sure - ly find you sleep - ing.

A - ran - ha Ta - tan - ha, A - ran - ha Ta - tan - ha,

All night by your bed I my watch will be keep - ing.

Soft - ly sound the ev - 'ning bells that mark the com - ing night;

D.C. al Fine

Na - ture sinks to peace - ful rest un - til the morn - ing light.___

Brazilian folk song
Words by Julia W. Bingham

BECOMING ACQUAINTED WITH THE MUSIC

Tutú Maramba, the Brazilian bogeyman, and Aranha Tatanha, his spider helper, are warned away from the child who is sung to sleep in this lullaby.

Listen to the recording and discover how the purpose of this song can be recognized in its

- tempo
- dynamics
- rhythm
- melody
- mode

When a song is used for a specific purpose, knowledge of that purpose leads to quicker understanding and learning of the music.

The alternation between minor and major modes creates a dramatic effect in the music. Follow the score while listening again to the recording and locate with ear and eye the minor and the major sections. Determine the effect the change in mode creates in the music and discover how each mode is appropriate to the text.

Observe the music sign *D.C. al fine* at the end of the score.

Discovering obvious dramatic characteristics makes a good starting point in studying a song.

STUDYING THE MUSICAL ELEMENTS

Although "Tutú Maramba" is longer than many folk songs, its form is quite simple. Sing the song with the recording to locate

- like phrases
- unlike phrases
- phrases that are similar

Songs are much more quickly and easily learned when like and unlike phrases are recognized.

221

Determine the song form. How does the repetition of the phrases affect the mood of the song?

Feeling the mood of the song through its melody and rhythm as well as through its text deepens knowledge and appreciation of musical sounds and their written notation.

Sing the song again with the recording to ascertain the general characteristics of the melody and rhythm. Determine how they contribute to the mood of the song.

Does the melody move, for the most part, scale-wise or chord-wise?

Is the rhythmic pattern, for the most part, even or uneven?

Aural recognition of harmonic structure is easier when the chord pattern is played and heard on the autoharp.

Prepare to sing "Tutú Maramba" with the autoharp by studying and playing the chord accompaniment, which reveals the harmonic structure of the music.

Observe that the first three phrases (AA′B) are in the minor mode and that they are harmonized with the G-minor, A_7, and D_7 chords.

Autoharp accompaniments are learned more quickly when students recognize that repetitions in harmonic structure occur with repetitions in melodic structure.

Observe that the fourth and fifth phrases are almost identical to the first two phrases except that they are in the major mode and are harmonized with the G-major, A_7, and D_7 chords.

Observe that the sixth, seventh, and eighth phrases (BAA′) return to the minor mode.

Observe that only the chord built on G is changed (G minor — G major) in alternation between the major and minor modes.

PLANNING A PERFORMANCE

Questions that give the opportunity to tell what is felt or thought about the music are especially stimulating to the class.

Practice the autoharp accompaniment. Set an appropriate tempo and dynamic level in the introduction (illustration 1) and sing "Tutú Maramba" with the autoharp. Listen particularly to the melody and decide which influence is strongest in this song — the Portuguese and Spanish, African, or Indian. The rich and colorful Brazilian folk music grew out of these cultures.

Illustration 1

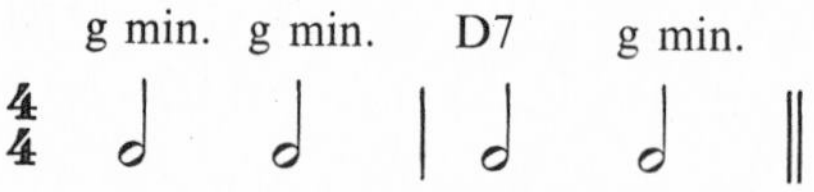

g min.
g min.
D7
g min.
4
4

Learning to select an appropriate rhythm pattern for instrumental accompaniment is as important as learning to select instruments with appropriate tone colors.

The simple autoharp accompaniment is especially appropriate for the quiet lullaby, particularly when the song is sung as a solo. When performing the song in a group, add a low-pitched drum, played softly, to the accompaniment. To emphasize the rocking rhythm of the music, use a pattern found frequently in the melody:

Illustration 2

DRUM
RH
LH
4
4

It is important to become acquainted with the score by playing melody patterns on instruments of the keyboard type. These patterns, however, should always enhance the musical effect and deepen appreciation of the music.

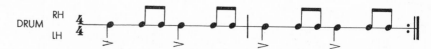

The bell sound suggested in the text of the B phrase may be played on the melody bells to add variety in tone color and to emphasize the complete change in melodic idea from phrase A to phrase B.

Learn the four measures of the B phrase on the melody bells. Listen for the interesting effects of the harmonic minor scale in downward motion (illustration 3a); of the major sound of the melodic minor in upward motion (illustration 3b).

Illustration 3

Determine the change in dynamics suggested by the text the second time the phrase occurs in the music.

Sing "Tutú Maramba" with autoharp, drum, and melody bell accompaniment.

Evaluate the class performance and determine whether the
- tempo was appropriate for a lullaby
- rocking movement of the music was evident in the interpretation of the rhythm pattern
- dynamic levels were effective

Study the form of the song to discover clues for dynamic interpretation. The dynamic level may be changed when a phrase is repeated, but such changes should be subtle in a lullaby and based on the meaning of the text.

Folk songs are most effective when sung simply, without affectation. Decisions on tempo and dynamics must be in keeping with the simplicity of folk-style singing.

Make final decisions on tempo, dynamics, and style of performance (accompaniment as well as vocal) and sing "Tutú Maramba."

Learning how to use dynamics effectively in instrumental accompaniments is as important as learning to choose the appropriate instrument.

Imagination and an understanding and knowledge of the function and structure of music are all important to expressive performance.

GOING DEEPER INTO STRUCTURE

Study illustration 4 to determine how the change from the minor to major mode is effected in the melody.

Listen while the major scale is played.

Listen while the harmonic minor scale is played.

Compare the effect of the major and minor scales.

With ear and eye, compare the structure of the major and minor scales.

A review of the scale pattern on which a melody is built emphasizes the importance of the tonal aspects of music and adds to the knowledge and appreciation of melodic structure.

Illustration 4

G-major scale   G harmonic minor scale

Compare carefully the A and A′ phrases to discover the subtle yet important change in the second (A′) phrase: the highest pitch in the song is found in the A′ phrase. This is a slight variation from the melody line of the first phrase. Sing the phrases to determine how the change affects the music.

Growth in understanding of the content and structure of a composition leads to the ability to recognize and appreciate the more subtle points in the music and to more effective performance.

223

OVERTURE TO *HÄNSEL AND GRETEL*

Included in the Overture to the opera *Hänsel and Gretel* by Engelbert Humperdinck is a beautiful melody, the "Children's Prayer," sung in the opera by Hansel and Gretel as they fall asleep in the forest. Listen to a recording of this Overture. (The recording may be stopped at the end of the "Prayer," or if the class chooses, the entire Overture may be played.)

Review the story of Hansel and Gretel with the help of the class.

BECOMING ACQUAINTED WITH THE THEMES OF THE MUSIC

Decide on the musical characteristics that best suggest the
- prayer of Hansel and Gretel
- Witch
- Dew Fairy
- song of the Gingerbread Children after they are released from the spell of the Witch

Making choices can be a game-like activity. The contrasts of musical features are often revealed in the comparisons necessary to make a choice.

As each theme is played on the piano, follow that theme in notation to discover which character it represents.

Illustration 1

Decide on an orchestral instrument that would express the spirit of each theme.

While following the notation, play or sing the themes until each is familiar to the ear and eye.

Listen to the Overture again for further clues about the
- character represented by each theme
- instrument that introduces each theme
- unifying theme
- principal characteristics of each theme

Compare class decisions about the themes with these observations:

Illustration 1d is the first theme, the prayer of Hansel and Gretel. It moves along the tonic (C) chord in an even, smooth-flowing rhythm and is introduced by the mellow tones of the French horn.

Illustration 1b is the second theme and represents the Witch. The melody moves by leaps and is played staccato by the trumpet in bold, piercing tones.

Illustration 1a is the third theme and represents the Dew Fairy. Moving principally on a scale line, it is played gently and quietly by the violins.

Illustration 1c is the fourth theme and represents the Gingerbread Children. It is a childlike dance with light, rollicking rhythm and is introduced by the woodwinds.

The "Children's Prayer" constitutes the unifying theme of the Overture. It is heard at the beginning and at the end and is combined with the song of the Gingerbread Children.

Listen to the Overture again and decide why it makes an important contribution to an opera performance.

The interest and concentration span of the class should be the guide in determining the length of time devoted to one experience. If interest is high, the activity may be extended or continued on another day.

Appendix

SAVEZ-VOUS PLANTER LES CHOUX *(Planting Cabbages)*

French folk song

1. Sav - ez - vous plan - ter les choux?
2. On les plante a - vec la main,
3. On les plante a - vec les pieds,

A la mo - de, à la mo - de,

Sav - ez - vous plan - ter les choux?
On les plante a - vec la main,
On les plante a - vec les pieds,

A la mo - de, de chez nous.

IL ÉTAIT UNE BERGÈRE *(The Shepherdess)*

French folk song

1. Il é - tait une ber - gè - re, Et ron, ron, ron, pe - tit pa - ta - pon, Il é - tait une ber -
2. Elle fit ___ un fro - ma - ge, Et ron, ron, ron, pe - tit pa - ta - pon, Elle fit ___ un fro -

gè - re Qui gar - dait ses mou - tons, Ron, ron. Qui gar - dait ses mou - tons. ___
ma - ge Du lait de ses mou - tons, Ron, ron. Du lait de ses mou - tons. ___

FAIS DO DO *(Go to Sleep)*

French nursery song. Words paraphrased by Eleanor Graham Vance

Go to sleep, my dear lit - tle sis - ter. Close your eyes and go ___ to sleep.

You'll find a sur - prise When you are a - wake, For Moth-er is bus - y mak-ing a cake.

A LA CLAIRE FONTAINE (At the Fountain)

French-Canadian folk song. English version by Ruth Martin

Just as the sun is set - ting, Cast - ing its part - ing ray,
A la clai - re fon - tai - ne M'en al - lant pro - men - ner,

I pause be - side the foun - tain, Watch - ing its shin - ing play.
J'ai trou - vé l'eau si bel - le Que je m'y suis bai - gné.

Refrain

Al - ways and al - ways I'll love you Though you are___ far a - way.
Lui ya long - temps que je t'ai - me, Ja - mais je ne t'ou - blie - rai.

SCHLAF, KINDLEIN, SCHLAF (Sleep, Baby, Sleep)

German folk song. Translated by V. S. Burrington

1. Sleep, ba - by, sleep, Thy fa - ther tends the sheep, Thy moth - er shakes the
2. Sleep, ba - by, sleep, Those white clouds are the sheep, They play a game of
3. Sleep, ba - by, sleep, See, there's one lit - tle sheep, A - round his neck a

dream - land tree And down fall pleas - ant dreams for thee. Sleep, ba - by, sleep.
hide and seek With twin - kling stars that shy - ly peek, Sleep, ba - by, sleep.
sil - ver bell,___ Tin - kle, tin - kle, sil - ver bell! Sleep, ba - by, sleep.

IN LAUTERBACH

German folk song. English words by Louise Kessler

1. In Lau - ter - bach hab' ich mein Herzel ver - lor'n, ohn' Her - zel da geh' ich nit heim.___
2. *In Lau - ter - bach vil - lage I met a lad, We danced un - til time to de - part.*

Drum geh' ich erst wie - der nach Lauter - bach nein, Und hol' mir ein Herz zu mein Rein'm!___
He whirled me and twirled me a - round and round, 'Twas then that I lost my young heart!___

Refrain

Tra la___ la la la,___ tra la la la la la,___

Tra la___ la la la,___ tra la la la la la.___

227

GLOCKEN JODLER

Austrian bell yodel as sung by Inge Peinlich of Vienna

Ho - da - ri ho - da - ro ho - da - ri - di - ri - a - ho

Ho - da - ri ho - da - ro ho - da - ri - di - ri - a - ho ri - di - ri - a - ho.

By permission of Cooperative Recreation Service, Inc.

LULLABY

Music by Johannes Brahms. Words from the German

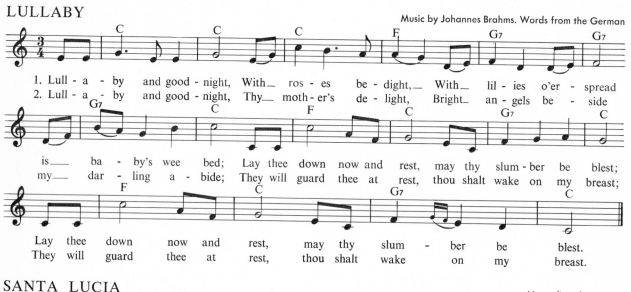

1. Lull - a - by and good - night, With ros - es be - dight, With lil - ies o'er - spread
2. Lull - a - by and good - night, Thy moth - er's de - light, Bright an - gels be - side

is ba - by's wee bed; Lay thee down now and rest, may thy slum - ber be blest;
my dar - ling a - bide; They will guard thee at rest, thou shalt wake on my breast;

Lay thee down now and rest, may thy slum - ber be blest.
They will guard thee at rest, thou shalt wake on my breast.

SANTA LUCIA

Neapolitan boat song

1. Now 'neath the sil - ver moon O - cean is glow - ing, O'er the calm
2. When o'er thy wa - ters Light winds are play - ing, Thy spell can

bil - low Soft winds are blow - ing; Here balm - y breez - es blow,
soothe us, All care al - lay - ing; To thee, sweet Na - po - li,

Pure joys in - vite us, And as we gent - ly row, All things de - light us.
What charms are giv - en, Where smiles cre - a - tion, Toil blest by heav - en.

Refrain

Hark, how the sail - or's cry Joy - ous - ly ech - oes nigh:
Home of fair po - e - sy, Realm of pure har - mon - y,

San - ta Lu - ci - a! San - ta Lu - ci - a!

228

LITTLE DUCKS

Folk song from Maryland

1. Six lit-tle ducks that I once knew, Fat ones, skin-ny ones, fair ones too,
2. Down to the riv-er they would go, Wib-ble, wob-ble, wib-ble, wob-ble to and fro,

But the one lit-tle duck with a feath-er in his back,

He ruled the oth-ers with a quack, quack, quack, quack, quack, quack.

He ruled the oth-ers with a quack, quack, quack, quack, quack, quack.

By permission of Cooperative Recreation Service, Inc.

I BOUGHT ME A CAT

Kentucky mountain folk song

1. I bought me a cat, and the cat pleased me, I fed my cat by yon-der tree;
2. I bought me a hen, and the hen pleased me, I fed my hen by yon-der tree;
3. I bought me a duck, and the duck pleased me, I fed my duck by yon-der tree;

First ending

Fine Second ending (repeat first ending, then to Verse 3)

Cat goes fid-dle-i-fee! Hen goes chim-my chuck, chim-my chuck!

Third ending
(repeat second ending, then first, then to Verse 4, etc.)

4. I bought me a goose

Duck goes quack, quack! Goose goes his-sy, his-sy!

5. I bought me a sheep 6. I bought me a pig 7. I bought me a cow

Sheep goes baa, baa! Hog goes squeel-y, squeel-y! Cow goes moo, moo!

8. I bought me a horse 9. I bought me a dog

Horse goes neigh, neigh! Dog goes bow-wow, bow-wow!

MI CHACRA *(My Farm)*

Argentine folk song. Translated by Olcutt and Phyllis Sanders

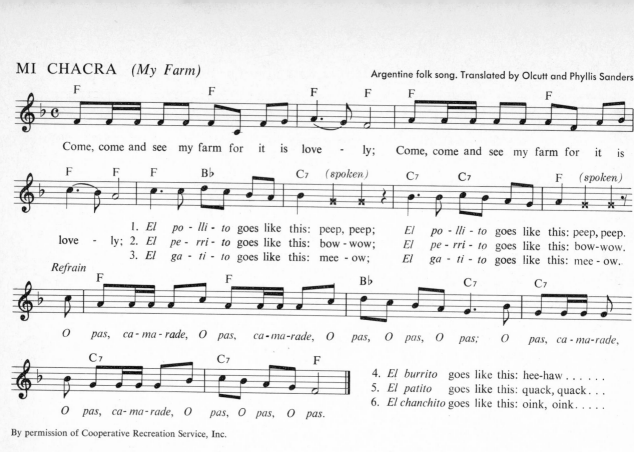

Come, come and see my farm for it is love - ly; Come, come and see my farm for it is

love - ly; 2. *El pe - rri - to* goes like this: bow - wow; *El pe - rri - to* goes like this: bow-wow.
1. *El po - lli - to* goes like this: peep, peep; *El po - lli - to* goes like this: peep, peep.
3. *El ga - ti - to* goes like this: mee - ow; *El ga - ti - to* goes like this: mee - ow.

Refrain

O pas, ca - ma - rade, O pas, ca - ma - rade, O pas, O pas, O pas; O pas, ca - ma - rade,

4. *El burrito* goes like this: hee-haw . . . . . .
5. *El patito* goes like this: quack, quack . . .
6. *El chanchito* goes like this: oink, oink . . . . .

O pas, ca - ma - rade, O pas, O pas, O pas.

By permission of Cooperative Recreation Service, Inc.

OH, DEAR! WHAT CAN THE MATTER BE?

English folk song

Refrain

Oh, dear! What can the mat - ter be? Dear, dear, what can the mat - ter be?

Oh, dear! What can the mat - ter be? John - ny's so long at the fair.

Verse

1. He prom - ised to buy me a trin - ket to please me, And then, for a smile, Oh,
2. He prom - ised to bring me a bas - ket of po - sies, A gar - land of lil - ies,

he vowed he would tease me, He prom - ised to bring me a bunch of blue rib - bons
A gift of red ros - es, A lit - tle straw hat to set off the blue rib - bons

D.C. al Fine

To tie up my bon - ny brown hair. _____
That tie up my bon - ny brown hair. _____

230

THE MERRY-GO-ROUND

Words and music by George Mitchell

Oh, how I like to go round and round All day long on a mer-ry-go-round.

Pranc-ing hors-es and kan-ga-roos, Gai-ly gal-lop-ing two by twos.

Oh, how I like to go round and round All day long on a mer-ry-go-round.

THE CAMEL

Words and music by Gladys Tipton

Fun-ny, hump-y cam-el, Take me for a ride._____

Back and forth and back and forth, And back and forth we go._____

OVER THE RIVER

Old song. Words by Lydia Maria Childs

1. O-ver the riv-er and through the wood, To grand-fa-ther's house we go;____
2. O-ver the riv-er and through the wood, Trot fast,___ my dap-ple gray!___

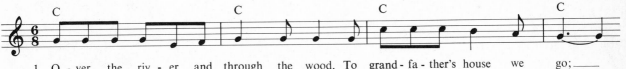

The horse knows the way to car-ry the sleigh, Thro' the white and drift-ed snow._
Spring o-ver the ground, like a hunt-ing hound, For this is Thanks-giv-ing Day!_

O-ver the riv-er and through the wood, Oh, how the wind does blow!____
O-ver the riv-er and through the wood, Now grandmother's face I spy!____

It stings the toes and bites the nose, As o-ver the ground we go.
Hur-rah for the fun! Is the pud-ding done? Hur-rah for the pump-kin pie!

BEFORE DINNER

Congo children's song. English words by Carol Hart Sayre

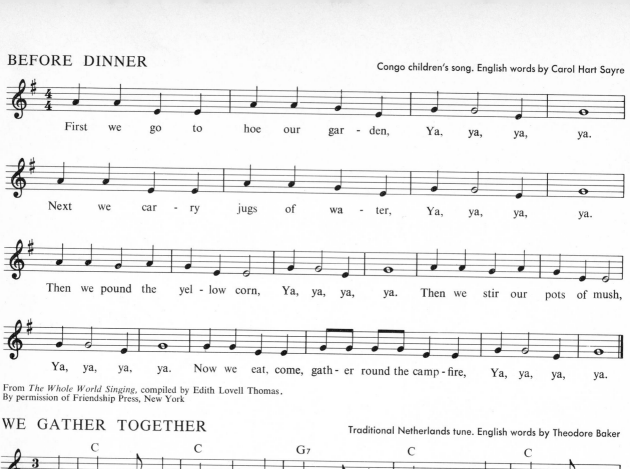

First we go to hoe our gar-den, Ya, ya, ya, ya.

Next we car-ry jugs of wa-ter, Ya, ya, ya, ya.

Then we pound the yel-low corn, Ya, ya, ya, ya. Then we stir our pots of mush,

Ya, ya, ya, ya. Now we eat, come, gath-er round the camp-fire, Ya, ya, ya, ya.

From *The Whole World Singing*, compiled by Edith Lovell Thomas.
By permission of Friendship Press, New York

WE GATHER TOGETHER

Traditional Netherlands tune. English words by Theodore Baker

We gath-er to-geth-er to ask the Lord's bless-ing, He chas-tens and

has-tens His will to make known. The wick-ed op-press-ing, now cease from dis-

tress-ing. Sing prais-es to His name; He for-gets not His own.

FIELDS OF HOME

Czech folk song. Words by Louis Adelman

1. Har-vest is the sea-son of brown and gold; Sum-mer la-bor soon will be done.
2. Har-vest is the sea-son of work and play; Work-ing out of doors, in the sun.

Rip-pling fields of gold-en wheat de-light the eye. Love-ly are the
Soon the gold-en shocks will all be gath-ered in. Pleas-ant are the

fields of home, Love-ly are the fields of home.
fields of home, Pleas-ant are the fields of home.

232

AMERICA

Music by Henry Carey. Words by Samuel Francis Smith

My coun - try! 'tis of thee, Sweet land of lib - er - ty, Of thee I sing;

Land where my fa - thers died, Land of the Pil - grim's pride,

From ev - 'ry___ moun - tain - side Let___ free - dom ring.

FOR HEALTH AND STRENGTH

Old English round

I   **II**   **III**   **IV**

For health and strength and dai - ly food We praise Thy name, O Lord.

SILENT NIGHT *(Stille Nacht, Noche de paz)*

Music by Franz Gruber. German words by Joseph Mohr

Si - lent night, ho - ly night, All is calm, all is bright
Stil - le Nacht! Hei - li - ge Nacht! Al - les schläft, ein - sam wacht
¡No - che de paz, no - che de a - mor! To - do duerme en de - rre - dor.

Round yon Vir - gin Moth - er and Child, Ho - ly In - fant so ten - der and mild,
nur das trau - te hoch - hei - li - ge Paar. Hol - der Kna - be im lok - ki - gen Haar,
Entre los as - tros que es - par - cen su luz, Bella a - nun - cian - do al ni - ñi - to Je - sús,

Sleep in heav - en - ly peace,___ Sleep___ in heav - en - ly peace.
schlaf in himm - li - scher Ruh',___ schlaf___ in himm - li - scher Ruh'!
Brilla la es - tre - lla de paz,___ Bri - lla la es - tre - lla de paz.___

DER TANNENBAUM *(O Christmas Tree)*

German folk song. German words by A. Zarnack

Fine

O Tan - nen - baum, O Tan - nen - baum, wie treu sind dei - ne Blät - ter!
O Christ - mas tree, O Christ - mas tree, How al - ways green your branch - es!

D.C. al Fine

Du grünst nicht nur zur Som - mers - zeit, nein, auch im win - ter, wenn es schneit.
Your leaves are green in sum - mer - time, And still they glow through win - ter snow.

233

WE THREE KINGS OF ORIENT ARE

Words and music by John Henry Hopkins

We three kings of O - ri - ent are, Bear - ing gifts we trav - erse a - far

Field and foun - tain, moor and moun - tain, Fol - low - ing yon - der star.

Oh, __ star of won - der, star of night, Star with roy - al beau - ty bright,

West - ward lead - ing, still pro - ceed - ing, Guide us to Thy per - fect light.

AWAY IN A MANGER

Music by Carl Müller. Words by Martin Luther

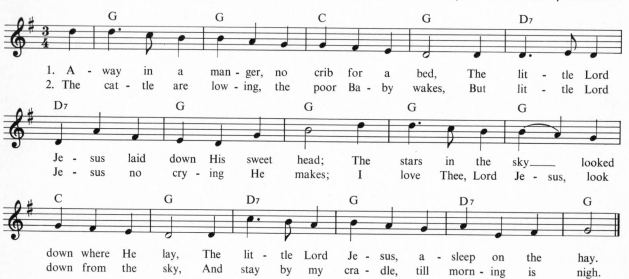

1. A - way in a man - ger, no crib for a bed, The lit - tle Lord
2. The cat - tle are low - ing, the poor Ba - by wakes, But lit - tle Lord

Je - sus laid down His sweet head; The stars in the sky__ looked
Je - sus no cry - ing He makes; I love Thee, Lord Je - sus, look

down where He lay, The lit - tle Lord Je - sus, a - sleep on the hay.
down from the sky, And stay by my cra - dle, till morn - ing is nigh.

JINGLE BELLS

Words and music by J. Pierpont

Jin - gle bells, jin - gle bells, jin - gle all the way!

Oh, what fun it is to ride in a one - horse o - pen sleigh! __

Jingle Bells

Jin - gle bells, jin - gle bells, jin - gle all the way!
Oh, what fun it is to ride in a one - horse o - pen sleigh!

LA PIÑATA

Spanish folk song. English words by Roberta McLaughlin

No quie-ro pla - ta ni quie-ro o - ro, Lo que yo quie-ro es que-brar pi - ñata.
We don't want sil - ver, we don't want gold,__ We want the good - ies piñ - a - ta will hold.

An - da - le Pe - dro no te di - la - tes Con la cha-ro-la de los ca - ca - hua - tes.
An - da - le Pe - dro, put on the blind - fold, We want the good - ies piñ - a - ta will hold.__

¡Pi - ña - ta! ¡Pi - ña - ta! ¡Pi - ña - ta!

From *Children's Songs of Mexico* by Roberta McLaughlin and Lucille Wood,
Copyright © 1963, Highland Music Company. By permission of the publishers.

SONG FOR HANUKAH

Jewish folk song

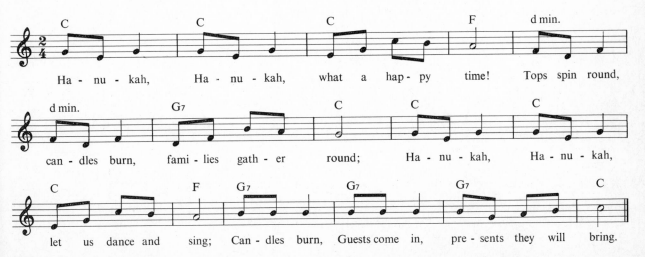

Ha - nu - kah, Ha - nu - kah, what a hap - py time! Tops spin round,
can - dles burn, fami - lies gath - er round; Ha - nu - kah, Ha - nu - kah,
let us dance and sing; Can - dles burn, Guests come in, pre - sents they will bring.

SKIP TO MY LOU

American singing game

1. Flies in the butter-milk, shoo, fly, shoo! Flies in the butter-milk, shoo, fly, shoo!
2. Little red wag-on, paint-ed blue, Little red wag-on, paint-ed blue,

Flies in the butter-milk, shoo, fly, shoo! Skip to my Lou, my dar-ling.
Little red wag-on, paint-ed blue, Skip to my Lou, my dar-ling.

POLLY WOLLY DOODLE

American folk song

1. Oh, I went down South for to see my Sal, Sing-ing Pol-ly Wol-ly Doo-dle all the day;
2. Oh, my Sal she is a __ maid-en fair,

My __ Sal, she is a __ spunk-y gal, Sing-ing Pol-ly Wol-ly Doo-dle all the day.
With __ curl-y eyes and __ laugh-ing hair,

Refrain

Fare thee well, fare thee well, Fare thee well, my fair-y fay,

For I'm goin' to Loui-si-an-a for to see my Su-sy-an-na, Sing-ing

Pol-ly Wol-ly Doo-dle all the day.

OLD FOLKS AT HOME *(Swanee River)*

Words and music by Stephen C. Foster

Way down up-on the Swa-nee riv-er, Far, far a-way,
All up and down the whole cre-a-tion Sad-ly I roam,

There's where my heart is turn-ing ev-er, There's where the old folks __ stay.
Still long-ing for the old plan-ta-tion, And for the old folks at home.

236

All the world is sad and drear - y, Ev - 'ry - where I roam;

Oh, broth - ers, how my heart grows wea - ry, Far from the old folks at home!

SWING LOW, SWEET CHARIOT

Spiritual

Swing low, sweet char - i - ot, ___ Com - ing for to car - ry me home,

Swing _ low, sweet char - i - ot, ___ Com - ing for to car - ry me home.

I looked o - ver Jor - dan and what did I see? ___ Com - ing for to car - ry me home.

A band _ of an - gels, com - ing aft - er me, ___ Com - ing for to car - ry me home.

GO DOWN, MOSES

Spiritual

Refrain

Go down, Mos - es, 'Way down in E - gypt land, ___

Tell ___ old Pha - raoh, "Let my peo - ple go." go."

Verse

When Is - rael was in E - gypt's land, "Let my peo - ple go."

Op - pressed so hard they could not stand, "Let my peo - ple go."

BILLY BOY

English folk song

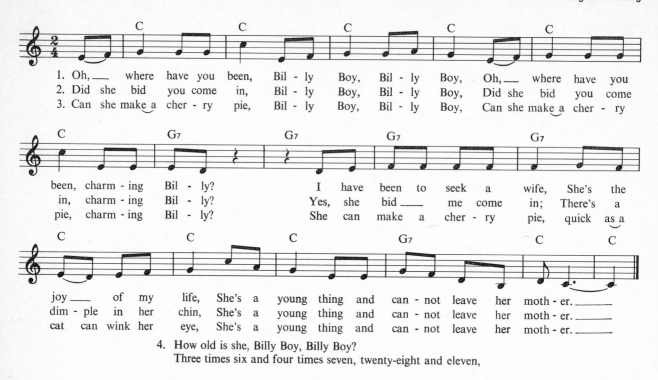

1. Oh, — where have you been, Bil - ly Boy, Bil - ly Boy, Oh, — where have you
2. Did she bid you come in, Bil - ly Boy, Bil - ly Boy, Did she bid you come
3. Can she make a cher - ry pie, Bil - ly Boy, Bil - ly Boy, Can she make a cher - ry

been, charm - ing Bil - ly? I have been to seek a wife, She's the
in, charm - ing Bil - ly? Yes, she bid — me come in; There's a
pie, charm - ing Bil - ly? She can make a cher - ry pie, quick as a

joy — of my life, She's a young thing and can - not leave her moth - er. —
dim - ple in her chin, She's a young thing and can - not leave her moth - er. —
cat can wink her eye, She's a young thing and can - not leave her moth - er. —

4. How old is she, Billy Boy, Billy Boy?
Three times six and four times seven, twenty-eight and eleven,

ON TOP OF OLD SMOKY

Kentucky folk song

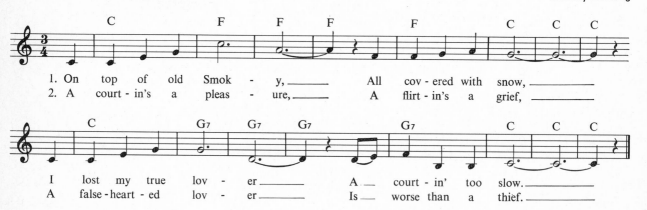

1. On top of old Smok - y, — All cov - ered with snow, —
2. A court - in's a pleas - ure, — A flirt - in's a grief, —

I lost my true lov - er — A — court - in' too slow. —
A false - heart - ed lov - er — Is — worse than a thief. —

LAVENDER'S BLUE

English folk song

Lav - en - der's blue, dil - ly, dil - ly, Lav - en - der's green. When I am king, dil - ly, dil - ly, You shall be queen.

Who told you so, dil - ly, dil - ly, Who told you so? 'Twas my own heart, dil - ly, dil - ly, That told me so.

DOWN IN THE VALLEY

Kentucky folk song

1. Down in the val - ley, the val - ley so low, _____
   Hear the winds blow, dear, ___ hear the winds blow, _____
2. Writ - ing this let - ter con - tain - ing three lines, _____
   Will you be mine, dear, ___ will you be mine? _____

Hang your head o - ver, hear the winds blow. _____
Hang your head o - ver, hear the winds blow. _____
An - swer my ques - tion, will you be mine? _____
An - swer my ques - tion, will you be mine? _____

From *The Singin' Gatherin'* by Jean Thomas, the "Traipsin' Woman" and Joseph A. Leeder,
©1939, Silver Burdett Company.

MORNING SONG (*Las mañanitas*)

Mexican folk song. Translated by Olcutt and Phyllis Sanders

With a morn - ing song we greet you As King Da - vid used to sing,
Es - tas son las ma - ña - ni - tas Que can - ta - ba el Rey Da - vid,

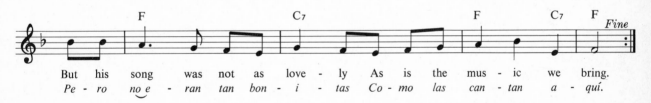

But his song was not as love - ly As is the mus - ic we bring.
Pe - ro no e - ran tan bon - i - tas Co - mo las can - tan a - quí.

Refrain
A - wake, then, O my be - lov - ed, A - wake, for the dawn is nigh;
Des - pier - ta, mi bien, des - pier - ta, mi - ra que y a - ma - ne - cío;

D.C. al Fine

Now the birds are sweet - ly sing - ing; The moon has gone from the sky.
Ya los pa - ja - ri - llos can - tan; La lu - na ya se me - tió.

By permission of Cooperative Recreation Service, Inc.

CLEMENTINE

American folk song

1. In a cav - ern, in a can - yon, Ex - ca - vat - ing for a mine,
2. Light she was, and like a fair - y, And her shoes were num - ber nine,

Dwelt a min - er, for - ty - nin - er, And his daugh - ter, Clem - en - tine.
Her - ring box - es with - out top - ses, San - dals were for Clem - en - tine.

Refrain

O my dar - ling, O my dar - ling, O my dar - ling Clem - en - tine!

You are lost and gone for - ev - er, Dref - ful sor - ry, Clem - en - tine!

SWEET BETSY FROM PIKE

American folk song

Oh, don't you re - mem - ber sweet Bet - sy from Pike,

who crossed the big moun - tains with her lov - er Ike,

With two yoke of ox - en, a large yal - ler dog,

A ___ tall Shang - hai roost - er and one spot - ted hog?

Refrain

Ri - choo - dle, ri - choo - dle, ri - choo - dle, ri - chay.

240

SACRAMENTO

Music by Stephen C. Foster. Words traditional

1. We've formed our band and we are well manned, Doo - da, doo - da!
2. Where the gold - en ore is ___ rich in store,

To jour - ney a - far to the Prom - ised Land, Doo - da, doo - da, day!
On the banks of the Sac - ra - men - to shore,

Blow, boys, ___ blow, To Cal - i - for - nia go!

There's plen - ty of gold, so I've been told, On the banks of the Sac - ra - men - to!

BENDEMEER'S STREAM

Irish folk melody. Words by Thomas Moore

There's a bow - er of ro - ses by Ben - de - meer's stream,
In the time of my child - hood 'twas like a sweet dream,

And the night - in - gale sings round it all the day long,
To ___ sit in the ro - ses and hear the bird's song.

That bow'r and its mu - sic I'll nev - er for - get,

But oft when a - lone in the bloom of the year,

I think is the night - in - gale sing - ing there yet,

Are the ro - ses still bright by the calm Ben - de - meer?

241

THE CRUSADERS

Silesian folk song. Words by Frederick H. Martens

1. "Blow, oh, ye trum - pets, blow! King, knight and serf we go,
2. Hark, still the trum - pets blare! Still rings the mar - tial air,

Bear - ing the cross to the Ho - ly Land!" Thus the cru - sad - ers cried,
Ech - o - ing down through the ag - es long; Their gal - lant deeds and brave,

Marched, suf - fer'd, fought and died, A dar - ing, daunt - less he - ro band.
Told in the print - ed page, Are liv - ing still in tale and song.

HOME ON THE RANGE

American cowboy song

1. Oh, give me a home where the buf - fa - lo roam,
2. How of - ten at night where the heav - ens are bright

Where the deer and the an - te - lope play,—— Where sel - dom is heard a dis -
With the lights from the glit - ter - ing stars,—— Have I stood there a - mazed and

cour - ag - ing word, And the skies are not cloud - y all day.——
asked as I gazed, If their glo - ry ex - ceeds that of ours.——

Refrain

Home, home on the range,—— Where the deer and the an - te - lope play,——

Where sel - dom is heard a dis - cour - ag - ing word,

And the skies are not cloud - y all day.——

242

NIGHT HERDING SONG

American cowboy song

1. Oh, slow up, do - gies, quit rov - ing a - round,
2. I've cir - cle herd - ed and night herd - ed too,

You have wan - dered and tram - pled all o - ver the ground; Oh, graze a - long, do - gies, and
But to keep you to - geth - er, that's what I can't do; My horse is leg wear - y, and

feed kind - a slow, And don't for - ev - er be on the go.
I'm aw - ful tired, But if you get a - way, I am sure to get fired.

Oh, move slow, do - gies, move slow, ___ Hi - oo, hi - oo - oo - oo! ___
Bunch up, lit - tle do - gies, bunch up, ___ Hi - oo, hi - oo - oo - oo! ___

OLD TEXAS

Oklahoma cowboy song

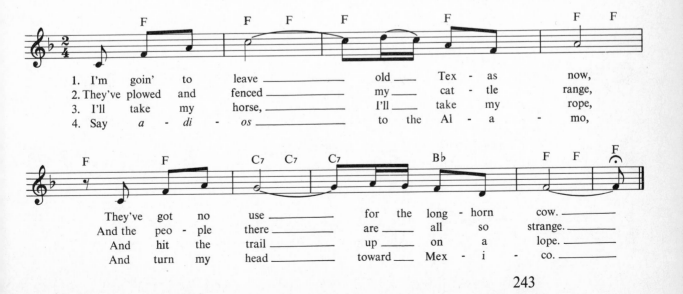

1. I'm goin' to leave ___ old ___ Tex - as now,
2. They've plowed and fenced ___ my ___ cat - tle range,
3. I'll take my horse, ___ I'll ___ take my rope,
4. Say a - di - os ___ to the Al - a - mo,

They've got no use ___ for the long - horn cow. ___
And the peo - ple there ___ are ___ all so strange. ___
And hit the trail ___ up ___ on a lope. ___
And turn my head ___ toward ___ Mex - i - co. ___

243

CIELITO LINDO

Mexican folk song. English words by Vivian Cooper

High in the Sier - ra Mo - re - na Lives _____ a fair maid - en,
De la Sie - rra Mo - re - na, Cie - li - to Lin - do,

Cie - li - to Lin - do. _____ Spar - kling eyes _____ cast a mag - ic spell, _____
vie - nen ba - jan - do _____ Un par de o - ji - tos ne - gros, Cie -

She's the fair - est, Cie - li - to Lin - do! _____
li - to Lin - do, de _____ con - tra - ban - do. _____

Refrain

Ay, ay, ay, ay! _____ Sing, ban - ish sad - ness! _____
¡Ay, ay, ay, ay! _____ Can - ta y no llo - res _____

Your swirl - ing shawl _____ and your mer - ry song _____
Por - que can - tan - do se a - le - gran, Cie -

Fill my heart with heav - en - ly glad - ness. _____
li - to Lin - do, los _____ co - ra - zo - nes. _____

ALL THROUGH THE NIGHT

Welsh folk song

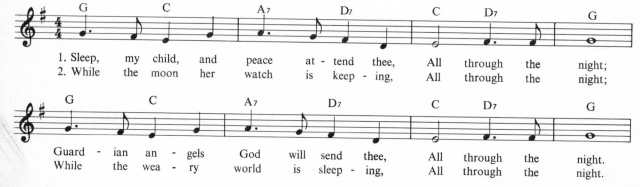

1. Sleep, my child, and peace at - tend thee, All through the night;
2. While the moon her watch is keep - ing, All through the night;

Guard - ian an - gels God will send thee, All through the night.
While the wea - ry world is sleep - ing, All through the night.

Soft the drow-sy hours are creep-ing, Hill and vale in slum-ber steep-ing,
O'er thy spir-it gen-tly steal-ing Vi-sions of de-light re-veal-ing,

I my lov-ing vig-il keep-ing, All through the night.
Breathes a pure and ho-ly feel-ing All through the night.

HUSH, LITTLE BABY

Folk song from southern United States. Collected by Jean Ritchie

1. Hush, lit-tle ba-by, Don't say a word,
2. If that _____ mock-ing bird won't _____ sing,

Pa-pa's going to buy you a mock-ing-bird.
Pa-pa's going to buy you a dia-mond ring.

THE LITTLE SANDMAN

Music by Johannes Brahms

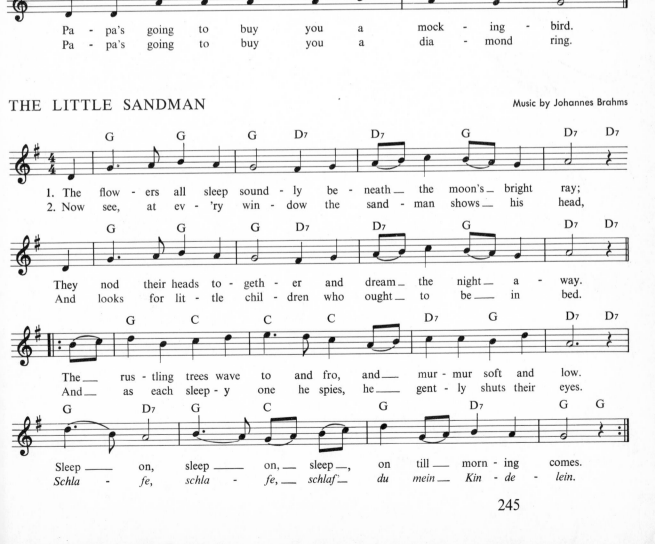

1. The flow-ers all sleep sound-ly be-neath the moon's bright ray;
2. Now see, at ev-'ry win-dow the sand-man shows his head,

They nod their heads to-geth-er and dream the night a-way.
And looks for lit-tle chil-dren who ought to be in bed.

The rus-tling trees wave to and fro, and mur-mur soft and low.
And as each sleep-y one he spies, he gent-ly shuts their eyes.

Sleep on, sleep on, sleep, on till morn-ing comes.
Schla - fe, schla - fe, schlaf' du mein Kin - de - lein.

Index of Terms

A cappella, 84, 102
Accelerando, 181
Accidentals, 62
Arpeggios, 22
Augmentation, 201
Autoharp
  fingering, 1, 151, 156
  illustrations of, 6, 9, 17
Autoharp effects
  accompaniment on lower
    strings, 174
  bagpipe, 123, 151
  banjo, 137
  guitar, 43, 111, 156, 183
  harplike strum, 26
  koto, 192
  plucking, 14
  strumming, 1
  'ud, 46
Basic tones, 133
Bass viol, 14
"Blues," "blue notes," 161, 162
Cadence, 11, 139, 145
Chord, 10, 11, 14, 20. *See also*
  Harmony
  "active," 11
  dominant, 19
  dominant seventh, 20, 43,
    139, 175, 216
  inversion, 134, 144, 190
  major, 133, 165
  minor, 133, 165
  "passive," 11
  primary, 54, 185
  root position, 178, 190
  secondary, 157
  seventh, 14, 20
  subdominant, 19
  tonic, 19, 43, 139
  triad, 14, 133, 165
Chromatic scale, 80
Climax (melodic), 97
Coda, 15
Color tone, 133
Consonance, 64
Consonant intervals, 34
Crescendo, 1, 98
D.C. al Fine (da capo al fine),
  41
Decrescendo, 1
Diatonic, 147
Dissonance, 64
Dominant, 19. *See also* Chord,
  dominant seventh

Dot, 19
Dynamics, 2, 4, 146
Endings, first and second, 31
Fermata, 155
Fifth, 133. *See also* Chord,
  dominant
First ending, 31
Flats, 28, 62
Form, 3, 9, 10, 24, 32, 33, 97,
  112, 186, 197
Fortissimo, 98
Fugue, 171
Glissando, 205
Half step, 28, 50, 80
Harmonic minor. *See* Minor
  scale, harmonic
Harmony, 4, 11, 14, 22, 28, 34,
  54, 64, 100, 107, 133,
  139, 142, 157, 162, 165,
  195, 212, 213. *See also*
  Chord
Interval, 28, 33, 34, 49, 51, 147,
  151. *See also* Scale
Inversion, 134, 144, 190
Key. *See also* Tonality
  major, 28, 110
  minor, 28, 29, 110
  signature, 28, 57
Leading tone, 195
Legato, 52
Major, 28
  chord, 133, 165
  key, 28, 110
  scale, 19, 28, 29, 39, 49, 52,
    149, 161, 195, 223
Major, relative, 73, 107, 110,
  215
Melodic minor. *See* Minor
  scale, melodic
Melody, 13, 22, 26, 53, 74, 84,
  97, 103, 181, 201
Melody bells (illustrated), 2, 6,
  10, 18, 26
Meters (introduced), 5, 9, 14,
  18, 23, 66, 153, 201.
  See also Rhythm
Meter signature, 14
Minor, 28
  chord, 133, 165
  key, 28, 29, 110
  scale, 28, 29, 149
    harmonic, 49, 107, 215, 216
    melodic, 223
    natural form, 149, 150, 215

Minor, relative, 28, 107
Mode, 29, 39, 110, 133, 149,
  150, 195
Monophonic, 3
Mood, 21, 52, 143, 155, 161
Motive (motif), 201
Natural minor. *See* Minor
  scale, natural form
Naturals, 55, 62, 202
Note values, 9, 19, 23, 31, 37,
  47, 201, 206
Octave, 147
Open fifth, 151, 211
Ostinato, 52
Pentatonic scale, 37, 39, 193,
  195, 197
Percussion effects
  conga drum, 40–42
  cymbals, 14, 36, 59, 60, 98,
    133,
  drum, 14, 17, 18, 36, 48, 59,
    93, 98, 143, 148
  finger cymbals, 17, 18, 48, 98,
    133, 192
  gong, 36, 192
  rhythm sticks, 93
  sand blocks, 93
  tambourines, 32, 98, 128, 137
  tone blocks, 36
  wood blocks, 36, 65
Period, 197
Phrase, 9
Piano, 98
Pizzicato, 120
Polyphonic, 3
Recorder
  arghool effect, 46
  fife effect, 185
  fingering chart, 22
Relative major, 73, 107, 110,
  215
Relative minor, 28, 107
Repetition, 10
Resonator bells (illustrated),
  10, 11
  "tremolo" style, 204
Rest, 15, 60, 83
Rhythm, 5, 9, 15, 18, 22, 23,
  31, 37, 41, 42, 47, 53,
  54, 62, 74, 102, 108, 155,
  161, 179, 189, 194, 206,
  208. *See also* Meters and
  Note values
Ritardando, 181

Rondo form, 186
Root, 14, 133
Root position, 178
Rubato, 181
Scale, 19, 39, 49, 52, 107, 147,
  149, 161, 195, 223
  chromatic, 80
  major, 19, 28, 29, 39, 56, 149
  minor, 28, 29, 149
    harmonic, 49, 215, 216
    melodic, 223
    natural form, 149, 150, 215
    pentatonic 37, 39, 193, 195,
    197
Second ending, 31
Sequence, 10
Sharps, 28, 55, 62
Slur, 67
Staccato, 52
Subdominant, 19
Suite, 112
Symbols, 14, 15, 18, 19, 23, 28,
  31, 41, 52, 54, 55, 57, 60,
  62, 67, 83, 98, 155, 201,
  202
Syncopation, 41, 208
Tempo, 1
Texture, 3
Third, 133, 149
Tie, 23, 67
Timbre. *See* Tone color
Tonality, 1, 6, 13, 19, 28, 81,
  193, 195
Tonal magnetism, 39, 195
Tone color (timbre), 2, 59, 97,
  146
Tonic, 19. *See also* Chord, tonic
Transpose, 129
Tremolo. *See* Resonator bells,
  "tremolo" style
Triad, 14, 133, 165
Trill, 52
Triplet, 161, 206
Unison, 3
Whole step, 50
Woodwinds, 113
  bassoon, 113
  clarinet, 113
  contra bassoon, 113
  English horn, 113
  flute, 80, 113
  oboe, 113
  piccolo, 80, 113
  saxophone, 113

Index of Instrumental Music by Composer

Bizet, Georges   "Prelude" from *L'Arlésienne:* Suite No. 1, 131
                        "The Top" from *Jeux d'Enfants,* **119**

Cailliet, Lucien   "Variations on the Theme — Pop! Goes the Weasel," 171

Copland, Aaron   "Circus Music" from *The Red Pony,* **63**

246

(Boldface numbers indicate the beginning of a lesson.)

Classified Index of Vocal Music

Index of Songs and Instrumental Music

*Available on a recording, Songs from The Craft of Music Teaching, from Silver Burdett Company.

2284-22
66